Sabbats
ALMANAC

Llewellyn's Sabbats Almanac:
Samhain 2016 to Mabon 2017

Cover art © Carolyn Vibbert
Cover design by Ellen Lawson
Editing by Ed Day and Aaron Lawrence
Interior Art: © Carolyn Vibbert, excluding illustrations on pages 37, 38, 73, 108, 110, 144, 146, 180, 183, 220, 250, 253, 286, 288, which are © Wen Hsu

You can order annuals and books from *New Worlds*, Llewellyn's catalog. To request a free copy call toll free: 1-877-NEW WRLD, or order online by visiting our website at http://subscriptions.llewellyn.com.

ISBN: 978-0-7387-3770-6

Llewellyn Worldwide Ltd.
2143 Wooddale Drive
Woodbury, MN 55125-2989
www.llewellyn.com

Printed in the United States of America

2016

JANUARY
S	M	T	W	T	F	S
					1	2
3	4	5	6	7	8	9
10	11	12	13	14	15	16
17	18	19	20	21	22	23
24	25	26	27	28	29	30
31						

FEBRUARY
S	M	T	W	T	F	S
	1	2	3	4	5	6
7	8	9	10	11	12	13
14	15	16	17	18	19	20
21	22	23	24	25	26	27
28	29					

MARCH
S	M	T	W	T	F	S
		1	2	3	4	5
6	7	8	9	10	11	12
13	14	15	16	17	18	19
20	21	22	23	24	25	26
27	28	29	30	31		

APRIL
S	M	T	W	T	F	S
					1	2
3	4	5	6	7	8	9
10	11	12	13	14	15	16
17	18	19	20	21	22	23
24	25	26	27	28	29	30

MAY
S	M	T	W	T	F	S
1	2	3	4	5	6	7
8	9	10	11	12	13	14
15	16	17	18	19	20	21
22	23	24	25	26	27	28
29	30	31				

JUNE
S	M	T	W	T	F	S
			1	2	3	4
5	6	7	8	9	10	11
12	13	14	15	16	17	18
19	20	21	22	23	24	25
26	27	28	29	30		

JULY
S	M	T	W	T	F	S
					1	2
3	4	5	6	7	8	9
10	11	12	13	14	15	16
17	18	19	20	21	22	23
24	25	26	27	28	29	30
31						

AUGUST
S	M	T	W	T	F	S
	1	2	3	4	5	6
7	8	9	10	11	12	13
14	15	16	17	18	19	20
21	22	23	24	25	26	27
28	29	30	31			

SEPTEMBER
S	M	T	W	T	F	S
				1	2	3
4	5	6	7	8	9	10
11	12	13	14	15	16	17
18	19	20	21	22	23	24
25	26	27	28	29	30	

OCTOBER
S	M	T	W	T	F	S
						1
2	3	4	5	6	7	8
9	10	11	12	13	14	15
16	17	18	19	20	21	22
23	24	25	26	27	28	29
30	31					

NOVEMBER
S	M	T	W	T	F	S
		1	2	3	4	5
6	7	8	9	10	11	12
13	14	15	16	17	18	19
20	21	22	23	24	25	26
27	28	29	30			

DECEMBER
S	M	T	W	T	F	S
				1	2	3
4	5	6	7	8	9	10
11	12	13	14	15	16	17
18	19	20	21	22	23	24
25	26	27	28	29	30	31

2017

JANUARY
S	M	T	W	T	F	S
1	2	3	4	5	6	7
8	9	10	11	12	13	14
15	16	17	18	19	20	21
22	23	24	25	26	27	28
29	30	31				

FEBRUARY
S	M	T	W	T	F	S
			1	2	3	4
5	6	7	8	9	10	11
12	13	14	15	16	17	18
19	20	21	22	23	24	25
26	27	28				

MARCH
S	M	T	W	T	F	S
			1	2	3	4
5	6	7	8	9	10	11
12	13	14	15	16	17	18
19	20	21	22	23	24	25
26	27	28	29	30	31	

APRIL
S	M	T	W	T	F	S
						1
2	3	4	5	6	7	8
9	10	11	12	13	14	15
16	17	18	19	20	21	22
23	24	25	26	27	28	29
30						

MAY
S	M	T	W	T	F	S
	1	2	3	4	5	6
7	8	9	10	11	12	13
14	15	16	17	18	19	20
21	22	23	24	25	26	27
28	29	30	31			

JUNE
S	M	T	W	T	F	S
				1	2	3
4	5	6	7	8	9	10
11	12	13	14	15	16	17
18	19	20	21	22	23	24
25	26	27	28	29	30	

JULY
S	M	T	W	T	F	S
						1
2	3	4	5	6	7	8
9	10	11	12	13	14	15
16	17	18	19	20	21	22
23	24	25	26	27	28	29
30	31					

AUGUST
S	M	T	W	T	F	S
		1	2	3	4	5
6	7	8	9	10	11	12
13	14	15	16	17	18	19
20	21	22	23	24	25	26
27	28	29	30	31		

SEPTEMBER
S	M	T	W	T	F	S
					1	2
3	4	5	6	7	8	9
10	11	12	13	14	15	16
17	18	19	20	21	22	23
24	25	26	27	28	29	30

OCTOBER
S	M	T	W	T	F	S
1	2	3	4	5	6	7
8	9	10	11	12	13	14
15	16	17	18	19	20	21
22	23	24	25	26	27	28
29	30	31				

NOVEMBER
S	M	T	W	T	F	S
			1	2	3	4
5	6	7	8	9	10	11
12	13	14	15	16	17	18
19	20	21	22	23	24	25
26	27	28	29	30		

DECEMBER
S	M	T	W	T	F	S
					1	2
3	4	5	6	7	8	9
10	11	12	13	14	15	16
17	18	19	20	21	22	23
24	25	26	27	28	29	30
31						

Contents

Ostara

Beltane

Litha

Lammas

Contents

Mabon

Introduction

NEARLY EVERYONE HAS A favorite sabbat. There are numerous ways to observe any tradition. This edition of the *Sabbats Almanac* provides a wealth of lore, celebrations, creative projects, and recipes to enhance your holiday.

For this edition, a mix of writers—**Melanie Marquis, Kristoffer Hughes, Kerri Connor, Michael Furie, Elizabeth Barrette, Suzanne Ress, JD Hortwort,** and **Stacy Porter**—share their ideas and wisdom. These include a variety of paths such as The Troth and Eclectic as well as the authors' personal approaches to each sabbat. Each chapter closes with an extended ritual, which may be adapted for both solitary practitioners and covens.

In addition to these insights and rituals, specialists in astrology, history, cooking, crafts, and family impart their expertise throughout.

April Elliott Kent gives an overview of planetary influences most relevant for each sabbat season and provides details and a short ritual for selected events, including New and Full Moons, retrograde motion, planetary positions, and more.

Sybil Fogg explores the realm of old-world Pagans, with a focus on Slavic customs such as Polish weddings during Mabon and lesser-known facets of symbols like decorated eggs and even storks.

Linda Raedisch conjures up a feast for each festival that includes an appetizer, entrée, dessert, and beverage.

Mickie Mueller offers instructions on craft projects that can also be incorporated into your practice.

Dallas Jennifer Cobb focuses on family matters and the incorporation of teenagers in Pagan traditions as related to each sabbat.

About the Authors

Elizabeth Barrette has been involved with the Pagan community for more than twenty-six years. She served as managing editor of *PanGaia* for eight years and Dean of Studies at the Grey School of Wizardry for four years. She has written columns on beginning and intermediate Pagan practice, Pagan culture, and Pagan leadership. Her book *Composing Magic: How to Create Magical Spells, Rituals, Blessings, Chants, and Prayers* explains how to combine writing and spirituality. She lives in central Illinois where she has done much networking with Pagans in her area, such as coffeehouse meetings and open sabbats. Her other public activities feature Pagan picnics and science fiction conventions. She enjoys magical crafts, historic religions, and gardening for wildlife. Her other writing fields include speculative fiction, gender studies, social and environmental issues. Visit her blog *The Wordsmith's Forge* (http://ysabetwordsmith. livejournal.com/) or her website PenUltimate Productions (http:// penultimateproductions.weebly.com). Her coven site is Greenhaven Tradition (http://greenhaventradition.weebly.com/).

Dallas Jennifer Cobb practices gratitude magic, giving thanks for personal happiness, health, and prosperity; meaningful, flexible, and rewarding work; and a deliciously joyful life. She is accomplishing her deepest desires. She lives in paradise with her daughter in a waterfront village in rural Ontario, where she regularly swims and runs, chanting: "Thank you, thank you, thank you." Contact her at jennifer.cobb@live.com or visit www.magicalliving.ca.

Kerri Connor is the author of *The Pocket Spell Creator: Magickal References at Your Fingertips, The Pocket Guide to Rituals: Magickal References at Your Fingertips, The Pocket Idiot's Guide to Potions, Goodbye Grandmother,* and *Spells for Tough Times: Crafting Hope*

When Faced With Life's Thorniest Challenges. High Priestess of the Gathering Grove, she has been published in several magazines and is a frequent contributor to the Llewellyn annuals. A graduate from the University of Wisconsin, Kerri holds a B.A. in communications and lives with her family, cats, and chickens in rural Illinois.

Sybil Fogg has been a practicing witch for over twenty-five years. She's been writing for even longer. Her real name is Sybil Wilen, but she chose to use her mother's maiden name in Pagan circles to honor her grandparents. She's also a wife, mother, writer, teacher, and belly dancer. Her family shares her passion for magic, dance, and writing. She lives in Saco, Maine, with her husband and children. Please visit her website: www.sybilwilen.com.

Michael Furie (Northern California) is the author of *Spellcasting for Beginners*, *Supermarket Magic*, and *Spellcasting: Beyond the Basics* published by Llewellyn Worldwide. Furie has been a practicing Witch for over twenty years. An American Witch, he practices in the Irish tradition and is a priest of the Cailleach. You can find him online at www.michaelfurie.com.

JD Hortwort resides in North Carolina. She is an avid student of herbology and gardening. JD has written a weekly garden column for over twenty years. She is a professional and award-winning writer, journalist, and magazine editor and a frequent contributor to the Llewellyn annuals. JD has been active in the local Pagan community since 2002, and she is a founding member of the House of Akasha in Greensboro, N.C.

Kristoffer Hughes is the founder and Chief of the Anglesey Druid Order in North Wales, UK. He is an award-winning author and a frequent speaker and workshop leader throughout the United Kingdom and the United States. He works professionally for Her Majesty's Coroner. He has studied with the Order of Bards, Ovates and Druids, and is its 13th Mount Haemus Scholar. He is a native Welsh speaker, born to a Welsh family in the mountains of Snowdonia. He resides on the Isle of Anglesey.

April Elliott Kent has been a professional astrologer since 1990. She is the author of *Astrological Transits* (Fair Winds/Quarto, 2015), *The Essential Guide to Practical Astrology* (Alpha/Penguin, 2011), and *Star Guide to Weddings* (Llewellyn, 2008). April's writing has also appeared in *The Mountain Astrologer* and *Dell Horoscope* magazines and in Llewellyn's *Moon Sign Book* and *Sun Sign Book*. She lives in San Diego, CA. Her website is BigSkyAstrology.com.

Melanie Marquis is a lifelong practitioner of magick, the founder of United Witches global coven, and a local coordinator for the Pagan Pride Project in Denver, Colorado, where she currently resides. The author of numerous articles and several books, including *The Witch's Bag of Tricks*, *A Witch's World of Magick*, *Beltane*, and *Lughnasadh*, and she's written for many national and international Pagan publications. She is the co-author of *Witchy Mama* and the co-creator of the Spellcaster Tarot. An avid crafter, cook, folk artist, and tarot reader, she offers a line of customized magickal housewares as well as private tarot consultations by appointment. Connect with her online at www.melaniemarquis.com or facebook .com/melaniemarquisauthor.

Mickie Mueller is an author, artist, and illustrator who explores the realms of magic with both visual mediums and the written word. Her mixed media artwork is created magically; she combines colored pencil techniques with paint that is infused with magical herbs that correspond to the subject, bringing the power of spirit into her magical artwork. Mickie's black and white illustrations have been published in various books since 2007, and she has illustrated tarot and oracle decks including Voice of the Trees oracle, which she also wrote, and Mystical Cats Tarot. She has also written for several of the Llewellyn annuals and the book *The Witch's Mirror*. She is a Reiki Master/Teacher, ordained Priestess, and loyal minion to two cats and a dog.

Stacy Porter is a Sea Witch. She has survived a Russian winter, studied politics in Africa, sampled the best gelato in Italy, and saved sea turtles in Nicaragua. Stacy holds a degree in International Studies with an emphasis in politics from Juniata College. She is a second-degree Priestess in the Ravenmyst Tradition, studying under Dorothy Morrison, Maggie Shayne, and Gail Wood. She is a certified yoga instructor, meditation guide, writer, and passionate advocate for those who don't have a voice. Stacy travels the world, as a mermaid and on two legs, teaching yoga, spreading magic, and daring the world to believe in their dreams. She lives by a lake on the east coast with her Jack Russell terrier, Mackenzie. Her writings regularly appear in *Elephant Journal* and you can follow her adventures on her website www.theavalonapothecary.com

Linda Raedisch is a papercrafter, house cleaner, and professional organizer who has somehow managed to find the time to write two books: *Night of the Witches: Folklore, Traditions and Recipes for Celebrating Walpurgis Night* (Llewellyn 2011) and *The Old Magic of Christmas: Yuletide Traditions for the Darkest Days of the Year* (Llewellyn 2015). Since 2011, she has been a regular contributor to the Llewellyn annuals. Linda lives in northern New Jersey, but enjoys the odd vacation on the west Baltic coast. She has eaten Danish hot dogs beside a fjord.

Suzanne Ress has been practicing Wicca for about twelve years as the leader of a small coven, but she has been aware of having a special connection to nature and animal spirits since she was a young child. She has been writing creatively most of her life—short stories, novels, and nonfiction articles for a variety of publications—and finds it to be an important outlet for her considerable creative powers. Other outlets she regularly makes use of are metalsmithing, mosaic works, painting, and all kinds of dance. She is also a professional aromatic herb grower and beekeeper. Although she is an American of Welsh ancestry by birth, she has lived in northern Italy for nearly twenty years. She recently discovered that the small mountain in the pre-alpine hills that she inhabits with her family and animals was once the site of an ancient Insubrian Celtic sacred place. Not surprisingly, the top of the mountain has remained a fulcrum of sacredness throughout the millennia, and this grounding in blessedness makes Suzanne's everyday life especially magical.

Samhain

Macabre Magick and Masquerade

Melanie Marquis

SAMHAIN, THE SABBAT THAT shares its date and many of its themes and traditions with Halloween, is one of my favorite holidays of the year. As nature prepares for winter's death and enters its slumber, our world whispers with the essence of the shadows, and everything around us seems to acquire a somber yet mystical ambiance. I love the magick of it all, from the masquerade to the macabre. I feel connected with the dead as we enter this dark stage of the year, which is a special blessing when there are loved ones that are dearly missed.

As a pre-Christian Celtic harvest rite marking the end of the growing season and signaling the beginning of winter, Samhain dates back all the way to the Iron Age. It was the start of the new year, a time to let go of the old and embrace a fresh start. Those who died throughout the year were believed to make their pilgrimage into the underworld on this night, and in response, the Celts would light fires and lanterns and leave out treats in hopes of aiding and appeasing the wandering dead. Since many of these roaming shadows were believed to be powerful and sometimes maleficent beings, Celts began wearing masks and costumes in imitation of the spirits or as disguises. Even after the Celtic world was Christianized, the costuming traditions of Samhain endured. On All Hallows Day, a Christian holiday honoring the dead created in the hopes of supplanting Samhain, children in Ireland and other parts of Great Britain would dress in costumes and travel from house to house singing songs and reciting prayers in exchange for apples, money, and other treats. These customs blended with the older Celtic traditions and morphed over time into our modern notions of All Hallows' Eve, better known as Halloween.

In the United States, the idea of donning costumes didn't catch on for quite some time. Victorian notions of morality discouraged raucous or nonconforming behavior, so Halloween was primarily celebrated privately with little community acknowledgment or involvement. Though private Halloween celebrations were common in the first decades of the 1900s in the United States, especially in Irish settlements, it wasn't until the early 1930s that store-bought costumes became widely available. Despite a brief respite brought on by the sugar rationing of World War II, trick-or-treating had become a national institution within two decades, and the Halloween costume had become a must.

I've always enjoyed dressing up, whether it is for Halloween or any day. There is something special about the magick of dressing up for Halloween in particular, though, that makes it the most fun. Perhaps it's the sheer number of people wearing costumes on Halloween that creates an atmosphere of mystery and mayhem that's downright contagious. Perhaps it's the opportunity to see and be seen wearing our most outrageous or extravagant or unexpected apparel. Perhaps it's simply the surprise of it all, the mystery of who lurks behind the mask. Dressing up in costume is empowering. With a simple mask or other guise, we become the very monsters we fear and the goddesses and heroes we wish to be. A costume can be a gateway to the magickal realm, transforming its wearer into something more than they are, something bigger or brighter or more fearsome and ferocious. Of course, a costume can also be just a bit of fun, encouraging playfulness and imagination—two qualities that incidentally prove very helpful in the magickal arts. Even for those unaware of the reality of magick, wearing a costume at Halloween provides the means for using fashion more intentionally, and thus more magickally. We think about the effect that a particular costume might produce. Do we want others to fear us or delight in us? Do we want to be mysterious or hilarious? Sweet and sexy or strange and creepy? The costumes we select do indeed have their magickal effects, whether or not the wearer is aware of the phenomenon. With so many "everyday" people utilizing fashion in more magickal, intentional ways than usual, it's no wonder that this time of year sparks within us our most imaginative and original ideas. From the silly and secular to the mystical and magickal, the costumes I choose each have their own form and function to best accompany different holiday activities and traditions.

At my house, Samhain dominates the whole month of October. While I'm admittedly a bit on the sloppy side in housekeeping and fashion, nothing *typically* motivates me to clean up both the house and myself like the promise of getting out all my spookiest decorations. I don my favorite cone-shaped witch's hat, complete with a wide brim and glittery orange spiderweb accents, to help kick the festive spirit into gear. The hat makes me feel almost comical, as I putter around the house arranging candles, brooms, cauldrons, and potion bottles like the stereotypical witch someone might see in a Halloween cartoon. Some might say I go a little overboard in the decorations department. I mean, I have bins of the stuff, in addition to all the magickal little extras that I pull out and display this time of year. I'm not sure what the neighbors think, but at least the kids don't seem to mind.

One of my most special "decorations" is an altar to the dead that I erect anew each October. I cover a portion of the mantle above my fireplace with a black cloth, and upon it I place photographs and mementos of my family and friends who are no longer living. I also place upon the altar fresh flowers and a glass of red wine or sometimes a cup of coffee, because I feel the spirits might enjoy these, or at least appreciate the gesture. Each day, I write a short note to one of my deceased loved ones and I place this on the altar. It helps me feel close, as if their spirits are with me and listening. I feel like it's a good way to show that I still care about them and that they are not forgotten.

Another essential Samhain decoration at my house is the jack-o'-lantern. Well, okay, maybe it's more like five jack-o'-lanterns. Originally carved not from pumpkins but from turnips and other tubers, jack-o'-lanterns are believed to help light the way for the wandering dead so they might more easily come calling. While my kids create jack-o'-lanterns that take the form of everything from pandas to puking pumpkins, I keep mine traditional with circular eyes, a triangle nose, and a friendly but jagged-toothed smile.

When Samhain finally arrives, I very much enjoy having a daytime picnic in the graveyard with friends both living and dead. For this activity, I again employ the magick of costume by painting my face like a skull in the traditional Día de los Muertos (Day of the Dead) style. I cover my whole face in grayish-white makeup, and then I blacken my eyes with eyeliner and eyeshadow, darken my cheeks, and pencil on a wide skeletal grin. Samhain is a time to remember and acknowledge the fact that death is a journey we all must eventually make. When we dress as the dead, we're showing our deceased loved ones that we are still all in this together and that we too are skeletons—on the inside. My friends and I like to honor the unknown dead as well as our friends and ancestors. We bring fresh flowers to put on the lonelier graves, and we try to spruce up the place as best as we can, picking up any litter and brushing the dust and fungus off of neglected headstones.

After this, I usually stop by my youngest child's school for the classroom Halloween party, where I might arrive as a shy mouse, a friendly bear, a playful monkey, or a cute kitty, depending on my mood. I love to dress up as animals! It makes me feel young again, little again—yet big and powerful all at the same time. Slipping on an animal costume instantly transports us to the primal realm, free from the constraints that typically come with wearing a human face.

It suddenly becomes semi-acceptable to grunt and growl, to bark and sing and purr, and to leap and run and roar as we assume our chosen character.

After a dinner of mashed sweet potatoes, black beans, spinach, and pumpkin pie that is eaten by candlelight, trick-or-treating dominates the evening. For this I go as my witchy self, usually with a long black dress, magickal jewelry, and somewhat elaborate makeup. I put on my makeup with magick in mind, lining my eyes in black to accentuate their darkness and adding a touch of enchanted glitter to my cheekbones to help cast the magickal aura I am aiming to project all the further. These days I draw a black widow spider on my cheek, just like my mom did every Halloween until she died. I feel like this symbol helps put me in touch with her spirit, allowing her to walk with me more easily on this sacred night. Sometimes I decorate my arms with the names of other deceased loved ones so they too might be invited to venture out with us for some trick-or-treating fun. I'm blessed to live in a neighborhood where even adults are often given candy, and where many a fool leave their candy dishes attended only by a "help yourself" sign! I try not to take advantage *too* much, but I usually end up with a good-sized handful or two of tasty goodies just for me.

After the fun of trick-or-treating, we return home and I contemplate the night of magick that lies ahead as the kids binge on candy. I try to make a plan and gather any ritual tools or magickal ingredients I might need, so I'll be ready for action as soon as the kids crash and I can count on some time uninterrupted. I wash off my makeup and put on additional jewelry, some of my older and more magickal pieces that I prefer not to wear out and about for fear of losing them. What I do for a ritual depends on my mood, current needs, and location. I usually do something a little different each year. Often I perform a masked ritual. Though a disguise in itself, a mask helps us strip away and step out of the other masks we wear, be they addictions, fears, insecurities, phony personalities, or other limiting beliefs and behaviors. Couple the potential of costume with the fact that there are friendly dead roaming among us just waiting to lend a helping hand, albeit a spectral hand, and you have a recipe for some powerful magick. Samhain is the perfect time to embrace and utilize the magick of masquerade and mediumship to your advantage. Try the Samhain ritual on page 43 to help you let go of fear, insecurity, or other blockages that are holding you back.

Cosmic Sway

April Elliott Kent

COMING JUST AFTER A New Moon in Scorpio, this Samhain is particularly rich in magic and imagination. The Sun is in an easy trine aspect to Neptune, and the power for summoning is strong—look for what you want to be brought to you after Neptune turns direct on November 19.

With Venus connected to Jupiter and Uranus, this is the right time to let go of past lovers and invite new ones to enter your life. Just beware of settling for what is familiar and comfortable instead of conjuring something extraordinary! Venus's square aspect to Mars on November 1 suggests lovers at odds, a battle of the sexes; you can be at peace together again by the time Venus trines Mars on November 26—but first, you must confront some deep hurts, secrets, or power struggles as Venus conjoins Pluto on November 22.

The Sun makes a conjunction with Saturn on November 24, and energy will likely be low or blocked in the weeks leading up to the exact aspect. Cooperate with Saturn by focusing on the long game; make gestures toward productivity and goal-setting, but don't expect success until after Thanksgiving.

Costume Changes

This Samhain season features more than the usual number of planetary sign changes. A planet changing signs is like an actor changing costumes; we feel the urge to "perform" that planet a little differently when it moves into a new sign.

The Sun, Mercury, Venus, and Mars all enter either Sagittarius, Capricorn, Aquarius, or Pisces between now and Yule. Sagittarius's costume is the bright, playful finery of Mardis Gras. Mercury in Sagittarius (Nov. 12–Dec. 2) encourages big thinking and grand ideas; the Sun in Sagittarius (Nov. 21–Dec. 21) insists that we can all be greater and do more than we think is possible.

Capricorn's costume is dark, simple, and serious. When Venus is in Capricorn (Nov. 11–Dec. 17), we are more serious, even businesslike in our personal interactions, and our taste runs toward classic style and things that are useful. Mercury in Capricorn (Dec. 2–Jan. 4, 2017), leading up to its first 2017 retrograde, promotes clear, careful, and systematic thinking.

Aquarius's costume is eccentric, with clashing patterns and unexpected touches, the costume of the wizard. Mars entering Aquarius (Nov. 8–Dec. 19) sets the stage for wizardry; but without enlightened command of your powers, you could end up like Mickey Mouse's apprentice sorcerer in *Fantasia*, who attempts some of his master's magic tricks but immediately loses control of them! Venus entering this sign (Dec. 17–Jan. 3) is advantageous for enjoying friendships, investigating new electronic gadgets, and indulging in pleasures that are quite different from what you would normally enjoy!

Finally, Pisces's costume is straight out of Stevie Nicks's wardrobe—flowing, gossamer, and sparkling. When we don Pisces's garb, we are ready to enter the world of enchantment. Mars here (Dec. 19–Jan. 28) can be frustrating for those who are pragmatic by nature, but enlightening for anyone who is prepared to let matters take their own—and often surprising—course.

Full Moon in Taurus—November 14, 2016

The Sun in Scorpio demands that we immerse ourselves in what is mysterious and unseen, and that can be a little bit frightening. But the Taurus Full Moon is the grounding response to Scorpio's call, tethering us to what is tangible and visible. "Feel free to explore other realms," Taurus reassures us. "When you come back, the Earth will be right back here where you left it." With Taurus's ruling planet, Venus, in capable Capricorn, part of what grounds us during this two-week period is the work that we do and the goals we've set for ourselves.

Grounding Exercise for the Taurus Full Moon

This one is simple, which is just how Taurus likes things: Find a bit of earth and get dirty! Walk barefoot on the beach and dig your toes in the sand. Finish clearing your garden and cover it with straw for the winter. Buy a potted plant and dig your fingers in the soil. Earth is made up of plants and animals and ancestors whose souls have passed into the invisible; it's what they've left behind to comfort, ground, and sustain us. Spending a little time in it is the best way to honor the Taurus Full Moon.

Sagittarius New Moon—November 29, 2016

Cuddled close to Saturn and in a hard aspect to Neptune, the Sun and Moon in Sagittarius send a blunt message at this New Moon: "Get real!" Neptune is the planet of faith, which lives in the heart; Sagittarius is the sign of belief in what can be understood with the mind. At this New Moon, create intentions related to truth. What are you hiding from yourself? From others? What are the tenets of your faith—as distinct from your religious beliefs—that is, what do you feel to be true about life without actually questioning it? As difficult as it may seem, be willing at this New Moon to question your faith.

Affirmations for the Sagittarius New Moon
I am honest with myself and with others.
I reach beyond my comfort zone to joyfully experience the unknown.
I embrace and am nourished by nature in all her forms.
When I am satisfied that I've examined all sides of a matter, I defend
my convictions with all my strength.

Full Moon in Gemini—December 13, 2016

The Gemini Full Moon, standing in opposition to both the Sun and Saturn, may find you feeling like a bird caught in a cage, facing intractable ideologues who insist on limiting your options to a single course of action. But this is not Gemini's way; Gemini Full Moon is the time to question everything.

Fortunately, the Full Moon also stands in a spectacular grand trine configuration with Mars in feisty, freedom-loving Aquarius and Jupiter in strategic Libra. Keeping busy and physically active along with a bit of traveling are the keys that will open your cage and set you free. This is one last opportunity to question your beliefs and convictions, to make sure you have really thought them through. Gemini's gift is flexibility, a quality that will serve you well at this Full Moon.

Gemini Full Moon Meditation

Most of us associate Gemini with communication—talking in particular. But this is the sign for listening, too. Like a bird flitting from flower to flower, Gemini's job is to gather information and insights and to spread them far and wide.

For this Full Moon meditation, choose one bird. What kind is it? Visualize its color, its size; listen for its song in your mind. Which trees does it prefer? Which flowers have the nectar this bird finds most delicious? Picture your avian friend in your garden, on your stoop, or perched on a wire outside your apartment building. It is listening; tell it your story. Then watch it fly away toward a distant land to share it with others.

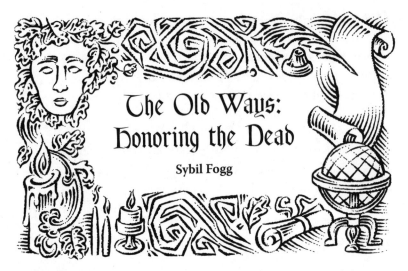

The Old Ways: Honoring the Dead

Sybil Fogg

SAMHAIN MARKS THE TRANSITION into the dark half of the year. The warm days are growing fewer and there is a marked crisp bite to the air. The nights are growing longer and we begin to turn our minds toward the darkness. And in the darkness, the veil becomes thin between the living world and where the spirits reside. Our thoughts move toward those who have come before us, those we have recently lost, and our ancestors. This is a good time of year to learn more about our family members of the past.

My father's family is of Lithuanian, Polish, Russian, or Belarusian descent. My great-grandfather came to America from a small village near Minsk in Belarus in 1913 or 1914. Whenever we wondered if we were Lithuanian or Polish (Belarus and Russian never seemed to be an option), we were told, "Take your pick." I don't really want to have to do that, so it seemed fitting to explore the Slavic region at Samhain and honor those ancestors from there. There is a wealth of culture and traditions from this area that are very pagan in their roots. The old ways are strong in this region of the world.

Samhain is the final of three harvest festivals. The weather at this time of year is often quite warm, lulling us before the storm of winter hits. This time of year was called Babie Lato in Polish, or

"Old Woman's Summer" (Hodorowicz Knab 219). This is when the fields were prepared for the long winter's rest and the final root vegetables gathered. As the earth went to rest, the year quieted down and people's thoughts turned inward, or even to the darker aspects of life and living—the end. The dark goddess roamed the land. In Poland she was known as Jagusia, Zośka, or Baśka.

> She was imagined to be a female, so tall and slender that she was unable to fit beneath the low ceiling of the cottages; thus she would stand outside the front door or before a window... This female was dressed in a white sheet, carried a scythe, and came three nights in a row, each time knocking on the window or door by way of giving notice. Nothing had the power to stay her since, if she wished, she could change shape and enter through the chimney or through a keyhole... No one escaped Death. (Hodorowicz Knab 257)

As frightening as she was, there were some clues to her looming. It was believed that a dog's howl announced her approach. If a bird flew into the house, a death was imminent. There was a belief that deaths occur in groups of three. If a mirror breaks, a death will follow. If a picture falls of a wall, a death in the house was coming. If an ill person hears a knocking, their death is imminent. Fortunately, the Polish also believe that the newly dead have various means of contacting the living soon after they have moved on. If a knock is heard or a door suddenly swings open, a newly deceased family member is reaching out (Anders-Silverman 56–57).

At the moment of death, a series of rituals involving the departing soul's protection began. The body was washed in an herbal bath (heated water filled with rue, myrtle, mugwort, or other herbs blessed for this occasion) so that the soul would be pristine for future travels. The deceased was then dressed in a "death shirt" that reached down to the ankles and must be made new without shedding tears, as crying would decimate the family line. A very tall hat, called a *duchna*, was made from the same material. Because knots were often used in curses and dark magic, the seamstress had to be careful to avoid knotting the thread as they worked.

Older men had black ribbons tied around their waist, neck, and wrists. Young men had green. Women's heads were covered with a kerchief. The very young or unmarried were dressed with red ribbons. The body was then immediately placed on a plank that was covered with straw and kept there for three days before being moved to the coffin. Finally, coins were placed in the hands of the departed so they would not have any reason to return.

It was believed that the soul stayed near the body for an unknown length of time, so comforts were left out where they would be easily found. These included furniture and food items. People would stop by and partake in the feast, sometimes staying for the duration of the wake.

꘎

The Lithuanian version of the death maiden is Giltinė. It was believed that she was a tall and gaunt blind woman carrying a scythe. She lurks at night and causes domestic animals to behave strangely as an announcement of her approach. Again, many odd occurrences announce death: bread will not bake properly, pictures and mirrors fall from crumbling walls, and people who dream of losing teeth are visited by dead relatives as they sleep.

Lithuanian funerals were often referred to as feasts for the souls of the dead. There was an abundance of flowing alcohol and food offerings to those who attended the funeral of their loved one. Offerings of beer were made to the goddess Žemyna at the onset of the funeral and then each person present was honored and offered their memories and condolences. The recently departed was regaled with songs and festivities. It was important to complete the feast of the funeral since it was considered ill omen to bring home any food ("Funeral Traditions").

It must be noted that these death maidens bear a strong resemblance to Russia's Baba Yaga, in the sense that they rule the darkest aspects of the year and part of life. The people of the old Slavic world accepted death and generally did not fear it. It was thought of as a natural progression through our time on the planet. Like the fertile and sleeping earth, we merely move from one realm to another.

Throughout the world, this time of year is often plagued with spooky stories and gatherings where people dress up and embrace the more frightening bumps in the night.

The Slavic countries are pregnant with folklore dedicated to the creatures of the night: werewolves, nightmares, vampires, ghosts, and ghouls factor heavily in their legends and myths. For instance, the Polish *zmora* or *mara* (where the word nightmare originated) is a kind of night woman who may take the form of a horse, but is the sleeping soul of a person that has left its body and feeds on the life force of others, causing fitful sleep and frightening dreams. As the nights grow longer and cooler and the veil thins, Samhain is the time of the year to embrace the darkness and celebrate the old ways of our people.

Bibliography

Anders Silverman, Deborah. *Polish-American Folklore.* Champaign: University of Illinois Press, 2000.

"Funeral Traditions," *Lithuanian Customs and Traditions*, accessed August 16, 2015. http://thelithuanians.com/bookanthology /funeral.html.

Hodorowicz Knab, Sophie. *Polish Customs, Traditions, & Folklore.* New York: Hippocrene Books, Inc., 1993.

Feasts and Treats

Linda Raedisch

WAIT! DON'T TURN THE page! I know what you are: you're a One Dish Witch and you're used to paging swiftly past the "Feasts and Treats" section of this almanac because you simply don't have time to cook. Thirty-minute meals are no help to you: you barely have thirty minutes to eat a meal, let alone prepare one, which is why none of this year's recipes are meant to keep you imprisoned in the kitchen for very long (except Ostara's Simnel Cake and Mabon's Chrysanthemum Tartlets). Many of the entrees require only one pot to cut down on the washing up.

No one did Halloween better than the Aztecs, whose autumnal Day of the Dead festivities thrive in modern Mexico as well as the American Southwest. Accordingly, I've chosen a Latin American theme for this year's Samhain menu, the first dish dedicated to Mexico's most famous ghost, La Llorona, or "the weeping woman."

I was introduced to the legend of La Llorona while I was living in Santa Fe, New Mexico. According to the version I heard, La Llorona drowned her two children in a river so she might be free to run away with a handsome Spanish soldier. The soldier soon spurned her, and the repentant mother has been haunting riverbanks in search of her lost children ever since. You'll know she's around when you hear the sound of inconsolable weeping. La Llorona is usually portrayed with a cascading black lace mantilla and, of course, a sodden handkerchief.

If there's a lesson to be learned from her story, it might be this: if La Llorona had had canned goods and cake mixes available to her, maybe she wouldn't have burned out on housekeeping in the first place!

Posole á La Llorona

No humans were harmed in the development of this recipe. But they might have been. I have heard that the original Aztec *posole*, a stew of parched corn, chilies, and meat, was originally made with human meat—the flesh of prisoners of war—and consumed in a ritual context. I have also heard that it's a popular cure for a New Year's Day hangover. Since Samhain is the Witches' New Year, I figured there's no better dish to keep warming on the stove throughout this sabbat. I'm sure La Llorona would have enjoyed cooking posole for her children before things went so terribly wrong.

Prep time: 25 minutes
Cook time: 45 minutes
Servings: 8

In the pot:
1 garlic clove, minced
½ small yellow onion, chopped
2 tablespoons olive oil
½ pound boneless pork rib meat or boneless pork chops, cut into half-inch cubes
Modest dash salt
Dash black pepper
¼ teaspoon ground chipotle chili
1 teaspoon curry powder
2 cups water
1 5.5-ounce can tomato juice
1 6-gram cube chicken bouillon

2 15-ounce cans white hominy, rinsed and drained (This is the posole or parched corn, but the can will probably say "hominy.")
1 4.25-ounce can diced green chilies

Toppings:
1 small lime
Grated Monterey Jack or Mexican blend cheese
Chopped fresh cilantro leaves

In a large, heavy pot, sauté garlic and onion in olive oil. Add pork
and seasonings and sauté until meat cubes are browned on all sides.
Add water and tomato juice. Bring to boil, add bouillon cube, and
then turn down to simmer. Add hominy and green chilies and let
simmer uncovered 45 minutes, stirring occasionally.

Not salty enough? Ask La Llorona to weep a little into the pot
when she passes through the kitchen.

Before serving, top each bowl with a squirt of lime, cilantro, and
grated cheese.

Horchata

Posole and chocolate cake would be impossible without corn, chilies, and chocolate—all crops native to Central America. The following recipe, however, originated in Spain. Horchata varies throughout
Latin America, but as far as I know they are all rice-based. Mexican
horchata always seems to contain cinnamon.

Having tried to do it myself and found it very messy, I think the
real reason La Llorona weeps is because she had to pound, soak,
and strain the rice to make horchata. Now there is an easier way!

Prep time: 5 minutes
Chill time: 2 hours
Servings: 6–8

½ cup sugar
2 cups plain unsweetened rice milk
2 cups plain unsweetened almond milk
½ teaspoon vanilla

¼ teaspoon cinnamon

Zest of ½ small lime (The zest is the green part of the peel which you can grate off with a cheese grater.)

Large jar with tight-fitting lid, or blender pitcher

Put all ingredients in jar or blender. Secure lid tightly and shake or blend vigorously. Chill for at least 2 hours, then serve in glasses over ice. If you want, grate a little more lime zest over each glass.

Horchata tastes best cold cold cold! But you don't want to be nursing a glass at a party only to find that your ice cubes have melted, diluting the sweet ricey goodness of your horchata. In order to prevent such misfortune, freeze a little of the horchata in an ice cube tray and use in place of ice cubes. Nor would a lump of vanilla ice cream go amiss.

Flanzana Cake

Flanzana: that's "flan" plus "manzana." *Manzana* is Spanish for "apple." *Flan* is Spanish for "flan," a sweet pudding you bake in the oven. Supposedly, the very best flan is made by Mexican nuns. Let's see if the Witches can give them a run for their money! This recipe is for a flan-topped cake because a cake is easier to pack up and take to a Halloween potluck than a sticky, quavering flan. As for the manzanas, well, what's Halloween without apples?

Prep time: 25 minutes

Bake time: 15 minutes for apples plus 45 minutes for cake

Servings: 8

Butter for greasing

1½ Golden Delicious apples

White sugar for sprinkling

6 large eggs (3 for flan and 3 for cake batter)

1 12-ounce can evaporated milk

1 14-ounce can sweetened condensed milk

½ teaspoon vanilla

1 box yellow cake mix

Water
Vegetable oil
9-inch layer cake pan
Electric mixer

Preheat oven to 300 degrees F. Line layer cake pan with nonstick foil. Generously grease bottom. (Yes, even though it's nonstick!)

Peel, core, and slice the apples into thin wedges. Place in cake pan, turning each one over so that all wedges are buttery on both sides. Arrange them artfully in one layer, overlapping as little as possible, sprinkle with sugar and bake for 15 minutes.

Set pan with apples aside to cool.

Now for the flan part: In a large bowl, beat eggs, evaporated milk, condensed milk, and vanilla with electric mixer until frothy, about 2 minutes. Mixture will be thin. No need to wash beaters: you can use them to mix the cake batter.

Pour flan over apples in cake pan. Set aside and preheat oven to 325 degrees F.

Prepare cake batter according to instructions on box (typically requiring eggs, water, and, oil). Pour just enough batter over flan to cover it. What to do with the rest of the cake batter? See the following recipe: La Malinche cake.

Bake Flanzana cake for 45 minutes or until top is golden brown.

Cool for 10 minutes, then turn pan over onto cake plate and remove foil. Slice and serve warm or at room temperature.

La Malinche Cake

According to some versions of the story, the original La Llorona was, in life, none other than La Malinche, an Aztec princess who became the mistress of Spanish conquistador Hernán Cortés. As an Aztec, La Malinche would have taken her chocolate a little bit spicy, a little bit smoky, and not too sweet, like the vein of chocolate in this cake. This cake came about as a way of using up the batter left over from the Flanzana cake. If you have decided to skip the Flanzana cake, you can go ahead and make a whole yellow cake mix, increasing the chocolate to 2 ounces and adding a pinch more cinnamon and chili powder. One yellow cake mix will make enough to fill 2 layer cake pans, giving you two La Malinche cakes.

Prep time: 15 minutes
Bake time: 30 minutes
Servings: 8

1 8-inch or 9-inch layer cake pan
½ tablespoon butter plus a little more for greasing
Leftover yellow cake batter from Flanzana cake recipe (see above)
1 ounce unsweetened baking chocolate
¼ teaspoon vanilla extract
½ teaspoon cinnamon
One small pinch chipotle chili powder

Grease cake pan and pour about half the leftover cake batter in it. Set aside and preheat oven to 350 degrees F.

In a small pot over very low heat, melt butter and chocolate, watching all the while. You can turn off the heat before the chocolate has melted, stirring until it is completely melted. Stir in vanilla, cinnamon, and chili powder. Give it a little taste to see if you dare add more chili powder. Pour remaining cake batter into pot and stir until well blended.

Spoon chocolate batter in blobs over yellow batter, swirling it in with the tip of a knife for a marbled effect.

Bake for 30 minutes or until knife inserted in center comes out clean. Let cool for 10 minutes, then turn out onto cake plate, marbled top up.

Crafty Crafts

Mickie Mueller

GROWING UP, ONE OF my first tools for divination was the popular novelty item the Magic 8 Ball. I would ask questions to the over-sized black billiard ball, rubbing it thoughtfully, shaking it up, and flipping it over breathlessly to see what wisdom it had to offer from the dice floating in its inky depths.

"Does Charlie like me?"

Reply hazy, try again.

Like many of the witches I know, Samhain is one of my all-time favorite sabbats. Back when we were kids, it was Halloween we were celebrating—outside under the moon, pointy witch hat in place, believing in the power of our own magical masked alter-ego to protect us from things that went bump in the night. Now we're grown-up witches celebrating the sabbat of Samhain, honoring our ancestors, working divination, and pointy hats are optional. During the time of the thin veil, divination is a very popular activity, and while we might have our standard tarot cards, crystal gazing, or pendulums, here's a new fun item you can add to your celebration that might just let your inner child out to play a bit.

Magic Divination Witch Bottle

Our device will not take the form of an 8 Ball, but that's okay. The precursor for the ball-shaped curio was actually invented in 1944 and was called a Syco Seer, which was closer to the shape of our Magic Divination Witch Bottle.

Time to complete: about 1 hour

Cost: $8 to $11 (if you already have a hot glue gun and paintbrushes, and print your own scrapbook pages)

Supplies

A small wide-mouth bottle (like the bottled coffee drinks come in, or an old-fashioned milk bottle with lid)

Green dry floral foam (not the wet kind that absorbs water)

2 mm foam sheets

Hot glue gun

Black food coloring

Distilled water

Glitter (optional)

Halloween scrapbook paper of your choice

Découpage medium

Fine tip permanent marker

Paintbrush

If you're using an iced coffee bottle, first consume that delish latte or Frappuccino, yum! Now wash out the bottle. Once your project is complete, you won't see anything but the cap and the base, so if there are expiration date numbers on the very bottom, you'll want to remove them with a little nail polish remover.

After using a straight edge to trace the line with a pencil or pen, use a serrated knife to carefully cut a one-inch cube out of the floral foam. Take a sheet of foam and use a ruler to measure out six squares, marking each one ¾" × ¾" with a pencil or pen. Carefully cut out the squares with a pair of scissors. Using the fine-tip permanent marker, write one answer on each square as neatly as you can. I used two positive answers, two negative answers, and two maybe answers, such as: *yes, count on it, no, not likely, maybe, ask again later.*

Carefully apply a square of hot glue to one side of the foam cube, then quickly glue on one of the foam squares with a *yes* answer written on it. Flip the cube over and repeat gluing the other *yes* answer on the opposite side of the cube. Glue on the *no* answers in the same way and then again with the *maybe* answers, until the cube is covered. Then put the cube aside.

Flip the bottle upside down on a piece of the craft foam and use an ink pen to trace around the mouth of the bottle. Carefully cut out the circle you just traced with a pair of scissors and push it inside the lid of the bottle. This is an important step as it creates a gasket that will keep the bottle from leaking. Put the bottle in the sink. Now fill the bottle to the top with distilled water and add three or four drops of black food coloring. Now is the time to add a bit of glitter if you want. Any color will do, and all you need is a pinch. If you don't have glitter but you want to add a bit of sparkle, use a pair of scissors and cut up some aluminum foil into tiny bits and drop them in. Now, put the cube in the bottle. It will bob around at the top, and that's just fine; just make sure the water goes all the way to the rim of the bottle as full as you can get it. Tightly screw the lid with the foam gasket in place onto the bottle and wipe the bottle dry. Now you're ready to decorate it.

You can use Halloween scrapbook paper from the store or, with a little research, you can find some nice ones online. There are some artists who create free printable scrapbook paper so this can be an inexpensive and simple option if you have a color printer. Tear a strip along the edge of the decorative paper about an inch wide. Then tear that strip into one-inch squares, retaining the one straight edge while the other edges are torn. Paint the bottle just under the edge of the bottle cap and about an inch or so down the bottle with découpage medium. Apply the torn paper, lining the straight edges up against the top of the bottle, overlapping the paper so there aren't any gaps in between. Repeat this on the bottom of the bottle,

lining up straight edges around the bottom edge. Leave the base of the bottle clear and uncovered so when you tip the bottle upside down, the foam cube pops up and you can read it. Tear the rest of the paper up and continue covering the entire bottle (except the very bottom) with découpage medium and squares of torn paper. Once you get past the curved parts of the bottle, you can use pieces larger than an inch, so if you have cool pictures on your scrapbook paper like big spider webs, skulls, or something, they will show on the middle of the bottle. When you're done, paint a coating of découpage medium all over the bottle. You can cut a piece of paper in a circle to cover the top of the bottle cap and découpage it on in the same way you did the rest of the bottle. Allow the bottle to dry.

You can then make a label for the bottle out of some of the scrapbook paper. Either hand write or print a label that says something like "Witch Bottle Oracle." You can either découpage it onto the bottle or punch a hole in it and tie it on. You can decorate your

bottle more if you like: glue gems on, tie a ribbon or raffia around the neck, and add charms to make it unique and fun.

Set it on a shelf next to your other Samhain décor. Ask your bottle a yes or no question as you shake it. When you flip it upside down, the answer will appear!

All One Family

Dallas Jennifer Cobb

As a younger woman, single and childless, I regularly went to rituals on Samhain, the most important of the greater sabbats. I loved communing with the spirits, honoring the dead, and making peace with the demons of my past. The rituals enabled me to converse with my shadow and understand the power of dark emotions. I remembered what I'd survived and felt assured that I'd survive hardship again in the future. I was aware of my own continuation of life, reminded that "just because something's come to an end doesn't mean it ceases to exist." Everything shifts and changes, but some small part of it always remains.

Change—that's the theme that binds these "All One Family" articles together. Over time, with changes in my family structure, my Pagan practice has changed. But the ghosts of my past dwell within me, and at Samhain they speak. As I write this, I am in touch with all the witches I've ever been.

When I had a child, my Pagan practice took a backseat to parenting. I devoted time to facilitating my daughter's trick-or-treat practice: making costumes and preparing treats. Sure, I worked some Pagan beliefs into the mainstream practice of Hallowe'en, recounting the story of Demeter and Persephone and reminding my daughter that the veils between the worlds were thin. But Samhain had changed into Hallowe'en, which was marked by going door-to-door requesting treats. Later, after my child was in bed, I did a small ritual, made an offering at the crossroads, and left treats for the roaming spirits.

Fast forward. These days, I'm living with a teenager and the scales of balance are shifting again. I'm rejoining large community-based rituals so beloved to my Pagan practice. As she becomes older and more independent, I can leave my daughter alone and go out. Sometimes she comes with me and sometimes she chooses not to.

Last Samhain as we carved pumpkins, she actually prompted me: "Tell me about Demeter and Persephone." Something has stayed the same, but everything else about the sabbat had changed. I didn't help her with a costume or go out with her. She spent the evening with friends, all dressed like zombie cheerleaders. Scary! They did some trick-or-treating, but were most engaged by a haunted house at the local abattoir. Their childish taste for sweets was replaced by a desire for thrill and fright. Gone was the little girl, replaced by a teenage shapeshifter.

As my daughter turns more toward her friends, I find it important to consciously create time to connect. That teen tendency toward individuation need not be alienation or isolation from parents, but it takes effort and thought from me to create time and space to connect.

With each sabbat as an anchoring point, I'll explore ways to stay connected with our teenagers as they are changing while sharing the Pagan practice. The practices offered for sabbat activities are easy and don't require special tools or supplies. If you're like me, it needs to be simple, or it simply won't happen. Let's make magic part of our daily lives with our teenagers.

❧

The sabbats offer eight finite points to consciously connect using ritual, symbolism, and engaged rites of passage. The Wheel of the Year represents a full cycle of the seasons and the sacred cycle of birth, life, death, and rebirth. Celebrating both the greater and lesser sabbats facilitates an understanding of beginnings and endings, balance and extremes, God and Goddess, and spirit and body.

If you're like me, you love your teenagers even when they seem possessed by evil spirits. And you need to welcome more magic back into your own life post-babying. With a bit of luck, and some of the ideas included in "All One Family," we can accomplish both and acknowledge the growing, changing, and individuating teenager in our midst.

I don't need to force my Pagan practice on my daughter, but I don't need to hide it either. When she was a "tween," she grew uncomfortable with my Pagan practice. Fitting in became more important than time with Mum. She resisted attending community rituals and celebration, events she previously loved. I was saddened, but I accepted her choice.

But lately, now that she's in her teen years, she's turned back toward me and toward the Pagan path. Maybe it's the recurring themes in much of modern teen literature and movies (vampires, witches, shapeshifters, and more), or maybe it's the rebellious need to move away from mainstream beliefs. It hardly matters. What matters is that there was an opening for me to connect with my daughter in a fun, meaningful, and sacred way. So I grabbed it. Like Demeter, I need to remember that my daughter may travel away from me, but she will also come back.

Practice: Loss and Love

Samhain is a great night to connect with teenagers. At an age when they know they aren't kids anymore, many feel reticent to celebrate Hallowe'en. They're too cool to put on costumes and too old to trick-or-treat.

This Samhain, recount the story of Demeter and Persephone. Talk about letting go of what we love, of loss, grief, and the resulting pain. Perhaps teens will identify with letting go of their "child self," the loss of innocence or the end of trick-or-treating. Invite them to pour the emotions into a pumpkin by carving a sad, tortured face.

Working together, one pumpkin each, scrape the seeds out, saying:

"The seeds represent Persephone, separated from Demeter. She's all alone." Separate the seeds from the stringy pumpkin mass, wash, and place in a bowl.

"But she's protected by her mother's love." Drizzle olive oil lightly over the seeds.

"Blessed by Demeter's salty tears." Sprinkle with sea salt. Stir.

"Persephone prepares to descend"—place seeds on parchment paper on a cookie sheet—"into the darkness." Place sheet in the oven at 300 degrees F for 45 minutes.

Then, as you turn to the task of carving pumpkins, gently ask: "What do you miss about being a child? What do you feel like you have lost? What do you mourn for?" Then just listen.

"Let's carve all those feelings of grief and loss into the faces of our pumpkins."

There is nothing quite so scary as knowingly choosing to leave behind the carefree innocence of childhood, and a ritual can help with big life transitions while marking the rite of passage. Let your teen pour those feelings into the face of the pumpkin so it becomes extra gruesome.

Later, when the seeds are cooked, share them, saying: "With every ending comes the promise of a new beginning."

As you eat, talk more about loss: ancestors who have died, friends who have left, classmates who have moved away, and lost loves and lost innocence. Hold one pumpkin seed and recount the sacred cycle: "A seed sprouts, grows, makes vines, leaves, flowers, and fruit. It is harvested, withers, and dies. Only then can it compost and be reborn as a tiny seed."

And remind your teens that regardless of what lies ahead of them in life, your love will be there for them, just like the fierce love of Demeter. That wherever they journey, your love will follow.

Samhain Ritual: Thirteen Wishes

Melanie Marquis

THIS RITUAL WILL ENABLE you to summon spirits of the dead in order to communicate with them, enlist their aid in breaking through any challenges and limitations you currently face, and to help make your wishes come true. Perform it on Samhain night, preferably in a graveyard or other haunted location for best results.

Items Needed

13 black tea light candles
1 small cauldron
1 sanitized sewing needle
9 strands black dog or cat hair (responsibly sourced by petting the
   animal, not yanked out or cut off)
1 charcoal block
Matches or a lighter
1 dried bay leaf
1 pinch dried mugwort
1 pinch dried sage
1 small piece dried mushroom
1 pinch dried marigold blossoms

Photographs, clothing, mementos, or other relics to represent the
   dead (optional)
1 mask, any variety
13 small scraps of paper
1 pen or pencil
13 small clear quartz crystals
1 goblet of water, wine, beer, or liquor

Arrange the thirteen black candles in a circle surrounding you. Place
the cauldron in the center. Light the candles. Prick your fingertip
with the sanitized needle and allow three drops of blood to fall into
the cauldron. Place nine strands of black cat or dog hair on top of
the blood, applying gentle pressure and stirring it up a bit until
the hairs are fully coated. Now is the time to evoke any deities or
other entities you choose to work with. You might call on the aid
of Hecate, Morrigan, Anubis, Kali Ma, or any other powers associated with darkness and death. Use a traditional evocation for summoning the deity of choice, or simply ask in your own words for the
entity to lend you its presence and aid. To call on Hecate, I use the
following evocation:

> *Hecate, Hecate!*
> *Lady of Darkness, I call on you!*
> *Hecate!*
> *Darkest Goddess!*
> *My mother!*
> *I call on you!*
> *Be here with me now and help me!*
> *I am your child and you are my mother!*
> *You are the queen of death and the night!*
> *Lady of Magick! Lady of Darkness!*
> *Hecate! Hecate! Hecate!*
> *Dark Mother, I call on you!*

Once you sense the presence of any entities you're evoking, it's
time to move on to the next stage of the ritual. Place the charcoal

block inside the cauldron on top of the blood and animal hair and light it on fire. Once the surface is glowing, blow out the flame. Take a pinch of the bay, mugwort, sage, mushroom, and marigold, and crumble it in your hand as you think of your intention. Your intention might be to contact a particular loved one who has passed on, or you might simply wish to commune with any spirits who are present and so inclined. State your intention as clearly as possible as you sprinkle the dried herbs onto the charcoal block.

Sit quietly as the herbs smolder. Think of your desire for an interaction with a spirit, your expectation that an apparition will appear. Wake up your senses and observe your surroundings. Do you sense any spirits present? If it's a particular spirit you are wishing to contact, try uttering its name followed by the plea, "Come to me!" If you've brought along any photographs or personal relics belonging to the dead with whom you are aiming to connect, hold these in your hands as you ask for the spirit to reveal itself. This revelation may come in the form of sights, smells, sounds, or sensations. Be open and aware, alert to any changes in the surrounding environment or in the thoughts and feelings that come to you. Spirit shows itself in many ways, and we can communicate with spirit in many ways, also. You may want to just sit quietly for a while and be open to any experiences that come to you, allowing any spirits present to express themselves however they will. You might pose questions to the spirit, asking for guidance regarding your fears, doubts, and dilemmas while paying attention to the answers you may receive in the way of visions or voices that seem to originate from outside your mind yet permeate it all the same.

For more detailed or precise communication, you might try utilizing a pendulum, spirit board, or tarot deck. To use the pendulum, suspend it between your thumb and forefinger, letting it dangle above the cauldron. Allow the pendulum to become still, then ask for any spirits present to make themselves known through your magickal device. If the pendulum starts moving to indicate the presence of a spirit, ask the spirit to show you "yes," and note the motion of the pendulum. Then ask the spirit to show you "no," and note the pendulum's course of movement. You may now pose "yes" or "no" questions to the spirit, allowing the pendulum to become still between each query while concentrating your attention intently to help ensure the clearest answers possible.

If you're working with a spirit board, place your fingertips on the planchette and wait for the spirit to guide it. The spirit may have plenty to say on its own, or you may want to ask questions to prompt more detailed responses. Respect the individual spirit with which you are communicating; for best results, be interested but not too pushy in what it has to say.

If a tarot deck is your tool of choice, spread the cards out in a loose pile and ask the spirit to guide your hands. You might pose questions and select cards to obtain the spirit's response, or you might simply select whichever cards you feel led to draw and interpret the messages accordingly.

Once you've finished communicating, whether through tarot cards, spirit board, pendulum, or other means, ask the spirit or spirits to stick around to help you in the magick you are about to cast. Put on the mask you've chosen. Any mask will do. You might simply tie on a piece of solid cloth that you can see and breathe through, or you might choose a ready-made masquerade mask, Zorro style. You might create your own mask that represents the very fears and doubts you are aiming to remove through the ritual. With your disguise in place, write on each of the thirteen slips of paper a fear, doubt, insecurity, or other issue that is holding you back from being all you can be. Pick up each slip of paper one at a time, read over it, and think about it objectively. How does each particular fear, doubt, or other issue prevent you from living life to the fullest? What is the cost of continuing to harbor this energy in your life? What would you advise someone else who had the same issue? Would you advise them to continue letting fear paralyze them, or would you urge the person to let go of these baneful patterns and move forward? Can you give yourself the same love and encouragement? Allow your desire to be done with this problem, and let desire flood your mind and heart. Light the corner of the paper in the flame of the northernmost candle, then quickly toss it into the cauldron. As the paper burns, you might think to yourself or say out loud:

This is nothing more than a mask I've worn, and I am no longer willing to wear it!

Repeat for each piece of paper, lighting each inscribed slip with a different candle until you've used every candle in the full circle.

Face the cauldron and say in your own words something to the effect of:

I am ready to let go of these fears!
I am ready to move past these blocks!
I am ready to break through these walls!
I am ready to take off these masks and be who I am!

Strip off the mask and cast it aside. Affirm that it is now a new era and you are ready to move forward. Now turn your attention to the thirteen crystals. Pick them up one at a time, and speak to each crystal a wish. Think of something positive you would like in your life, perhaps something to fill the space of the fear or doubt you have just disintegrated. You might think of thirteen different wishes, one for each crystal, or you might simply repeat a single wish thirteen times. As you make your wishes, place each crystal in the wax of one of the thirteen candles, starting at the north and again making the full circuit. Sit quietly and enjoy the peace of the moment as you wait for the candles and the smoldering mixture in the cauldron to burn down and extinguish themselves. Thank the spirits for their presence, then pour some water, beer, liquor, or wine on the ground to further express your gratitude.

Notes

Yule

Alban Arthan: The Midwinter Solstice

Kristoffer Hughes

THE MULCH OF LEAF and bark crunches beneath his feet as each footfall—felt, sensed, and intentional—calls to the land. Skeletal trees bathed in the shadows of pre-dawn stand as silent sentinels, sleepy witnesses to the changing color of the sky. Where the trees part, they frame the distant mountains. White mists clothe their cold feet, and above their heads a pale gold appears and the rays of the midwinter sun gleam brightly. Into a cauldron of iron the man casts a handful of herbs, and as the smoke rises, words of praise, of hope, and gratitude tremble from his lips.

This is the beginning... anticipation and the silence before the dawning of light. This is the true beginning of the Celtic year, for within the period of greatest darkness hides the potential of light, the promise of hope, of new life and growth. This is difficult to comprehend when the majority of nature slumbers, protected against the merciless energy of winter, the cold, frost, ice, and snow.

The old standing stones upon the moor wait in expectation of a new dawn. The memories of ancestors swim within them as they recall generations of people who flocked to them in anticipation of the sun's rebirth. A hum of energy streams through the sacred landscape as the sun begins its journey toward the north.

This is the beginning... for upon the dawn of the winter solstice it all happens in a moment, and light is victorious, and death and darkness flee before the tiny bright ball that rises on the distant horizon. Slowly we emerge from the womb and tomb of the Samhain season, blinking in the new light that struggles to gain a foothold on the brightening horizon, and we turn our faces to greet the dawn and embark upon the journey of birthing.

Alban Arthan—A Druid Feast

The festival of Midwinter in the Welsh Celtic tradition is referred to as Alban Arthan, which marks the beginning of the season of hope, the initiation of the period of light and growth. It begins at dawn, normally on or around the 21st of December each year as the sun enters the astrological sign of Capricorn. In Celtic lore, the ancestors began the year on the morrow of the shortest day of the winter, that is, on the turn of the sun. This is the day of Alban Arthan or Midwinter Day. This Welsh, Druidic term for the season was coined by the legendary Iolo Morganwg in his 18th-century collection of bardic wonders, *Barddas,* and is now commonly used throughout the Druidic and Pagan movement to denote this festival.

The term itself is split into two components: *alban,* meaning "high point, regal, or supreme," suggesting that the four Albans are the peaks or topmost sections of any season. They are the crescendo of energy, and the orgasmic climax of a particular cycle. *Arthan* is derived from *arth,* meaning "bear," and refers to the constellation Ursa Minor (the little bear) that holds Polaris, the pole star, within its constellation. Coincidentally, the Ursid meteor showers have been visible from the northern hemisphere for the past century during the time of the winter solstice.

Alban Arthan heralds the midpoint of winter, and as the wheel sighs to a stop, the land falls under an ancient spell of silence and anticipation. The festivals that have long since marked this season have a myriad of names: Yule, Winter Solstice, Hanukkah, Kwanzaa, and Mistletide. They may be cultures apart, but they all share a commonality in that they invoke the powers of hope, warmth, and community. In the bleak midwinter, lights are hung about houses and trees or anything permanent enough to be adorned and decorated with festive cheer. But why do we do it? What is actually going on behind the scenes and between the words that we associate with the winter holiday season?

The Dance of Earth and Sun

It is remarkable to consider that our blue planet is three million miles closer to the sun during the dead of winter than it is in the height of summer. Poles apart, the northern hemisphere succumbs to the grip of winter, the southern hemisphere bathes in warm sunlight. So how can we be closer to the sun when we are in the grip of cold and darkness?

The magic of our planet's peculiar orbital dance around the sun has little to do with the seasons here on earth. Our planet does not orbit the sun in an upright position but instead she pole dances, literally! Her poles turn their countenance to greet the sun, bowing their white faces toward or away from our star at a staggering tilt of twenty three and a half degrees. It is this exquisite dance of our poles that is the reason for the seasons. Our distance from the sun itself is of no consequence.

On the stage of life, and in the drama of the seasons, it is the magic of movement that turns the Wheel of the Year. During the height of midwinter, the earth reaches the furthest extent of her tilt away from the sun. She is almost leaning on her back, with the North Pole staring out into the depth of space; here the sun does not rise, and the nights bite long and cold. But further south we experience the delicious cold pinks of sunrise and sunsets, colors that are influenced by the angle of our planet and our view of the light.

The incoming solar energy is greatest in the southern hemisphere around December the 21st, and it is at its weakest in the northern hemisphere. It is this energy that is responsible for the magic of life here on our blue planet. And this is what we are moved to celebrate during the midpoint of winter.

When the Sun Stands Still

The word "solstice" is derived from two Latin words, *sol*, meaning "sun," and *sistere*, meaning "to stand still," which is exactly what appears to happen. At your locale, chart the rising of the sun each morning during the weeks following Samhain. As the year nears its midwinter point, you will notice that for around three days the sun appears to stop at a certain point on your horizon. This is the solstice phenomenon, the point where nature itself seems to hold its breath. Will it or won't it? Will the sun move again? Will it turn on its heels and journey once more and bring summer?

It was this element of the unknown that caused our ancestors to erect enormous temple structures that marked the passage of the sun and its declination at the winter solstice. In our increasingly cynical world, our society pays little heed to the movement of the sun, our technologies have served to distance us from the songs of the seasons. In our centrally heated homes, stockpiled with food transported from the farthest reaches of the globe, we are secure in our technology and no longer in awe of the passage of the earth as she spins around the sun. But in stark contrast, our ancestors were utterly reliant on this knowledge—it was a matter of life and death.

When the wheel stops, we pause and take stock of the year that has passed and contemplate the year that is to come. As the sun stalls on its course through our skies, something within us remembers that this time is significant and the hopes and loves of countless generations sing from your genes, from the rivers and hills of the land. The sleeping trees stir to the call of this season and in the tomb of earth, deep in the dark soil, the plants that will stir the world into spring sense a calling so loud, so powerful that they cannot do anything but respond—but in time, all in good time.

For now we pause and watch as the wheel stops and the sun stands still. Our breaths catch in the pit of our throats, and a sense of anticipation moves the spirit to call to the sun—*come back, come back!*

The Great Wheel

As the secular world bows beneath the mighty hand of materialism and the blatant commercialism of the holiday season, others are taking a different view—I am talking to you. The Pagan traditions invoke a sense of being an inexorable part of the wheel, not simply an observer. This is why the study of the Wheel of the Year is a fundamental practice of the Pagan traditions; this is not passive observation, but rather active participation, and it moves us to an understanding that we are not separate. We are a part of the great wheel.

The opening paragraph of this article is not a depiction of fantasy; it describes my own personal ritual on the morning of the winter solstice. It is oddly devoid of flashing swords and flouncy robes—it is me with nature, as a part of nature, singing the praises of the sun as it rises on the morning of the shortest day. My prayers ask for its passage north again, toward growth and summer, and the trembling words are words of gratitude for the myriad of life forms its power brings.

Have you ever been out there on the eve of a dark and moonless solstice, the eve of the shortest day and longest night? Have you ever stood in the deepest darkness of a wild and forlorn place and felt this night, been there with it, danced with it, your body moving to the subtle rhythms of the earth? Have you taken time out of the glorious festivities to be with the night itself? If not, I encourage you to do so, to take an hour to stop and stand in the darkness and be fully present. Feel that energy, the sheer anticipation that only occurs upon this night, anticipation that most of us recall feeling as children three days later on Christmas Eve. This night has a hunger for new life. The world grows weary of the depth of dreams and sleep, and it calls for sunshine, for the warming rays to caress the voluptuous curves and folds of our green and sleeping earth. And we feel it too. It is here within us, this wonder and sense of expectation that we feel at this time of year. The crackle of energy sparks and flows through us as we sense a shift to the normal pattern of things.

Midwinter, Yule, the Winter Solstice—what memories do they call? In my position in the northwestern corner of Wales, on a small island that floats gracefully in the Celtic Sea, I am reminded of cold, crisp mornings. The warmth of our hearth is accentuated by candles that flicker and seem to mimic the power of the sun, and the air of our home is filled with the scent of cinnamon and pine, oranges and cloves. Spells and prayers are cast with words of power and intent onto the burning logs of the season, changing through fire into smoke as they ascend through the chimney to the realm of the gods. The air is filled with potential and anticipation.

This excitement and sense of apprehensive expectation masks the fact that we are aware that the merciless nature of winter is not over, and our spells reflect this, for the worst is almost certainly to come. We must face storms and plummeting temperatures, the death and diseases of winter. There is promise nonetheless, and although this season stretches from the edge of solstice to the very beginning of February, we are aware of how long this season feels. And so we gather together as communities, families, circles of friends, and groves and covens to mimic the power of the sun and imbibe warmth and joy into the heart of humanity.

Come join us on a journey in celebration of light...

Cosmic Sway

April Elliott Kent

THINK OF WINTER AND two visions come to mind. One is bleak with cold, bare merciless landscapes, hunger, and hardship. The other is cozy with a blazing fire, a table groaning with delicious food, and loved ones gathered close. One represents obstacles and the other, success. Warmth, food, love, and safety in winter means we've managed, through some mixture of perseverance and good luck, to get things right.

Similarly, we can look at Yule, our annual festival of light, as a celebration of survival. It begins each year when the Sun enters Capricorn, the sign that symbolizes the pursuit of goals and the determination to overcome all odds to rise to the top. On this day, the Sun is at its lowest point in the noonday sky; tomorrow, it begins its rise until it reaches its noonday peak at Midsummer.

This Yule celebration begins with Moon high overhead in Libra, just past last quarter. A quarter Moon indicates the strength and motivation to push ahead, but Libra, unlike Capricorn, doesn't like to work alone. This is a Yule that invites teamwork, partnership, and togetherness.

Mercury Retrograde—Dec. 19–Jan. 8, 2017

Two days before Yule, Mercury turns retrograde, appearing to move backward in its orbit. Mercury's retrograde periods have been blamed for all manner of tribulations, from lost house keys to natural disasters. But I don't think it's necessary to blame Mercury retrograde for anything. In fact, I find these three-week periods, three times each year, extremely helpful—but we need to understand what they're for and how to use them.

Mercury rules thought processes and perception, writing, information gathering, short trips, and useful technology for daily life. Mercury's retrograde periods are good times to look within and canvass your true thoughts without external influence. Review what you've said, written, and learned to see whether more understanding can be brought to it. It's the right time to repair, refurbish, and perhaps reevaluate your need for your trusty technological devices.

Mercury retrograde rewards us when we don't push too hard to keep a particular schedule or timetable and when we're not trying to move forward with new agreements or projects. We can get into trouble at these times when we're overscheduled and pushing ahead with something that requires we have all the facts. Wait awhile; more information is coming.

Saturn Trine Uranus—December 24, 2016

This is the first in a series of exact trine aspects between Saturn and Uranus (the other two are on May 18 and Nov. 11, 2017). But while the energy of the aspect will be especially strong around these dates, its larger influence will be felt throughout the coming year.

Saturn and Uranus move through the zodiac very slowly, so when they connect with each other, it's serious business. Saturn represents authority, structure, and rules while Uranus symbolizes rebellion and destruction of all those things. The last major aspect between them was in 2008 and 2009, and that was a difficult aspect that coincided with a worldwide financial crisis and dramatic political change.

The trine aspect is much less likely to disrupt the status quo. The last Saturn–Uranus trine was in 2002 and 2003, and you are likely to find similarities between the issues of greatest interest to you back then and those that occupy your mind today. The good news is that when Saturn and Uranus join forces, you can fulfill some of your most brilliant goals because you're able to summon the discipline and perseverance needed to make them a reality!

New Moon in Capricorn—December 29, 2016

The final New Moon of the calendar year brings the Sun and Moon together in Capricorn in an exciting, opportunity-filled aspect to Mars and Neptune. As you draft your resolutions for the new calendar year, include both practical and quantifiable goals and include those that bring you into closer alignment with your softer side.

At this New Moon, Jupiter in Libra is in close opposition to Uranus, turning around after a long retrograde period. Your biggest, most revolutionary dreams are eager to be brought forth in the year ahead. Nothing less than your own personal Mount Everest will do! Why climb it? Because it's there!

A New Moon in Capricorn Ritual: A Blessing for Your Climb

Create a New Moon altar on a stone surface in your home, such as a hearth or granite countertop. (A heavy flagstone or several bricks from your garden will work in a pinch.) Assemble offerings to the spirits: a bit of cake, fruits, chocolate. Spread grains of rice around your offerings. Add representations of the goals you have set for the year ahead. It might be a photo of an inspirational person, a place you hope to visit, a student on graduation day, or a couple in love. I personally add a candle to every ritual altar, and for this one, choose an earthy color—a rich green, cedar, or even black. Burning some juniper incense would be a nice touch, too. And find a small bell to use in your ritual.

Upon awakening on the day of the New Moon, light your candle and sit quietly in front of your altar. Focusing on your most important goal in as much detail as you can, imagine that you are standing at the bottom of a mountain, mustering your energy for the climb. When you have pictured this, ring your bell. Then on each of the sabbats, imagine reaching a marker that says you are an eighth of the way farther along in your journey. Finally, picture yourself at the top of the mountain, having achieved your goal, and add a placard that reads, "Yule 2017." Ring the bell a final time.

Full Moon in Cancer—January 12, 2017

This is a tremendously powerful lunation, with the Sun and Moon in a tight configuration with Jupiter (growth and daring), Uranus (sudden change), and Pluto (lessons about power). With Mercury now direct, the time is right to charge ahead with your resolutions for the new year. Be forewarned, however, that the energy of this Full Moon, which is very strong for initiating action, is not terribly supportive for sticking with things while they grow roots. Your best course of action is to generate lists and plans of action now, use the nourishing symbolism of the Cancer Full Moon to incubate them, and "plant" them at the next New Moon.

Aquarius New Moon—January 27, 2017

Here is the moment to put your New Year's resolutions into practice with the New Moon in Aquarius, a fixed sign. Mercury in a close aspect with Uranus and Pluto suggests mental acuity as long as you aren't derailed by romantic intrigue (Venus and Mars conjunct in Pisces).

Aquarius is called the sign of friendship, but it's probably more appropriate to call it the sign of friendly associations. Even the most solitary of us may find the short, dark days of midwinter hard to handle on our own. Most resolutions have a better chance of sticking when you have a little support and encouragement!

On this New Moon, which falls just a few days before Imbolc, stick your head out of your burrow and look around. Is there a Meetup group in your area that's devoted to one of your interests? If not, perhaps it's time to start one! Or maybe you could gather some friends for a Groundhog Day party and watch the beloved Bill Murray film of the same name!

The Aquarius New Moon cycle is the best time of the year to become more closely connected with your community. Even if you tend to be a bit of a loner, know that your tribe is out there somewhere, waiting for you. It's time to put some effort into finding them, and helping them find you.

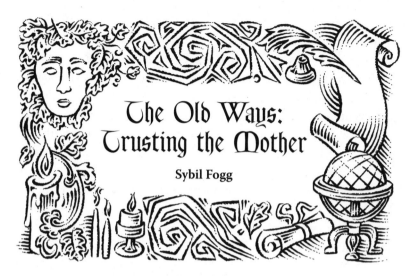

The Old Ways:
Trusting the Mother

Sybil Fogg

YULE IS THE TIME of year when the days are the shortest and the sun is beginning to creep back into the world. It is not hard to imagine that back in ancient times it felt like the sun was disappearing forever and that the world would be enveloped in black. But then there was that reprieve, that sliver of brightness that slipped through, growing stronger and more poignant, reminding us that the sun was still out there waiting to blanket our days in warmth. Because of this darkness, many cultures hold festivals and holidays of light at this time of year. The nights become more tolerable when we surround ourselves with family, friends, and celebration.

Food was in short supply by the winter solstice and faith was given to the great mother for the promise of fresh crops in the spring. To demonstrate their faith, people would dig into their stores to create great feasts. This was a tradition of many cultures, including those of the Slavic people. Many of the feast traditions still follow today as part of various Christmas rituals.

In Poland, feasting is still an integral part of the December holidays. The large dinner on Christmas Eve is called Wigilia and means "to keep vigil." In the old world, much of the day was spent in preparation or in waiting for the culminating feast. It was traditional for the activities surrounding the meal to begin right after midnight. The first task was to collect water in which to bathe. It was believed that water on this day was blessed and could keep illness at bay. During the bathing rituals, coins were thrown into the basins. This ensured prosperity for the family in the coming year. It was important to prepare the household for a time of celebration by completing at least three days worth of chores, so that no one would have to break from the festivities to chop wood or do other serious work.

The work might be backbreaking at first, but it is to prepare the home for feasting and gathering. This was also the time the holiday tree was brought in and decorated. There was much belief wrapped up in the tree as the early Pagans believed that the trees were inhabited by gods. The spruce tree was believed to foretell the upcoming weather based on the distribution of cones. Fir trees were particularly magical, having the power to protect against evil. Branches were used to dispel sickness and keep those in the home healthy during the winter months. It was important to the early Polish to bring as much evergreen into the home during solstice time. Boughs were decorated with apples, nuts, and colored bread *oplatki* (wafers).

Lithuanians celebrated similarly during Kūčios (Christmas Eve). Both countries served a twelve course feast, one for each month. Traditionally, the feast lacked red meat since Christmas Eve was once a fasting time. Dairy and hot dishes are also absent from the table. As we dig deeper into pre-Christian traditions, this semi-vegetarian celebration might mark a lack of access to meat in the cold winter months, though plenty of fish dishes were served up. Traditional foods included fish, vegetables, and bread. Herring was a very popular dish, served with a variety of tomato, mushroom, or onion based sauces. Other dishes included eel, borsch, mushroom or fish soup, potatoes, kissel, sauerkraut, cabbage, mushrooms, noodles with poppy seeds, cranberry puddings, a variety of breads, and honey.

The Yule season was called Koliada in Russia and was a time where life and rebirth were celebrated, as it was believed this time of year was chaotic, when the film between the living and dead was thinning and spirits may walk the earth once more. It felt as though time was coming to an end. The god Veles was honored at this time. Veles governed the earth, water, and the realm of the dead (the underworld). He was often associated with dragons, cattle, musicians, magic, money, and was a trickster god. His foil was the supreme thunder god, Perun. The two were believed to battle, Perun always winning, and Veles taking a mighty serpent form and shedding his skin to be reborn.

Fortune-telling was a popular pastime of the winter holidays in old Russia. This was a time when young women used mirrors and candles to catch a glimpse of their future husband. As ghosts were moving amongst the living, this was also a perfect time to ask questions of the deceased. If a person shed all that was protecting them (rings, belts, plaited hair), they could inquire about their futures. It was also customary to use candles and wax poured in snow for divination.

As with their Slavic counterparts, feasting was a popular tradition of the solstice. Showing the Mother Goddess that she was trusted to provide once the ground warmed again was practiced by many. As we turn our faces to the cold of winter, stringing up our lights as a mark that the sun will return and the God indeed will be reborn, why not call on our ancestors from Eastern Europe and build a ritual around the Yule feast?

Consider preparing your home to be sustained for at least three days. Cook, clean, and bathe in the sacred waters and practice some divination. Do not be afraid to create a feast from what is left in your stores. Wake up early to bake the bread for the day and sweep the cobwebs away. This can be done mentally and spiritually as well as physically. What thoughts are no longer helpful and could be done away with? Let them go.

Yule is the darkest point of the year for many of us. But within it, a tiny light glows. That light comes from within, and it is fed by those who have come before us and will be grown by those who will come after. Bask in the traditions of the old ways. Trust that the earth will become fertile and abundant with crops. Our ancestors' light is the ember we need.

Bibliography

Dice, Elizabeth A. *Christmas and Hanukkah*. New York: Chelsea House, 2009.

Dixon-Kennedy, Mike. *Encyclopedia of Russian & Slavic Myth and Legend*. Santa Barbara: ABC-CLIO INC., 1998.

Hodorowicz Knab, Sophie. *Polish Customs, Traditions, & Folklore*. New York: Hippocrene Books, Inc., 1993.

Ivanits, Linda J. *Russian Folk Belief*. New York: Routledge, 2015.

"Lithuanian Traditions: Christmas." *Arizona Chapter of Lithuanian-American Community*, accessed August 20, 2015. http://www .lithaz.org/arts/xmas.html.

Stallman, K. Sophie. *My War, My Life*. Minneapolis: Mill City Press, Inc., 2013.

"Wigilia," accessed Aug. 20, 2015. http://www.polishamericancenter .org/Wigilia.htm.

Feasts and Treats

Linda Raedisch

This Yule, we're going into the forest to see what the fairy-like wood-wives and Dames Blanches might be preparing for their feast. The Germanic wood-wife is content with simple fare, but the vengeful French Dame Blanche, who haunts thorny ditches, is gathering ingredients for something a little more *haute cuisine*.

Cheese Fondue

We begin our Yuletide journey high above the tree line in a stone shepherd's hut that's abandoned for the winter. The only way to keep warm is to sing songs and put on a pot of bubbling cheese and wine. You don't have to have a fondue set: you can cook the fondue in a heavy pot and keep it hot over a tea warmer with 3 tea lights inside. Ordinary forks work just as well as fondue forks for dipping in.

I've made this fondue for 6, and we all seem to fill up before we can empty the pot.

Prep time: 15 minutes
Cook time: 10–15 minutes
Servings: 6–8

For the fondue:

½ garlic clove (for anointing the pot)

1½ cups dry white wine

Juice of ½ lemon

2 cups grated Gruyère cheese

2 cups grated Fontina cheese

3 tablespoons white flour

¼ teaspoon white pepper

⅛ teaspoon nutmeg

Accompaniments:

1 crusty loaf French bread, cut or torn into chunks

1 small jar pickled pearl onions

1 small jar cornichons

(If you anticipate one of your guests demanding a salad, you can throw some arugula leaves around.)

Rub the cut side of the garlic clove all over the inside of your pot. Pour in wine and heat on low until very hot but not boiling. Squeeze in lemon juice.

In a bowl, toss cheeses and flour together with hands. Add handfuls of cheese to the hot wine while stirring. When cheese is all melted, stir in pepper and nutmeg.

Bring hot pot and heat source to table and invite everyone to dip bread in. The fondue will slide off the onions and cornichons, but they taste wonderful when crammed in the mouth with the hot cheesy bread.

A French friend once told me the crust left at the bottom of the fondue pot is a delicacy, but I have not found it so.

Nürnberger Mocha

Once you've polished off the leftover wine from the fondue, you'll need something to keep your eyes open while you watch for the creamy white petals of the black hellebore, or Christmas rose, to open at midnight, as Germanic legend says it must. The black hellebore is native to the Berchtesgadener Alps—the only mountains, as far as I know that contain the name of a witch: the old winter witch Berchta. The inspiration for this recipe comes from a little farther north, the city of Nürnberg, which is famous for its Lebkuchen, a spiced Christmas cookie.

Prep time: 5 minutes
Cook time: 7 minutes
Servings: 4

1 quart 2% milk
⅓ cup sugar
⅓ cup pure cocoa powder
Pinch black pepper
4 teaspoons instant coffee
Cheesecloth or tea ball
1 cinnamon stick
3 cloves
3 cardamom pods
1 tablespoon grated nutmeg

In a large pot with flame off, stir a little of the milk into the sugar, cocoa, and pepper. Cocoa powder is very stubborn, so you will have to stir vigorously. When the cocoa is thoroughly mixed into the milk, turn heat to low. Add rest of milk, instant coffee, and spices (except for nutmeg). If you have a tea ball, you can put the spices in there, snapping the cinnamon stick into smaller pieces to fit. You can also knot your spices into a piece of cheesecloth.

Stirring gently the entire time, heat mixture until hot and starting to froth. Remove spices or pour through strainer before serving. Sprinkle grated nutmeg over each mug.

Flaming Yule Log

It's a shame about that old cherry tree. It just never recovered from last summer's lightning strike, and by Christmas Eve, it was clear that it had to come down. We honored it by cutting a section of the trunk for our Yule log. And here it is, in all its flaming glory!

Yes, the usual *Bûche de Noël* or Yule log is made from a rolled cake, but the idea of rolling up a cake terrifies me, as it does most One Dish Witches. Technically, this is a Yule stump rather than a Yule log, but it tastes just as good, and has actual flames coming out of it—or could they be will-o'-the-wisps? It's the sort of thing a Parisian *pâtissière* might come up with after getting lost in Germany's Black Forest.

Why three tea lights? They are in token of the 3 crosses that German woodcutters used to leave on fresh-cut tree stumps. When the Wild Hunt came charging through the forest, the wood-wives could take shelter in the space inside the three crosses. If the wood-cutters were lucky, the wood-wives would leave gifts of gold behind when they departed.

And yes, busy Witches: you *may* substitute a chocolate cake mix for the from-scratch instructions. I recommend using store brand mix since these tend to be just a little bit drier and denser than brand name mixes and therefore easier to frost.

Prep time: 30 minutes
Bake time: 30 minutes
Decorating time: 20 minutes
Servings: 8 big pieces

2 8-inch or 9-inch cake pans
¾ cup (1½ sticks) butter, softened
1 cup white sugar
2 hefty tablespoons Nutella
1 teaspoon vanilla extract
3 eggs
⅔ cup pure cocoa
2 cups white flour
1¼ teaspoons baking soda
½ teaspoon baking powder
For the frosting:
½ cup (1 stick) butter, softened
1-pound box powdered sugar

⅓ cup whole milk
½ teaspoon vanilla extract
2½ teaspoons pure cocoa powder
1 tablespoon instant coffee powder
1 teaspoon pure cocoa powder
1 ounce (square) unsweetened baker's chocolate, melted (add last!)
1 Comb

Other:
¾ cup tart cherry preserves
1 empty aluminum tea light holder
3 red tea lights
Gold-wrapped chocolate coins

Grease and flour cake pans. Set aside. In large bowl, cream together butter, sugar, Nutella, and vanilla. With electric mixer, beat in eggs until well blended. Stir in cocoa by hand. Preheat oven to 350 degrees F.

Using the electric mixer again, mix flour, baking soda, and baking powder into your wet mixture, adding the dry ingredients a little at a time. Batter will be fairly stiff. Spoon batter into cake pans, spreading evenly.

Bake for 25–30 minutes or until knife inserted in center comes out clean. Cool for about 10 minutes before turning cakes out of pans to cool completely.

Now for the frosting. In another large bowl, cream together butter and a little of the powdered sugar. Continue adding powdered sugar a little at a time, alternating with the milk until you have achieved the consistency of a thick but easily spreadable frosting. (You may not need all the milk.) Use an electric mixer to blend in the vanilla and ¼ teaspoon cocoa and smooth any lumps out of the frosting. Don't lick the beaters yet; you're going to use them again.

Spread the flat top of one cake layer with a layer of frosting. Stir cherry preserves in a small bowl to loosen them up, then spread preserves over frosting. Put second cake layer on top and spread a little more frosting smooth over it. Run a comb lightly around it to make "tree rings." A long-handled hair pick works nicely.

Back to the frosting bowl! Beat the melted square of baker's chocolate into remaining frosting.

Once you have frosted the sides of the cake, put it in the refrigerator a few minutes to chill.

Use the empty tea light holder like a cookie cutter to cut three holes in a triangle formation on top of the cake. (A cheaper tea light tends to pop more easily out of its holder.) Insert your red tea lights in the holes. Pile some small gold coins in the center of the triangle and scatter more around the edges of the cake plate. When ready to serve, light the candles.

Crafty Crafts

Mickie Mueller

My family loves to decorate outdoor trees to feed wildlife for Yule. We've done it in different ways throughout the years, with strings of popcorn, peanut butter and birdseed on pine cones, balls of homemade suet, and even dried fruit tied with bright colored ribbons. It can be a truly spiritual experience during the shortest day of the year, when the sun is at its lowest, to see birds and squirrels gather around your outdoor tree to dine on a feast you made for them with your own hands. Make your Yule gift for nature as you embrace your stewardship to the earth, giving back the gifts that you receive all year. We found our favorite way to make birdseed ornaments; I hope it will be your favorite too.

Winter Solstice Birdseed Tree Ornaments

The best thing about these outdoor ornaments is that they don't melt if the weather gets unseasonably warm, which has happened to us. Nothing says Yule like sticky peanut butter and birdseed dripping all over your tree. Yuck! But you can use these even if you live in a warmer climate; they add a festive touch and allow you to celebrate Yule by connecting your spirit with nature while helping the critters this winter. Tie them onto your outdoor tree with bright red or gold ribbon or raffia. Apartment dwellers can hang them from trellises, or they can create a hanging outdoor mobile by stringing them onto a grapevine wreath to hang on the porch.

Time to complete: 1 hour to make (24 hours to dry, plus a couple hours in the oven)

Cost: $10 to $12 (if you already have the household staples like syrup, flour, aluminum foil, and cookie cutters, etc.)

Supplies

One package of unflavored gelatin, such as Knox (vegetarians and vegan friends, you can use a substitute like Vegan Jel or agar if you wish)

½ cup hot water

3 tablespoons corn syrup (pancake syrup works too)

¾ cup flour

4 cups of birdseed (which may include dried fruit, raisins, dried berries, or peanuts)

Baking parchment paper or aluminum foil

Cooking spray

Open-ended cookie cutters (I like ones shaped like stars, moons, suns, etc., but just use ones you like)

Bamboo skewer or chopstick

Gold, silver, or red ribbon or raffia, cut into 10-inch pieces.

Add the packet of gelatin to the hot water and stir until it's dissolved, then stir in the corn syrup until completely mixed in. Next add the flour, mixing it well until it forms a smooth white paste-like consistency. Pour this into the large bowl of birdseed. Stir the mixture with a wooden spoon and keep mixing until all the birdseed is covered with the liquid mixture. It will become somewhat like loose dough. You might need to get your hands in there to get it good and mixed up.

Cover several cookie sheets with either baking parchment or aluminum foil. Spray the inside of the cookie cutter with the cooking spray and lay it on the cookie sheet. Work as if you were making

cookies: plan ahead and try to fit as many on the cookie sheet as you can comfortably. A great tip: spray a little cooking spray on your fingertips to keep your fingers from sticking to the birdseed dough as you work! Fill the cookie cutter with the birdseed mixture no more than an inch thick and pack it in tightly with your fingers; the more firmly packed, the better they stay together. Push in the skewer or chopstick to form the hole that you'll hang it from. You might be tempted (as I was) to put the hole near the edge, but the best place for the hole is actually right in the middle of the ornament. If you put the hole too near the edge, birds can peck at the top of the ornament and free it, and the ornament will fall. Putting the hole in the middle gives your ornaments more staying power since the birds will eat all around the edges making their way toward the center.

Carefully remove the cookie cutter and repeat the steps until you have used up all the birdseed mixture, occasionally spraying the cookie cutter again with cooking spray. Let them dry for about twenty-four hours.

To make sure they're completely dry after air drying, bake them right on the cookie sheet for three hours at 180 degrees F. Once they cool, you can run the ribbon through the holes and tie them off. If you're making them ahead of Yule, resist the urge to store them in airtight containers, and instead keep them out in the open. Storing them in an airtight container can cause them to mold, but they should be fine in the open air. I placed mine in a pretty basket lined with tissue paper until the grandkids arrived to help decorate. When you're ready, you can hang them on your outdoor tree or anywhere you want to add some Yule cheer and magic while sharing your abundance and love with the creatures of the land.

A nice addition to your outdoor Yule tree would be old fashioned strings of popcorn and cranberries, along with your birdseed ornaments. These are really easy to make. Just get a bowl of popcorn, a needle, and long thread. String the popcorn on one at a time. You can add cranberries occasionally too for a pop of color, and the birds and squirrels love both popcorn and cranberries. Another favorite at our house is strings of lights on outdoor trees. You can use regular electric lights, or if you're lucky, you can find some strings of solar lights that capture the suns energy and light your tree at night, perfect for Yule when we celebrate the return of the sun!

No matter how you choose to display them, your birdseed ornaments will look charming and will be appreciated by the local wildlife. If you don't use something natural to hang them, like raffia, keep an eye out as the ornaments disappear, and gather up the ribbons from the trees as soon as the ornaments are gone.

All One Family

Dallas Jennifer Cobb

ONE THING I LOVE about the Pagan path is that it provides an alternative to the overly consumerized holidays of mainstream life in North America. The sabbats don't require us to go out and buy "stuff," but instead encourage us to gather from the surrounding natural environment what is needed for ritual.

Modern teens get sucked into consumerism so easily. Preyed upon by the "cradle to grave" marketing campaigns of multinational companies, they're taught that they need to wear designer labels to be cool, dress in the latest fashion to be accepted, and own the newest technology to be part of popular crowd. The bottom line: they must buy and consume in order to be loved.

Gone are the days when I could dress my little darling in frilly dresses and sparkly tights. And gone are the days when I was the center of her world. These days I live with an iPhone toting alien, dressed in dark colored "cool" clothes. She insists that her "girls" are the center of her world. Friends come first.

But underneath that polished teenage persona, I still see the sweet, loving child that I raised her to be. And Yule reminds me to make time to connect to her essence, not to buy her love, but to cultivate a deep and meaningful bond between us. As we approach

Yule, I initiate discussions around the downfalls of consumerism, over-consumption, and corporate greed. These topics were met with eye-rolls and impatience.

"You don't understand, Mom, there is a lot of pressure on me at school. I have to be cool. To fit in. To be one of the crowd. It isn't just about buying stuff, it's about securing my social status. You don't want me to be the odd one out. Remember how I was bullied?"

Despite the bullying awareness and prevention that is so popular in schools these days, bullying was widespread and persistent throughout elementary school. The bullying was often a result of her being "different." As she moved into the teenage years, I watched her opt to become more mainstream in order to fit in. The bullying lessened, but I worried about the pressure to conform and dreaded my daughter becoming someone she was not.

But last year, something changed. Involved in Student Council and Leadership, my daughter started to find her "people," her place of belonging. A group of high functioning kids with high IQs, EQs, and social awareness. Mentored by a strong school principal, the group started to learn about youth activist role models like Save the Children founder Craig Kielburger.

At leadership-building rallies like We Day, my daughter and her peers met youth leaders who were overcoming huge obstacles. These leaders told stories of coping with poverty, disability, racism, sexism, depression, and illness by using tools like community-building, generosity, compassion, and service. My daughter easily identified with the struggles and the process of overcoming oppression and the status of being an outsider that many of the speakers described. There stories awakened her identification, empathy, and compassion and inspired her to become an activist.

Practice: Changing the Tides

At Yule, I borrowed some of the ideas from the "Me to We" campaign: focusing on giving, building, sharing, and collaboration and cooperation. While she focused on overcoming hardship, I reminded her of the deep symbolism of rebirth associated with Yule: transition, rebirth, the return of life, the growth of light, and the changing of the tides.

I encouraged altruism. Instead of focusing solely on what she wanted for Yule, I suggested that she think of a way to give to a local person or organization in need. She could give her time, money, goods, wisdom, or energy. It was up to her. But I wanted her to learn about giving, not always expecting. To my surprise, she identified a local shelter for women and children fleeing abuse. Not only did she undertake fundraising for the shelter but she took the idea to her leadership team at school, which then organized a school-wide food drive to benefit residents. When she came to me and shyly suggested that maybe I could make a donation instead of buying her a gift, I knew she was in touch with the spirit of the sabbat.

Talking to my daughter about the people who use the services of the shelter, I made a point to make the link back to the Yule themes. At a time of great transition, the women and children using the shelter were leaving the darkness behind and moving into the light. Just as the fir tree represents life amidst death, the gifts we give at Yule represent our abundance even in this time of scarcity.

Teaching teenagers to give is a gift we give them, one that will bring them joy and satisfaction for a lifetime. Yule is a time to reflect on the gifts of the Goddess.

This Yule, talk to your teens. Help them to understand the human component of rebirth. Engage their compassion, empathy, and care and direct them toward giving to or serving people at time of transition. Whether they buy and wrap toys for children through a children's aid society, or help serve a seasonal meal in a shelter, they will be paid in gratitude and awareness.

When you dress your Yule tree, hang symbols of fertility, protection, light, and nature upon the tree. Each one is an affirmation that engages the law of attraction: the more we express our gratitude for all that we have, the more we magnetically charge that goodness and draw more to us.

So as you place a big radiant star atop your Yule tree this year, make a wish for your radiant youthful teen god or goddess. Make a wish for the light to grow in their heart, the bright light of compassion, care, generosity, and goodwill. For these are what this season is all about.

Yule: The Midwinter Ritual

Kristoffer Hughes

THE RAIN BEATS HEAVILY against the window, a portal onto a dark and unknowable landscape. The tempest howls and whistles at the door, commanding entry into the warmth of company. Within a shadowed room three candles glow warmly about a circle of friends. Each one is lost in thoughts, their attention directed to the calennig in their hands. In turn the participants whisper words of power that tremble from their lips:

By apple red and almond white,
I cast this spell upon this night!
By might of triple evergreen,
Oh spirits present and unseen,
By warmth of glowing candle flame,
Luck and fortune thus we claim!

The calennig (kal-ENN-ig) is an old Welsh term that is derived from the Latin word *kalends,* meaning "the beginning of a new month or year." The English word "calendar" shares the same etymological root. In Wales, the calennig is an ancient winter ritual that may be traced as far back to the fourth century and the Celto-Romano period of the British Isles. The Romans introduced the

Mediterranean apple to Britain, a much larger species than the small native crab apple. Whilst the actual significance of this ceremony has been lost to the mists of time, it is being successfully reintroduced into Welsh and Pagan culture.

Traditionally, the calennig is a new year gift that is claimed to bring good luck and fortune for the year ahead. It consists of a bright red apple studded with almonds which sits atop three small legs made of twigs. In recent times, cloves have been used to replace the almonds. A candle is stuck into the top of the apple and evergreens decorate its base. Children would wander from house to house carrying their calennig, knocking on doors and singing a verse in return for cookies and cakes.

In modern Paganism, the calennig represents a myriad of symbols associated with the longest night and shortest day. The apple, long associated with the otherworld, symbolizes our connection to the ancestors and the dead. The candle atop the apple is symbolic of the returning light, the sun born from darkness. The almonds represent promise and faithfulness, as it is the first tree to flower in spring, and is traditionally associated with the powers of awakening and watchfulness. The evergreens of holly, ivy, and mistletoe remind us of the animistic principles in nature and our connection to them and the qualities of protection, friendship, and magic. The calennig is kept year round, and whilst the apple and greens may well shrivel and dry, it is believed that luck and fortune will remain so long as the calennig remains upright.

So this Alban Arthan, why not bring a little Welsh magic to your celebrations by performing this simple yet beautiful ritual with ancient roots? This ceremony can be performed by a group of people as well as solitary. The main working of the ritual is the creation of the calennig itself. With this in mind, you will need to consider the space afforded to you and how many participants will be present. Be creative—this is a fun ceremony that should be radiant with joy and laughter. Place the required components around the central cauldron, which, if there are twenty or more people present, will be quite a spectacle! The only thing that will limit the effectiveness of this ceremony is your imagination.

Items Needed

1 cauldron
1 small candle (the small Christmas tree variety is perfect)
4 additional candles (either pillar or jarred or whatever you have in your magical cupboard) to represent the powers of land, sea and sky, and one to sit in the cauldron
An array of evergreens and pinecones
3 twigs approximately 4 inches long
1 large red apple
A small, sharp knife
13 split almonds
A sprig of holly
A sprig of ivy
A sprig of mistletoe

And so it begins...

Delineate sacred space in that manner by which you are accustomed or...

With your cauldron taking center stage with candle within, arrange the calennig components around it. Place the 3 additional candles around the edge of your circle at equal distances from each other. Take some evergreens or pinecones to delineate your circle and approach the candle that represents land and say these or similar words:

Powers of the land, we/I call to thee. Powers or stability and strength, nurture and security arise and come unto us. Creatures of the land, hear this call. Gods and spirits of this land, witness and protect this rite.

Light the candle and lay a trail of evergreens from this candle to the next, which will represent the sea. Say these or similar words:

Powers of the sea, we/I call to thee. Powers of tide and flow, of emotion and feeling, lover of moon and keeper of secrets, arise and come unto us. Creatures of the sea, of lakes and rivers hear this call. Gods and spirits of the sea and water, witness and protect this rite.

Light the candle and lay a trail of evergreens from this candle to the next, which will represent the sky. Say these or similar words:

Powers of the sky, we/I call to thee. Powers of breath and expression, of inspiration and vitality, come unto us. Winged ones, creatures of the air hear this call. Gods and spirits of the sky, witness and protect this rite.

Complete the circle by trailing the evergreens or pinecones to the candle that represents land. Turn to face the center and with both hands outstretched toward the cauldron, say these words or similar:

Powers of the center, of potential of the fire within and the fire without, powers of creation and all-knowing, arise and come unto us, witness and protect this rite.

Light the candle that sits within the cauldron.

Now take the apple and hold it in your power hand, i.e., the hand that you normally write with. Close your eyes and reflect on the previous Samhain season, considering your ancestors and the quality of darkness and rest. Hold the apple aloft and say these or similar words:

Ancient ones of shadows deep,
Sacred dead your wisdom keep.
Here within this apple round,
Otherworldly powers found,
Calennig bring by ancient lore,
Magic from the days of yore.

Now take the three twigs and either force each one into the underside of the apple or create three small slits with the knife to ease their entry. As each twig represents the powers of land, sea, and sky, respectively, call to these powers as you insert each twig. The ultimate aim is to create a stool-like appearance. Fiddle with them until they support the apple firmly on sturdy little legs.

Now take the knife and make thirteen small incisions around the apple, each one representing the passage of the moon. Holding the almonds in your power hand, close your eyes and consider the powers of emergence, of awakening, and promise and how they reflect the qualities of Midwinter. Hold the almonds aloft and say these or similar words:

Blessed fruits of sacred tree,
Imbibe, imbue thy might in me,
Awaken, bring to us the sun,
Now that light o'er dark is won.
Calennig bring by ancient lore,
Magic from the days of yore.

Carefully insert each almond into the apple's flesh, rounded end first. If you wish, continue to recite the above verse until the task is complete.

Now make three small slits around the top of the apple and take the sprig of holly, close your eyes, and consider its attributes. It is strong and majestic, the red berries glisten against the snows of winter. It is protective and resilient. Hold the holly sprig aloft and say these words or similar:

Oh radiant king in forest deep,
Oh holly stir the world from sleep,
Protect and guard, your luck abound,
Within the wood you are thus crowned.
Calennig bring by ancient lore,
Magic from the days of yore.

Insert the sprig of holly into the top of the apple. Now take the ivy and consider its properties of friendship, resilience, and potential and call to it thus:

Blessed ivy, stout and strong,
Guide us through cold winter's song,
Climb, ascend to summer's light,
Keep us through the longest night.
Calennig bring by ancient lore,
Magic from the days of yore.

Insert the sprig of ivy into the top of the apple. Take the mistletoe and consider its properties of healing and magic and call to it:

All heal, all heal, green and white,
By shout of ancient Druid rite,
Between the realm of sky and earth,
Bestowed within the gift of birth.
Calennig bring by ancient lore,
Magic from the days of yore.

Insert the sprig of mistletoe into the top of the apple. Affix the small candle to the very top of the apple; a little melted wax will help position it securely.

Consider the meaning of this night and light the candle to mimic the rebirthing of the sun. Now hold your calennig aloft in both hands and say these words or similar three times:

By apple red and almond white,
I cast this spell upon this night!
By might of triple evergreen,
Oh spirits present and unseen,
By warmth of glowing candle flame,
Luck and fortune thus we claim!

Your calennig is now complete. Remain in your sacred space and revel in celebration and frivolity. Finally, bid farewell to the powers of the cauldron and extinguish the candle therein. Turn to the three candles that sit about the circle, acknowledge their powers, and extinguish them. Keep your calennig as close to the center of your home as possible or near the hearth until the twelfth night, and then find it a home in a quiet corner. When the wheel turns to Midwinter once more, offer your calennig to fire and thank it for its presence in your life, a reminder of the powers of nature and the sun.

The rite is done and the wheel resumes its perpetual turning through the seasons.

A blessed Alban Arthan to you all.

Notes

Imbolc

Imbolc: The Winter Blues

Kerri Connor

DURING THE WINTER SEASON, a settling peace falls over the land. The world is fallow, quiet, and dormant. The growing season has come, thrived, blessed us with abundance, and gone. The world around us has closed down and shifted energies from an external one of growth and change to an internal one of thought and introspection. Even busy cities are transformed when the snow begins to fall, muffling the sounds of traffic, enterprise, and life while blanketing the world in white. The slate is wiped clean, and for a brief while, the world looks new, crisp, and pristine.

The holidays celebrated at this time of year take on a different tone than summer holidays. Many celebrate Halloween as the last chance to get outside with things like corn mazes, hayrides, and, of course, trick-or-treating. All things that define the summer's end of Samhain, which for Pagans is really a highly introspective sabbat.It is different than the more boisterous sabbats of the summer, such as the high energy Beltane or the secular and exploding Independence Day. Next on the list is Thanksgiving, a time for Americans to reflect on the past year and express their gratitude for their many blessings. After Thanksgiving comes Yule and Christmas, a time of celebrating families and personal beliefs. It is a time and promise of rebirth and life. The sun begins to grow stronger, yet we are only at the very beginning of winter.

While the days are growing longer, our weather is growing colder. It can become a confusing time for many people. Those who suffer from seasonal affective disorder (SAD) usually begin feeling their affliction in the fall, and it may last all the way until April or May. Even people who don't fully suffer from SAD can feel the effects to a lesser degree. The darkness of cloudy days combined with the lack of daylight hours is often depressing.

February is often not only the coldest but the snowiest month, as well. The groundhog pokes his head out of his hole on the 2nd and really, whether he sees his shadow or not, there will still always be six weeks until spring begins. But frankly, the weather doesn't necessarily care what the date on the calendar says. The beginning of spring is just that, the beginning. It's when things THINK about warming up, but this doesn't always mean the weather actually does warm up. Living just outside of Chicago, I have seen snow in the middle of May in just the past few years.

While winter doesn't technically begin until the winter solstice, or Yule, the cold and snow can begin months before then. By the time February rolls around, some areas have already been dealing with four full months of winter, and the people who live there know they probably have another two to three months to go. Winter is long and can be drawn out for several months.

Cabin fever sets in, particularly in February, since this is when the weather intensifies so much. We want the days to warm up, the sun to come out, and the gray to disappear from view. We want to clear away the filthy exhaust-covered snow. What was once a beautiful white blanket is now dingy, dirty, and trampled. This time of year can make us feel the same as the snow—dirty, overused, and mushy. We want to be able to open our curtains, drapes, and blinds to let in a cleansing bright light and open our windows to a crisp clean air. But these things don't exist yet. More than likely, the windows are sealed in plastic wrap to help keep the freezing cold and wind at bay. You may even have doors blocked off or entire rooms that have been closed off to help keep your home and family warm. The fact that February is a slightly shorter month than the rest actually becomes a comfort as you tick off the days waiting for this month to end. Once March rolls in, there is generally a feeling of promise that the cold, snow, and boredom really does have an end in sight. But at the beginning of February, particularly as early as Imbolc on the 2nd, the light at the end of the tunnel just doesn't seem to exist.

As cabin fever grows, we want to become more active. We want to stop focusing so much on the inward and start focusing on the outward again. We want to grow. We want that life-giving energy to surge through us. We want to plan our gardens, our vacations, and our projects for the summer. We want to clear our minds and feel refreshed and renewed in preparation for the uplifting spring days just ahead. Once spring does arrive, we are so relieved and happy, we experience a type of euphoria. We feel that "love is in the air," and while it may not always be a romantic type of love, love is definitely in the air. It just may be that it is our very love of life that has us in such an ecstatic mood. It is the love of the sunshine, the love of fresh air, and the love of the world around us waking up and reminding us once again that we are alive and vibrant beings.

Even if you live in an area where the cold doesn't take over and freeze everything, there are still some aspects in common with those struggling to stay warm. The natural energies at this time of the year are directed toward clearing, planning, and recharging, and so bringing these elements into your Imbolc ritual just makes sense. Now is the time to get ready for the warm spring. Now is the time to get ready for new life and new energy. Now is the time to go ahead and start making those plans that you can't wait to implement, but there is an order to follow to implement those plans with the most success.

The first step is to tie up loose ends. While you may be in a hurry to move on from the introspection of winter, you first need to make sure you are truly ready to move on. Personal introspection can be very difficult work. It's hard to look deep inside. Often we learn things about ourselves that we don't want to face or don't want to know. Ignoring these things doesn't change them. It doesn't make them go away. These aspects must be faced and worked through, and this is what the energies of winter are good for.

There are many different tools you can use to assist yourself in working through this type of introspection. You may want to explore different types of meditation, perhaps guided meditations with a specific purpose would be helpful to you, while others may find a more open, free-thought type of meditation to be more beneficial. Tarot cards or other types of oracle cards may give you ideas of areas of introspection you need to explore. Working with the chakras may lead you to discover blockages and the underlying causes of them. Self-help workbooks that are designed to help you get to know yourself better are another option. Adding yoga to your daily routine not only gives you a great way to get some physical exercise during the cold winter months, burning up and grounding excess energy, it is a great way to put your mind into a meditative and relaxed state. Yoga helps connect your mind with your body and can help you discover issues that need to be dealt with. Journaling helps you explore your thoughts and emotions and can point out things like inconsistencies in your thinking or just the opposite—areas where you are extremely steadfast. Shamanic journeying may also be useful to opening your mind to your subconscious and your desires or anxieties that reside there.

While it may be tempting to just shut down during the winter months, don't fall into that trap. Remember that even though the natural world outside of us may look like it isn't doing anything, that simply isn't true. The plants and the animals are all doing their own type of internal work. They are using stored energy to get them through the winter months. Their growth patterns are being planned and ours should be too. Complete your inner workings.

Take care of the internal business that you need to so you will be ready and able to move on when the time does come.

Internal work brings about change, and this change often brings about internal clutter. Learn to let go of that which no longer serves you, whether it is ideas, beliefs, emotions, habits, or people. Unclutter your mind and take out the trash. Cleanse yourself in order to give yourself the freshest start possible. Imagine yourself as a foundation. You will be building on this foundation, so you need it to be as clutter free and swept clean as possible. Any debris on the foundation when you start building will get in the way of giving you a secure, strong, and sturdy base.

Once you have cleared away what you need gone, it's time to move on to your planning stage. What do you plan to build? Do you need to create new, healthy habits? Do you want to plan a garden or other physical project? Whatever you are going to build, you need to plan it out first. Make a blueprint. Write down your goals. Create an actual working plan that you not only follow but use to evaluate progress and check off completed steps and goals.

Finally, in order to set your constructed plans in motion, there is one very important component you need—energy. Even the best laid plans will get you nowhere without the energy and strength to implement them. The winter can leave us feeling sapped and depleted of energy, just as the trees seems to be, but their energy is stored deep inside their roots, and so is ours. We simply need to learn how to dig deep to find those energy reserves and bring them to the surface. As the strength of the sun grows, so does the energy of the natural world around us, and so does our own. Once that energy starts building, it gains momentum that in turn helps build more energy, more easily. This energy then gives us the power and the strength to pull ourselves out of the darkness and into the light. We are able to implement our plans, face our challenges, and forge a path into our new future, making necessary changes and growing as we go along.

With practice, you will find yourself overcoming the boredom of winter. You will battle off the confines of cabin fever. You will be able to take your own place in the natural world as it prepares to burst forth with renewed life. The flowers that are waiting to burst through ground and snow; the animals that are stirring in their dens, ready to end hibernation, take up the hunt and feed after a long sleep; the buds that have already begun forming on the trees to eventually burst into leaves—all of these are forms of energy ready to begin a new chapter of life, right along with you. In the Imbolc ritual you will find on page 115, you will learn how to clear, plan, and recharge through exercises you can implement not only into your ritual but into your daily life as well.

Cosmic Sway

April Elliott Kent

A BRIGHT CRESCENT MOON, approaching a dazzling conjunction with Mars, illuminates the night sky as we welcome Imbolc, a festival of light. Look for the Mars and Moon in the west a couple of hours after sunset and consider their combined symbolism: emotional ferocity and the determination to protect what is ours, and the desire to let intuition guide us toward getting what we want for ourselves.

Within a few days of Imbolc, on February 3, Venus leaves gentle, empathetic Pisces to join Mars in feisty, independent, yet strangely romantic Aries. Imbolc is also a fertility feast, and while Aries is not traditionally considered a fertile sign, it is excellent for encouraging the sort of unions that make conception possible! Venus's retrograde period, however (March 4–April 15), is a less than ideal time for initiating lasting romantic relationships or business partnerships, so look before you leap.

The lunations of this Imbolc season bring two eclipses: the February 10 Full Moon (lunar eclipse in Leo) and the February 26 New Moon (solar eclipse in Pisces). Eclipses occur twice each year when the Sun and usually the Moon are close to the Lunar Nodes, points where the Moon's orbital path meets the Sun's. Eclipses tell us where you need to make a change, which usually involves letting go, leaving your safety zone, and embracing an uncertain but potentially rewarding course of action.

Full Moon/Lunar Eclipse in Leo—February 10, 2017

Lunar eclipses have an impact on relationships of all kinds, but this one is likely to bring particular changes in the realm of romantic relationships. Venus and Mars are in a conjunction in the sign of Aries, symbolizing sexual chemistry and excitement. But they are also approaching a square aspect to Pluto, which favors deeper unions based on true, deep understanding, rather than those entered impulsively and based only on desire. This lunar eclipse also sets the stage for Venus turning retrograde a few weeks from now; read more about that later in this article.

However, if you're trying to accomplish just about anything that is daring, bold, and visionary, you could hardly hope for better celestial conditions to push it out into the world. The eclipse occurs near the Moon's North Node, which suggests a change for the good in the direction of your fondest dreams. You need only find the courage to follow. Look to previous years when eclipses fell near this same degree of Leo, including 1989/90 and 2008/09. What were you pursuing then? This may be the time when you bring those matters to fruition and a satisfying conclusion.

Pisces New Moon/Solar Eclipse—February 26, 2017

This eclipse occurs at the Moon's South Node, so it's a "letting go" eclipse. In particular, it's time to let go of any feelings of persecution or victimization. Anything difficult that's happened to you has served its purpose, which is to make you more empathetic, compassionate, and emotionally available to others. If instead you have become bitter or mired in helplessness and self-pity, this eclipse will give you another chance to shift the way you view your life and your troubles.

So many opportunities are available now, with an exciting, ongoing configuration of Jupiter (opportunity), Uranus (thrilling changes), and Pluto (the ability to remake our lives). It would be a shame to waste it by clinging to what was or will never be, instead of opening your arms wide to embrace a brighter future.

Recent years when eclipses fell near this point include 1988/89, 1997/98, 2007, and 2016. Are you holding on to things that happened then? And can you find the strength and faith to let some of them go?

Venus Retrograde—March 4–April 15, 2017

When Venus is retrograde, it's difficult to get a clear picture of what is happening in our relationships and what we should be doing to improve our financial condition. These are important times to review why past relationships failed so that current ones can be made stronger. Venus's retrogrades are considered poor times to begin new relationships, but they are excellent for connecting with important people from the past. They are also poor times to make large purchases; usually, there is something you are unaware of that will make you regret the purchase over time.

Venus is retrograde in the same sign about every eight years. Venus is in Aries (and very late Pisces) during this retrograde period. It was most recently retrograde in this sign in March of 2009, 2001, 1993, and 1985. What do you remember most about these periods of your life? These years might hold the key to personal connections and pleasures that will be revisited during this Venus retrograde period.

Aries—Venus retrograde in your Sun sign invites you to find pleasure in individual pursuits, activities you enjoy on your own, and anything that helps you feel more attractive and appealing to others.

Taurus—This is a period when spending time alone, resting and retreating from the world as much as possible, will connect you with a deep sense of value and pleasure.

Gemini—Friends from the past may appear, particularly those with whom you shared a love of art or music. Find enjoyment in socializing and collaboration.

Cancer—Reconnect with mentors from the past, learn more about your parents and family history, and review ways to beautify your home and workplace.

Leo—This is a time when you are preparing to take a great leap of faith into a new adventure. You may consider returning to school, traveling, or even moving to somewhere very new.

Virgo—This is a very practical sign, but this is a retrograde period designed to put you in touch with your mystical side. Reconnect with the unseen.

Libra—This retrograde period is crucial for your closest relationships. How is the past holding you back in this area of your life, or how could it help you move forward?

Scorpio—How can you find more pleasure in your work and in your daily life? Reflect about what you truly value and enjoy in your work, and evaluate whether you need to make a change.

Sagittarius—This is a very likely time to reconnect with soulmates from the past, such as those friends and lovers who taught you how to open your heart. It can also be a rich time to complete unfinished creative projects.

Capricorn—Not a good time to initiate serious renovation or redecorating, but an excellent time to collect ideas about what you'd like to do with your home in the future. Reconnect with your family, or dig into your family history.

Aquarius—This retrograde is good for repairing relationships with siblings or neighbors, finishing writing projects, and reviewing important household paperwork.

Pisces—This retrograde is connected to your property and possessions. You may need to spend some money on necessary repairs during this period, but it will repay itself over time. Review how you're spending and investing your money.

Full Moon in Virgo—March 12, 2017

When the Full Moon is in Virgo, the Sun is in Pisces. It's a gentle time of year, as we emerge drowsily from winter's sleep. But Jupiter, Pisces's traditional ruling planet, is locked in an opposition aspect with Uranus, a wake-up call, so no one is sleeping very deeply. The Full Moon in Virgo shines a light of vigorous and thoughtful usefulness—particularly as it's in square aspect to Saturn. Faith and empathy are not enough, says Virgo: they must also be accompanied by good works. Add Mars in Taurus, a sign very friendly to Virgo, and an out-of-sign trine to Saturn, and there is work to do and energy with which to do it.

The Old Ways: The Sacred Flame

Sybil Fogg

EARLY FEBRUARY IS OFTEN associated with an almost primal desire for winter to come to an end. Alas, we are often only in the middle of it. The days are growing longer, but the icy cold holds the northern hemisphere in a tight grip. In the past, food stores were shrinking and becoming inedible. The promise of the warmth of spring seemed far off, but the people celebrated anyway, showing their faith that the sun would grow stronger, the snow would melt, and the ground would be ready for planting. To demonstrate that they truly believed the days would grow warmer and brighter, light became an integral part of the celebrations in early February. The middle of winter is a dark place in Slavic countries. A lighted candle represented the warmth and protection of fire and the sun's strengthening power.

As the candle held protective qualities in old Poland, it was brought out at this bleak time of year to purify the home, fields, and people both living and dead. Candles were decorated with ribbons and symbols and then blessed before a priest (when Christianity took hold). These candles were brought home and used in various ways for protection and divination and were called *gromnica* (from the word *gromny,* meaning "loud" or "thunderous").

On February 2, people would honor the Great Mother by burning one of these candles throughout the night until the sun rose in the morning. The candle would then be kept in a safe place so that its magic could be called upon throughout the year as needed.

One of the more sacred uses of the gromnica was in the blessing of women following childbirth. This tradition finds its roots in ancient Jerusalem when it was believed that women were "unclean" after giving birth and could ruin the crops in the field. Women were therefore isolated for approximately six weeks following the birth of a child. Upon the end of this time period, a procession would begin from the home of the woman, who would carry a gromnica blessed on Candlemas, through the village to the house of worship.

Another protective use for the gromnica called for the head of a family to lead the household in a procession around the home while holding the thunder candle and making signs with it. The family would then be protected from wolves and other wild animals. It was also common to place the gromnica in windows during storms to protect the home from lightning. The gromnica would also be placed in the hands of the dying to assist in their journey to the next world.

Candlemas was known as Sretenie (meaning "meeting" and "joy") and is celebrated in Russia on February 15. This is a time of year that was viewed as a meeting of winter and spring. As with Yule, Russian fascination with the magical and mysterious realms led to a variety of divination practices at this time of year. Many superstitions ascribe weather signs to determine what the remainder of winter will bring, similar to Americans waiting on a groundhog. Russians looked to nature for signs of how winter would change to spring. For instance, if the sunset was bright on Sretenie, then the icy days were over. If there was no sun in the evening, a cold wave was sure to hit before spring would make her appearance. These omens would spill over to fortune telling for the coming harvest as well. A thaw on Sretenie predicted a strong season for wheat. Snow ensured a rich cop.

Following candle magic traditions, fortune-telling with candles was popular in old Russia. A fun form of divination called for girls to place little candles in walnut shells, light them, and float them in a bowl of water. The girls would circle the bowl, keeping a keen eye on their specific shell. A series of rules abounded; the first candle to go out showed who would marry first. Unfortunately, if one sunk, that girl would never marry (though perhaps there were some who hoped for this future). Other fire scrying included staring into flames and smoke, dripping wax into water, or burning paper and reading the shapes that appeared.

A rather frightening divination was to use a candle and mirror. In a dark room right before the clock struck midnight, a girl or boy would stare intently into a mirror illuminated only by the candle. As the clock struck twelve, the reflection of the future partner would appear over their shoulder.

This would also be a good time of year to honor Gabija, the Lithuanian goddess of fire and the hearth. Gabija lives in the hearth and is the sacred fire. It is important in the cold months of winter to not let the fire go out. In ancient traditions, Gabija was tended only by the women of the family. It was of utmost importance to not allow her to be left unattended since an unattended flame is dangerous. Therefore, when the family sleeps for the night, Gabija must be put to bed as well. Steps involved in bedding the goddess for the night include covering the coals with ashes and leaving a bowl of clean water nearby in case Gabija wanted to bathe. Salt and bread offerings were left as well as gentle requests to not wander.

Although Gabija was the flame, she can take other forms, often that of a cat, stork, or rooster, but also as a woman clad in a red gown. She must be kept content because although fire is helpful in cooking and warmth, fire is also destructive. If angered, it was believed Gabija would go wandering, treading flames. It was therefore crucial to never be disrespectful to the fire. People were careful to not carelessly toss garbage or anything unclean into the fire. The hearth and stove were kept very clean, and the flame could only be put out with pure water. Gabija was the protector of the home and property.

February marks the center between winter and spring. We can feel the hopefulness of the warm months approaching in the breeze that touches our lips. We can feel the fire rekindling in our soul. Inspiration comes from the gently growing warmth. Why not call upon our ancestors and tend our sacred flame? Spend some time decorating and blessing candles, and then use them to smudge the household. Sit still with one and look to the future. Don't forget to leave out offerings to Gabija, the goddess of the flame, and honor her at this time of year when the fire is growing stronger and more sacred than ever. Don't let the fire go out! Blessed Be.

Bibliography

Dixon-Kennedy, Mike. E*ncyclopedia of Russian & Slavic Myth and Legend*. Santa Barbara: ABC-CLIO INC., 1998.

Gilchrist, Cherry. *Russian Magic: Living Folk Traditions of an Enchanted Landscape*. Wheaton: Quest Books, 2009.

"Gromnica," *Wikipedia,* accessed August 28, 2015. http://pl.wikipedia .org/wiki/Gromnica.

Hodorowicz Knab, Sophie. *Polish Customs, Traditions, & Folklore*. New York: Hippocrene Books, Inc., 1993.

"Russian Holiday Calendar," *Passport Moscow*, accessed August 28, 2015. http://www.passportmagazine.ru/article/1437/.

Feasts and Treats

Linda Raedisch

THIS YEAR, I'M PLAYING up the Irish flavor of this sabbat, with the first recipe dedicated to the Irish Aoife. I won't lie to you—Aoife wasn't a good witch. She turned the Children of Lir into swans. Aoife was a queen of the Tuatha De Danaan, the "people of the goddess Dana," a magical race who inhabited Ireland before the Irish and subsequently retreated to the land of Faerie. These days, even the Tuatha De Danaan must be finding it hard to get good help. I'm sure that Aoife, now keeping her own kitchen in the hollow hills, would heartily approve of the concept of One Dish Witchery.

Aoife's Irish Breakfast Frittata

I have not yet been to Ireland, but my uncle has. While there, he dutifully snapped a picture of his breakfast: fried eggs, sausages, and sliced tomatoes, inspiring what my household calls Irish Breakfast for Supper. Busy witches like Aoife don't have time to hang around the stove watching over eggs, so this recipe is made—you guessed it!—all in one dish. It works just as well for supper as for breakfast.

Prep time: 35 minutes, provided potatoes are already cooked
Bake time: 30 minutes
Servings: 8

1 hot Italian turkey sausage
Potato masher (but not for the potatoes!)
4 small or 2 medium Yukon gold potatoes, cooked, peeled, and sliced 2 scallions, chopped
½ cup chopped fresh cilantro
3 eggs
½ cup heavy cream
Dash black pepper
¾ cup grated cheddar cheese
1 large tomato

Fry sausage in skillet until thoroughly cooked. Mash sausage with potato masher until crumbly.

Grease a 9-inch or similar-sized baking dish.

Spread sliced potatoes in baking dish. Sprinkle sausage crumbles, scallions, and cilantro over them.

Preheat oven to 350 degrees F.

In a medium-sized bowl, whisk eggs together with cream and pepper. Whisk for about a minute then pour over potatoes. Top with cheese and bake for 25–30 minutes or until frittata no longer quivers. Put tomato slices on top during last few minutes of baking or serve on the side. Let frittata cool a few minutes before slicing and serving.

Fairy Mimosa

It's always twilight in the fairy realm, so it's always time for a drink! The mimosa—champagne and orange juice—was probably named after a bright yellow-flowered variety of the *Acacia dealbata* tree. This one calls for pink grapefruit juice to approximate the color of a February sunset.

Prep time: 2 minutes (longer if you struggle opening the wine)
Servings: 8

1 bottle sparkling white wine, chilled
1 quart pink grapefruit juice, chilled

Fill glasses with equal parts wine and juice. And don't forget to toast Queen Aoife!

Aoife's Irish Coffee Dessert

This tiramisu-like dessert is what I imagine the repentant queen serving to King Lir to soften his mood when he finds out why his children never came home for supper. The only baking needed is for the ladyfingers, which the kind Irish fairies have already made and left for you to find in the produce section of your supermarket, near the berries.

Prep time: 25 minutes
Chill time: 4 hours
Servings: 8

2 3-ounce packages of ladyfingers (that's 24 "half fingers" each)
¾ cup mascarpone
2½ cups heavy cream
3 tablespoons instant coffee powder
6 tablespoons powdered sugar
2 tablespoons whiskey
Electric mixer
Sieve
¼ cup pure cocoa powder
About 2 tablespoons grated milk chocolate (You can grate an ordinary plain chocolate bar or shave off curls with a small sharp knife directly over the whipped cream. Chocolate sprinkles are also acceptable.)
Plastic wrap
8-inch spring form (A spring form is essential if you want to be able to cut this dessert like a cake. If you're okay with scooping it out, you can use a similar size straight-sided dish and put the ladyfingers only on the bottom and in the middle.)

If the fairies have not yet halved the ladyfingers, do so now, cutting each in half lengthwise with a serrated knife. Arrange ladyfinger halves, cut side in, standing up in a fairy ring inside the rim of the spring form. Break and scatter more fingers in the bottom of the pan. It's okay if they don't cover the bottom completely. Set aside.

In large bowl, stir mascarpone, coffee powder, 4 tablespoons powdered sugar, and whiskey together with a spoon until smooth and a uniform light brown in color. Pour in 2 cups cream and blend on low until all ingredients are well blended. Increase speed to medium to whip it up well.

Drop half of mascarpone mixture into pan in blobs. Spread with the back of a spoon, making sure there are no gaps between filling and ladyfingers. Tap a dusting of cocoa powder over this then add another layer of broken ladyfingers. Cover with rest of mascarpone mixture.

In a clean bowl, beat ½ cup heavy cream with 2 tablespoons powdered sugar. When it's stiff, spread over top of dessert.

Cover with plastic wrap and chill for 4 hours.

Top with grated chocolate just before removing spring form ring. Cut and serve.

Crafty Crafts

Mickie Mueller

THE SEASON HONORS THE beginnings of the thawing of the earth, so a lovely way to celebrate is with a craft project that echoes the theme. I've actually had my water pipes freeze right before two different Imbolc coven gatherings at my house, so I have very deep magical associations with Imbolc, ice, and the concept of thawing—it's been very personal. I like to honor the coming thaw with fire and ice lanterns, which is much nicer than frozen water pipes!

Imbolc Fire and Ice Lantern

These easy-to-make and nearly cost-free ice lanterns can be made in your freezer or outside if it's cold enough. Add some creative additions and you'll have a lovely magical candleholder made of ice. If it's cold enough to make them outside or if you have a large enough freezer, you can make enough of them to line your walkway.

Time to complete: 10–12 minutes (12 hours to freeze)
Cost: Under $5

Supplies
Two plastic containers, one an inch larger all the way around
Water
Duct tape

A freezer (or a weather forecast of less than 32 degrees F)
Rocks

Choose your plastic containers; they can be bowl-shaped, square plastic storage containers, two sizes of butter tubs, or both a large and a single-serving-sized yogurt container. In the sink, fill the larger container with water, then drop the smaller container into the larger one and weigh it down with a couple rocks until the tops of each container are close to even. Tear off two pieces of duct tape and run them crisscrossed across the top of both containers to hold the smaller one in place so it doesn't float over to one side.

Place it in the freezer for about twelve hours (or outside if possible). Once it's frozen solid, remove the tape. Run cold or lukewarm water over the outside of the large container to release it from the lantern. Pour a little cold or lukewarm water inside the small container and pull it free from the ice lantern. Now all you have to do

is set your lantern outside and drop in a tea light candle. When the candle is lit, the ice glows with candlelight, welcoming guests and symbolically melting the ice of the cold earth and bringing warmth and light to the land.

Set it on the porch at dusk with a candle inside and as the ice melts, you symbolically make way for the coming spring. If it's cold outside, you can make several to line your walkway.

Tips

The ice usually has some clear parts and some frosty looking sections, which can look really cool, but if you want the ice to be very clear, boil your water and then allow it to cool before pouring it into your mold. If you want to add food coloring, you can tint your lanterns different colors. Sprigs of evergreen or berries added to the mold can add interest. If you don't want to use real candles, you could use electric lights set inside glass candle holders. Add some magic by focusing any obstacles into the water before you freeze it, and as the ice melts, may your obstacles also melt away!

Fire and Ice Globes

Here's a second kind of ice lantern that I just love. I've made these for a couple years now and I probably will continue to make these year after year. (You can also use the same method to make big ice marbles that you can decorate your yard with if you just freeze them solid.)

Supplies

Round balloons
Water
A round bowl or a 13" × 9" cake pan
Freezer (or freezing temperatures outside)
Pin
Tea light candles or glow sticks

If you want to create colored ice globes, add a couple drops of food coloring in the balloon before you fill it up with water. Fit the

lip of the balloon securely over your sink faucet. Supporting it from the bottom, turn on the faucet and allow the balloon to slowly fill with water. Once it's as full as you want it, turn off the faucet and remove the lip of the balloon from the faucet while firmly holding the neck of the balloon closed. Keeping it in the sink, tie the balloon closed in the same way you would if it were filled with air.

Place the balloon in a round bowl that keeps it from tipping over so the knot stays at the top. Now you can freeze it either in your freezer or outside if it's cold enough. If you want to make more than one, try using a cake pan lined with a towel and wedge them together in the pan—they will hold each other up.

Check the balloon about once every hour and poke the top of the balloon with your finger to break the ice forming there but leave the rest of it undisturbed. Freeze for five to six hours depending on how big your balloon is. Put the balloon back into the sink and poke it with the pin. The balloon tears away from the ice and it looks pretty cool! Peel off any leftover balloon; you might need to chip away a bit at the top of the ice with a butter knife. Tip it over and pour out the water into the sink and continue to shape the hole so it's large enough to allow a tea light through it. If you make the hole a little larger, it will help keep the melting ice from extinguishing the candle. If you prefer to, you can use glow sticks instead of candles, and the ice won't melt as fast.

If there's snow outside, these globes sit nicely in the snow. If there's no snow and the bottoms aren't flat enough to stand up, you can hold your lantern and basically sand it back and forth on a concrete walkway to create a flat spot for it to sit upright.

Have fun with these charming ice lanterns, and may they warm your spirit this Imbolc and welcome the thawing of the earth while you dream of the season of growth and renewal.

All One Family

Dallas Jennifer Cobb

ANOTHER OF THE GREATER sabbats, Imbolc, also called Candlemas, represents the quickening of life, a time when seeds deep within the earth begin to receive temperature messages which awaken them. They get ready to sprout. *Imbolc*, in the Gaelic translation, roughly means "ewe's milk" or "in the belly." I like the "in the belly" interpretation because it makes me think of that little seed, down there in the belly of the earth, awakening and getting ready to perform miracles.

Imbolc is also a celebration of waking the light of the soul. After a long winter and much darkness, we too feel a deep stirring. We notice the days getting longer and the light lasting those extra few minutes. And like the seeds that have laid dormant, we awake deep inside. Our soul awakens, anticipating spring and the rebirth which is coming.

We might see those brave snowdrops poking their flowers up through the snow, and the sight of them assures us that we will make it. We sigh, knowing that we will make it through the last cold, cruel weeks of winter, and we will survive until spring.

The Imbolc celebration invites us to banish winter and welcome spring. We think of the Goddess, renewed and reborn. No longer the Dark Crone, the Hag, she is reborn as the Flower Maiden, young, fertile, and ready to conceive the Sun God.

Why not use the symbolism of Groundhog Day, also celebrated on February 2, to craft a ritual you can do with your teen. In the same way that the groundhog comes out into the light to take stock, look around and decide what to do, encourage your teenager to do the same. Whether it's an intention made at solstice, Yule, or a resolution written at New Year's, suggest that your teen pull it out, examine it in the light of the growing sun, take stock, and decide what to do. Just like the groundhog.

The curious thing about intentions and resolutions is that all we really need to do is to make them. Like a small seed planted in the psyche, they are always with us. And with temperature and light signals being sent at this time of year, chances are that something has already begun to sprout. Imbolc is a time for lighting our own light, illuminating what is inside of us and seeks to grow. We review our intentions and resolutions, we make lists, and then we look outside ourselves and prepare to do the work needed to make our little seeds grow.

Like sprouting seeds, our intentions must be warmed by the glow of our commitment to them, and watered with the daily attention of action. This is how we fulfill our potential.

Practice: Quickening the Seeds

Ask your teenager to go and find what they wrote down at Yule or New Year's Eve. Gather together and suggest that you both review your Yule intention or resolution. It is not necessary to share the exact nature of the intention, since we know that we sometimes seek to do very private work during the dark days.

Share the process around the intention. Talk with one another about what you remember feeling when you set that intention or resolution. What prompted it, what was the seed that inspired it?

Now, take stock. Each of you must ask yourself honestly what has grown, changed, or transpired since you set the intention. Be honest and take note. Share your observations with one another, taking time to actively listen to each other. After, offer reflection on where you might see growth with the other person's intention. Sometimes we need the outside perspective to help us to see what we might have otherwise ignored. Like the snowdrop flower popping up amidst the snow, some growth is harder to see because it blends in. Be one another's eyes, and look for evidence of growth in each other. And like we do when we are outside and spot the early blooms of brave flowers in the snow, be genuine with your joy when you discover growth. Clap your hands and exclaim: "Look at that. What a miracle!"

On a piece of paper, take a moment to record what your intention or resolution looks like now. Write down what you observed about the growth of your intention and what the other person observed as well. Make note of the incremental growth and shift that has happened toward your goal in the short time since Yule. Write today's date.

Like a little groundhog, blinking in the bright light, we need to take a good look around. We have looked back, so now let's take a look forward. Quickly write down a list of five things you can do that will help you grow your intention and actualize your goal. Make sure that at least one item is small and easy to accomplish. My usual trick is to make the number one item on the list: "make a list." That way, once I have written the five items, I can go back and check off number one. Quick and easy progress is always encouraging.

Teach your teenager that making a list is part of the work. Preparation paves the way to success. In the same way that writing down the intention did, writing the list of steps toward your goal will actually sow the seeds of success and initiate growth, movement, and change on a deeper layer of our psyche.

When you are done writing and the seeds are sown, hug your teen and affirm all the light you see growing within them. Then, turning away, each of you take your lists back to your altars or safe spots, and tuck them away. Our quickening seeds are growing.

Imbolc Ritual: Cleanse & Transform

Kerri Connor

IMBOLC IS WHEN WE celebrate and honor Brigid, the Celtic Goddess of smithing, poetry, and fire. She is also revered for being a goddess of healing. If you prefer to work with a different goddess, that is up to you, but be sure to use one that will fit your purpose. On the surface you may think, "Smithing? What need do I have of that?" But smithing is really all about transformation and change, and that is what you really will be working with. You may also be healing some old wounds when working through clearing, so this also makes Brigid an ideal candidate.

This ritual is going to take place in three different stages with three different activities and at least two different locations. You will begin with a ritual bath, then a planning journaling session, and finish with a recharging meditation. The last two stages will take place at your altar in your sacred space.

Items Needed
For the ritual bath:
Angelica
Frankincense
Horehound

Hyssop
Lemon peel
Myrrh
Cheesecloth
White rose petals
A white candle
For your altar:
A red candle to represent Brigid
Sandalwood oil
Bergamot oil
Black pepper oil
A notebook or journal designated for spiritual purposes only
A writing utensil
A fire-proof container or incense burner designed for self-lighting
   charcoal tablets
Self-lighting charcoal tablet
Lighter
Your preferred method of energy raising—drumming, dancing,
   chanting—whatever works best for you
Any other altar decorations and ritual supplies you generally use

You will begin by preparing the ritual bath. Add equal amounts of angelica, frankincense, horehound, hyssop, lemon peel, and myrrh to a piece of cheesecloth and bundle it up and tie it into a knot. Place it into the bathtub where the water will be able to flow easily through it from the faucet. As the tub fills, scatter the white rose petals on the water and light the white candle, placing it in a safe location.

Remove your clothes and as you step into the bath, ask Brigid (or whoever you decide to work with) to join you. (If you want to call quarters, do so before entering the bath.) This is a cleansing bath. It's a bath to help you clear away the grime in your emotions and your mind. Allow this bath to wash away the heaviness you have been feeling—the sadness, the boredom, the oppressiveness of winter that has been piling on for months. Inhale the scents around you, particularly the lemon peel, frankincense, and myrrh. Each of these have cleansing, purifying qualities. Let the feeling of clean wash over you and visualize the "dirt" washing away. Picture what exhaust-covered snow looks like. It's dirty and dingy, but when clean hot water is poured over the snow, it melts away, revealing the grass below just waiting for the rays of the sun to wake it up and bring it back to a lush green life. You are the waiting grass. You need to melt away the cold, dirty snow and warm up your roots for your growing season. Feel the change take place inside of you. Really feel it. Feel the relief of becoming clean and pure once again. This may become very emotionally, and that's good. Let out your built-up frustrations. Splash the water if you feel like it. Kick and scream. Any mess you make can easily be cleaned up later—it is, after all, just water. Cry if you feel like it. Let out feelings of boredom, help-lessness, frustration, powerlessness, sadness, and any other negative feelings you need to let go of. Just let them out, then pull the bath-tub drain plug and let those feelings be sucked right down the drain. Send them out of you and on their way.

Exit the tub and get dressed, or if you prefer, proceed to the next part of the ritual skyclad. You may just want to throw a robe or cloak on to keep you warm without interrupting the flow of your ritual and energy too much.

Proceed to your prepared altar area. If you want to cast a circle or call quarters, do so now. Light the charcoal tablet and place it in a safe location. Light the red candle and place in a safe location as well. Drip a few drops of the sandalwood oil onto the lit charcoal. Pass your journal through the smoke the oil gives off and say:

Bless this work I do today.

Pass the writing utensil through the smoke and say:

Bring to fruition, these words I write.

Take a seat in front of your altar and get comfortable. Take a few deep breaths to relax and center yourself. While preparing for this ritual, you have had some ideas come to you about what you would like to work on and what you would like to plan. Take the time now to meditate on those thoughts and explore them more fully. You may want to title one page "brainstorming" and another "final thoughts." You may want to use a list or outline format. You may want to draw what you want to see come to fruition. Take as much time as you need to think about and write about your plans. Be as concrete with your thoughts as possible. Don't just say, "I want to be happier," write about what you need in order to be happier. Do you need a plan to have more free time in order to pursue pastimes that bring you joy? Dissect how that happens, and then write about it. Perhaps becoming more organized mentally and physically with your surroundings would help free up time. Put real thought into what you want and need and what steps you need to take to get there. If you really have no ideas, perhaps that is precisely what you need to work on—getting to know yourself better and what you want out of life. Write about the steps you are going to take in order to do that. When you need a boost, add a couple more drops of the sandalwood oil to the charcoal tablet. When you are finished with the planning portion, place your journal back on the altar and say the following:

Brigid, goddess of transformation, lend to me your strength, to bend, to ply, to shape my wishes and desires into realization. Your blessings are appreciated and I give my thankfulness and devotion in return.

Begin the final part of this ritual by sprinkling a few drops of both the bergamot and black pepper oils onto the charcoal tablet. Both have energy raising properties. Remain standing through this part of the ritual until the end. You are going to raise energy to recharge and rejuvenate your spirit. If you like drumming, do that. If you prefer to dance, do that. (Just have music ready to go if you want it.) Whatever it is you like to do to raise energy, spend time doing that and do it knowing you are doing it just for you. Often when we raise energy it's for some far greater purpose such as sending healing out into the world. But this time it is all for you. If you want to sing, drum, and dance around naked, go for it! Raise the energy, keeping in mind that your intent is simply to raise energy for you. When you hit the point of release, let it go and collapse to the ground. Roll around on the floor and let the excess energy soak into the carpet or whatever is beneath you. Feel the release of pent-up emotions and feelings. Feel the energy you built up giving new life to your spirit. Release everything. You may find yourself wanting to laugh; this is common, so let yourself laugh. Let the energy and endorphins breathe new life into your spirit and soul. When you have come down from your energy high and are fully grounded, state purposefully:

So Mote it Be.

Often these are just words to end a ritual or spell, but don't let that be the case. Fully feel these words as you say them, and then allow them to come true.

Notes

Ostara

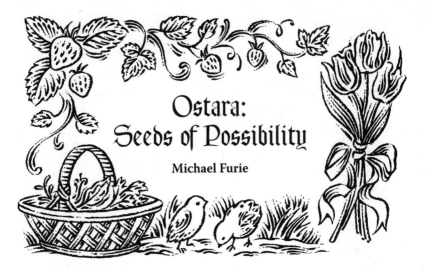

Ostara: Seeds of Possibility

Michael Furie

LIGHTING THE FIRE, THE witch proclaims, "When equal night meets equal day, the power of winter is chased away; the earth awakens from her slumber, life-force builds in greater numbers; waxing light breaks free from the storm, the world revives, green and warm." The fire leaps up, confirming the energy of the sacred day: Ostara, the vernal equinox.

Depending upon tradition, this holiday can be celebrated for a variety of reasons. One of the four seasonal markers, this sabbat occurs between Imbolc and Candlemas on February 1 and Beltane on the 1st of May. The exact date of Ostara varies since our modern calendar is imperfect, but the day falls roughly around March 21 each year. According to generally accepted lore, the point of vernal equinox marks the awakening of the Great Goddess from the slumber of winter. When the eight sabbats as a group are related as a cyclical story of the Goddess and God (telling of the yearly life course of the God through the agency of the Goddess and how this is reflected in nature), the time of the spring equinox is when the Goddess is fully awakened and the God is beginning to reach maturity. His growth is mirrored by the increasing heat and light of the sun. This rush of solar energy in turn vitalizes the earth, cultivates the atmosphere, and brings forth the full flowering of spring. The spiritual interaction of the Goddess and God is therefore reflected in the changing of the seasons in the natural world.

Aside from this mythos, which is intricately woven throughout all eight of the sabbats, there is also the individual legend of Ostara (or Eostre), the Saxon goddess that has given her name to the vernal equinox. Though her origins are steeped in mystery, Ostara is venerated as a goddess of spring, dawn, fertility, and the vibrant earth. This equinox, being the station of blossoming greenery, has become her official feast day to her followers. Since she is a goddess of new growth and life, practices to honor Ostara on this day can include such activities as gathering wildflowers, decorating eggs, the planting of herbs and seeds, and taking a walk in nature; all of these should be conducted with an attitude of reverence and joy.

This holiday is rich with spiritual significance and also natural and astronomical influence. The sabbat of Ostara is, among other things, the celebration of the vernal equinox, when the earth's polar tilt has reached the point in its cycle when the light of the sun is directly focused over the equator, the middle latitude region of the globe. When this occurs, the hours of daylight and darkness are basically equal. In one hemisphere, it is the season of spring, and simultaneously in the opposite hemisphere, it is the season of autumn. The interesting point about this, at least to me, is that unlike winter (when sunlight is farthest away from a given hemisphere) or summer (when sunlight is more directly over a given hemisphere), spring and autumn are only differentiated by what went before and what comes next. There are essentially only three main astronomical occurrences in regard to the seasonal shifts: upper solstice, middle point, and lower solstice. This cycle reverses and then there is another middle point and on to upper solstice and so on. When the midpoint is followed by shorter hours of daylight, then it is autumn, but when it is followed by the lengthening of daylight, it is the spring equinox.

The fact that they are basically the same phenomena (the sunlight directly over the equator) actually underscores their importance. The spring equinox begins the time of the greatest growth activity whereas its counterpart, the autumnal equinox, ushers in the time of the greatest dissolution activity. It is worth noting that both of these times occur when the sun is not at either extreme but at its midpoints in the yearly cycle. With spring in particular, there is such an incredible display of greenery, abundance, and new life all beginning at the magical point in the cycle when the levels of heat and light are ideal to sustain this delicate unfolding. As the season progresses, the majority of newborn plants and animals grow and become hardy enough to sustain themselves through the increasingly warm and dry weather.

Astrologically speaking, the spring equinox occurs when the Sun leaves Pisces, the last sign, and enters Aries, the first sign of the zodiac. Aries is a cardinal (initiator) sign whose element is fire. The Sun moves out of Pisces, a mutable (changing) sign whose element is water, and into Aries; thus a balance of fire and water are represented in the equinox. The element of earth is also astrologically represented since the peak of the spring season occurs when the Sun is traveling through Taurus, the fixed earth sign. Additionally, many Pagans associate spring with the element of air since it is a time of year that is frequently windy. Clearly, each of the elements are represented; the equinox shifts from water to fire, then moves into earth, and as it shifts away, it travels through air (Gemini) and out to water at the next season (Cancer on the summer solstice). As I see it, the vernal equinox is all about growth and rebirth through the interplay of the elemental forces. It is a vital convergence of life forces that signal to the natural world to fully awaken from its slumber and undertake the vital processes that ensure survival.

My own practice is somewhat different from the standard Ostara celebrations. Though I observe traditional elements of the holiday, such as doing the work of "turning the wheel," kindling a fire, honoring the growth of plants and animals, decorating eggs, and the like, part of my personal focus is bidding a bittersweet farewell to the cold half of the year. Being a priest of the Cailleach (the pre-Celtic Crone Goddess most strongly associated with winter), I have more than a fondness for the dark half of the year—Samhain to Beltane being her active time. Additionally, in the area where I live, the summer temperatures regularly reach into the 100 degree Fahrenheit range, and temperatures average in the mid-90s from April through the third week of October before the heat finally breaks. This being the case, cold weather (and rain) becomes a precious commodity: a gift from the goddess to soothe away the harshness of summer. Given the fact that I view summer in less favorable terms than most people, my view of spring also takes on a different, almost opposite dimension than the prevailing perception of the season.

Being the season that precedes the heat of summer, spring is all about moving forward and shifting into a higher gear and racing ahead, though the dark half of the year is not finished yet. In the Celtic dynamic of Cailleach and Bride, the Cailleach takes power on Samhain and begins to create the dark half: freezing the land with her hammer and keeping Bride, the goddess of the light half, imprisoned in her lair. The Cailleach has free rein through most of the wintertime, but Bride is freed by Angus, the god of love and son of Cailleach, on Imbolc and attempts to regain the land. Battles ensue between the goddesses, creating the tumultuous weather of late winter. As Cailleach tries to hold back the spring, the final battle is won on the vernal equinox (or March 25, for consistency), and Bride, aided by Angus, reclaims dominion over the land. Though Cailleach escapes their grasp and retains her power, causing some storms to rumble their way during the remainder of April, she is frustrated by the increasing heat and growth. On Beltane Eve, she throws down her hammer and transforms herself into gray stone to endure the light half of the year.

Not every Pagan follows this path, and there are variations of the tale even among those who do; regardless, it serves as a powerful reminder of the delicate balance between dark and light, cold and hot, winter and summer, and autumn and spring. Though the forces of spring are counter to the forces of autumn, they are in fact opposite sides of the same coin: equinox. The warring sides are linked together by the force of love. In this case, the son of Cailleach is the mate of Bride and the god of love. His power (love) was born of Cailleach (the year beginning in winter) and given freely to Bride, showing the yearly progression of emerging from the darkness and into the light. Cailleach holds the power of the cold and Bride holds the power of the warmth, while Angus represents the progression from one to the other; he is, in a sense, the progression itself. In my own practice, though, I acknowledge the inevitable shift to warmer weather; during the spring equinox, I honor the Cailleach and send energy to her with the purpose of helping to minimize the heat of the light half of the year, helping to turn the wheel but not to an extreme.

Participating in the seasonal shifts is a time-honored practice. In some traditions, it is a major portion of the sabbat celebrations. To raise energy and release it out to the deities and then draw energy back down into our circle and to the earth to promote positive change is a wonderful, transformative experience. It lends a greater depth to the sabbat beyond celebration or spell work, and it brings us a glimpse of the cosmic connection, the divine and the powers of creation. We all continually create our own futures by our energy, intent, and experiences, but to do so consciously and for a greater purpose than ourselves is empowering. This can be accomplished in a variety of ways such as using a circle dance to create a cone of power, chanting, using guided meditations, or working with magical implements to raise and channel the energies.

Any actions taken now with a reverent attitude and a desire to connect can actually be part of making this magical connection to the season. Coloring eggs, though greatly associated with the Christian holiday of Easter, has Pagan roots. Eggs are a symbol of life and fertility, two themes that are paramount in spring. Decorating them in beautiful colors, images of the spring, or even of desired magical outcomes and then adding them to the sabbat feast can be a festive act of food magic perfectly in tune with the season. Another method of springtime food magic, much more of a long-term effort, would be to plant a magical garden of edible herbs and vegetables. Planting magically charged seeds creates plants that are pre-energized to work toward your goals. If you then use these plants in your meals, they can impart their influence into your life.

Ostara seems to be one of those holidays that tends to get overlooked or lumped in with Easter since there are some surface similarities to that holiday, but Ostara is a rich and distinct event with lore and practices all its own, and if we choose to connect to it, we are able to harness a great amount of earth and cosmic energy to create positive, growth-related change and restore balance in our lives. Whether we are seeking new opportunity, celebrating the burgeoning display of color and life, preparing ourselves for the heat of summer, or breaking free from the snows of winter, Ostara is a vibrant sabbat that can pave the way to prosperity, possibility, and advantage as we move through the rest of the year. It is a powerful time filled with the strength of Aries, the force of each of the four elements, and the divine influence of the deities of spring.

Cosmic Sway

April Elliott Kent

THROW OPEN THE WINDOWS and welcome spring! The Sun entering Aries at the vernal equinox signals that it's time to break soil and prepare it to receive new seeds. The nature of the tool we will use to do it is described by the condition of Mars, the planet that rules Aries; at this vernal equinox, Mars is in Taurus. The tempo of this Ostara season starts at a slow, steady pace, but not necessarily because that is our choice. Indeed, the Sun, Mercury, Venus, and Uranus all in Aries compel us to think quickly and act just as fast.

But Mars in Taurus knows better. Mercury (April 9–May 3) and Venus (through April 15) will be retrograde for much of this Ostara season, favoring a return to past ideas and projects. And the chart for the vernal equinox includes the Moon in a close conjunction with Saturn; for the first few weeks of the period, there is the feeling of being pinned under something heavy, unable to break out and move forward. Don't despair. Saturn adds a heavy load when he is trying to strengthen us for new challenges.

But by April 21, as Mars moves into Gemini and Venus has finally turned direct, the soil that was broken at Ostara begins to loosen up. By the time we reach the Taurus New Moon, we'll be well on our way to more fecund and productive times.

Changes in Direction

You probably have heard about Mercury retrograde, but did you know that all planets (other than the Sun and Moon, which astrologers call "planets" for the sake of convenience) have periods of retrograde motion?

Venus and Mars turn retrograde every couple of years, Jupiter for about four months each year, and Saturn about five. Uranus, Neptune, and Pluto are retrograde for about half of each year. The retrogrades of the slower-moving planets are generally most noticeable right around the time they are changing direction, either to move retrograde or direct.

This Ostara season is notable in the number of planets that are changing direction. Saturn (April 5), Mercury (April 9), and Pluto (April 20) will all turn retrograde, while Venus (April 15) will turn direct after her latest retrograde period. (Mercury will turn direct just after Beltane.) Between April 5 and May 3, many matters are in a state of flux, and it may not be the best time for making final decisions or permanent changes in your life.

New Moon in Aries—March 27, 2017

The New Moon in Aries is when the spirit of Ostara is probably at its strongest. With our energy renewed, it feels like time to put boots on the ground and get to work. At this New Moon, the enthusiasm is represented by a dynamic configuration of Mercury, Jupiter, Uranus, and Pluto, a combination that favors decisive action of all kinds.

However, the Sun, Moon, and Venus (still retrograde) are in a wide square to Saturn at the New Moon. The square aspect indicates the urge to act. Saturn indicates caution and roadblocks.

This New Moon ushers in an especially intense week of mounting tension and frustration between Saturn preparing to turn retrograde (April 5), the Sun making one of two annual square aspects to Pluto (April 8), and Mercury turning retrograde (April 9). Delaying all action between this New Moon and the next Full Moon is unrealistic, but at the very least, build in contingency plans in case you encounter unexpected obstacles. After the 15th, you might even find that what you had hoped to accomplish no longer seems worthwhile.

Full Moon in Libra—April 10, 2017

This is a Full Moon that brings recent tensions to the surface, possibly in a fairly explosive way. The Sun is in a conjunction with unpredictable Uranus, in opposition with the Moon and Jupiter in Libra, and all four square Pluto. Sudden, unpredictable actions bring an exaggerated reaction, triggering power struggles.

Venus, the planetary ruler of Libra, will turn direct five days after the Full Moon. For a month and a half, Venus retrograde has prompted introspection about what we really want. If you are involved in a relationship of any kind in which one person is feeling stifled, controlled, or simply needs a change, those feelings must be confronted now and the relationship renegotiated.

Mars in Gemini—April 21, 2017

Mars is one of the easiest planets to recognize in the actions and moods of the people around you. That's because it describes how we actually behave, and that doesn't always reflect our desires (Venus), emotions (the Moon), or thoughts (Mercury). As Mars changes signs on April 21, notice the changes in the people around you and the tempo of how work gets done. The change from Taurus to Gemini can be pretty striking—whereas Taurus is deliberate and measured, Gemini is spontaneous; Taurus likes to pursue a single plan at any given time, while Gemini is happiest when multitasking. Taurus doesn't say much, and Gemini loves conversation!

While Mars is in Gemini, you'll accomplish more with words than by example. Tell people what you plan to do and ask them for their help. Work (Mars) on your communication (Gemini). Conflicts will usually center around poorly chosen words, vague communication, or differences of opinion.

New Moon in Taurus—April 26, 2017

Though it falls a few days before Beltane this year, the New Moon in Taurus, symbolized by the bull, marks the true beginning of that season. In Irish tradition, this feast marked the beginning of summer when cattle were sent out to pasture. Rituals were performed to encourage growth and protect cattle and crops. Protective bonfires were built, and people and their cattle walked around the fires, sometimes leaping over them.

In astrology, Taurus is associated with contentment, fertility, protection of resources, and delight in the physical world. The New Moon in Taurus asks us to affirm all that brings pleasure and prosperity, to delight in what we have, and to take good care of what has been entrusted to us.

This is a fairly gentle New Moon chart, but there is a significant (and challenging) aspect between Venus, the ruler of Taurus, and Saturn. This aspect implies that we can generally have what we need and want during this New Moon month, but we will have to work for it. In doing so, however, we are likely to more greatly appreciate what we get.

So be willing to work, although there's no reason not to ask the universe for a little help. A friend swears by this very simple prosperity ritual, originated by astrologer Lynne Palmer.

Taurus New Moon Exercise: Draw upon Universal Abundance

This is a particularly appropriate ritual for the Taurus New Moon since Taurus is one of the two financial signs (Scorpio is the other). But you can actually try this one at any New Moon, and it couldn't be more simple.

Using a check from your check register (or, if you don't use checks, simply draw one on a piece of paper), write a check payable to yourself in an amount you wish to receive before the next New Moon. Sign the check, "The Law of Abundance."

The amount you choose might be for something practical or something you simply desire. The key is to choose an amount that you believe you could reasonably expect to receive in the next month. Then take Saturn's advice and work as hard as you can to help it come to you!

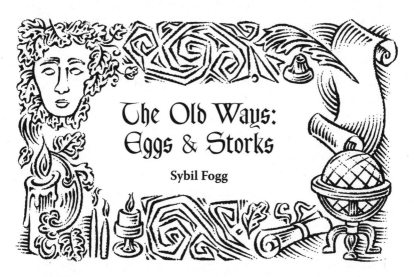

The Old Ways: Eggs & Storks

Sybil Fogg

MARZANNA, WHO CARRIED THE *plague with her, once traveled in a boat down the Vistula to reach the city of Warsaw, which had previously escaped her ravages. She stepped ashore and walked up the main street. Her long black hair flowed down her back, and a gentle breeze swirled her skirts about her tiny white feet. She was very beautiful, but those who knew her for what she was quickly turned their eyes away. To look her in the face would be to ask for doom.*

Those who were unfortunate enough to gaze upon her blushing complexion or who paused to look at her emerald green eyes would feel as if a fist had clenched their heart. Unable to speak a word, they returned to their homes, bringing the plague with them. (Asala 87)

The Polish goddess Marzanna—also called More (Lithuania), Morena (Russia), or Morana (Czech), or Mara, Maržena, Morana, Mora, or Marmora—is associated with the seasonal death and rebirth of nature, nightmares, the darkness of winter, and death. For sure, winters are hard in the Slavic countries, where they are long and cold. The winds alone can creep through clothing and chill the skin, howling like pained lovers drowning in the dark. Fall back through the centuries, and the winter months brought even more trepidation to those trying to battle through, their cupboards bare, the firewood in short supply, and hoping to see the spark of life that signals spring is on its way.

Marzanna wore many guises: one was of a beautiful woman with pale skin and either black or blond hair; her teeth were like that of a wolf, and she had claws for hands. Other names for her were Frost Maiden and Winter Witch. She was known to prey on the elderly and children who were most vulnerable in the winter. She also came for those who were afraid, often appearing as a crone, stealing through their dreams and wrecking their sleep with night terrors. She was closely associated with the Baba Yaga and is one of the oldest Slavic goddesses.

The Polish people still call on an old tradition to say goodbye to winter and Marzanna on the spring equinox. They start making a straw effigy of the goddess on the autumnal equinox, adding to it throughout the six months leading up to spring. Often women of the household would add something each moon cycle. The poppet ranged from the size of a small doll to life-sized. On the vernal equinox, the entire village would parade the Marzanna doll through the village to a riverbed. Along the way, she will be dipped into puddles and melting snow. Oftentimes, she was accompanied by a pine tree decorated with flowers and ribbons. Once the procession ended and all had gathered, Marzanna was set on fire and burned with sacred herbs. Afterward, she was drowned in the river water. There were many superstitions surrounding this ritual. As Marzanna was considered a powerful sorceress and bringer of doom and death, it was bad luck to look at her once she was in the water. One must be careful not to stumble or fall down on their way home, or they would be plagued by bad luck in the upcoming season. This ritual ensured a strong planting season and set winter to bed.

As Marzanna left to sleep through the warm months, she was replaced by her sister goddess, Devana (also known as Vesna, Zhiva, Živa, Siva, Sieba, Razivia, and Diva). The Polish goddess of springtime fertility, Devana was often depicted as being full-breasted, large-bellied, naked, covered by plant life, and having extremely long hair decorated with flowers. People were exultant to have Devana return to their world and of course bring with her the fertile earth ready to burst with life. It was believed that on the spring equinox, Devana came down the mountainsides singing beautiful songs that only some people could hear. The smell of springtime emanated from her, and everyone she passed felt comforted and hopeful. The people feasted, played games, and celebrated in her honor.

Revered and well-loved, Devana was closely associated with the willow tree in old Poland. This is one of the first trees to awaken in early spring, so it would have had great significance to those just coming out of a long, cold winter. Celebrations were held in late March into early April to honor Devana and the willow tree. It was a traditional custom for boys to waken girls early in the morning by pouring water over their heads and striking them on the legs with decorated twigs made from willow branches.

Even earlier customs focused on gift giving, particularly decorated eggs. Still, there was the threat of a soaking if no eggs were ready to be offered. As the day progressed, girls would find themselves dragged to rivers and ponds and soaked again and again. There are even tales of girls being carried in their beds to the water and thrown in, bed and all. Girls could "buy" their way out of a soaking by offering the decorated eggs. These were considered magical talismans that ensured a strong harvest, fertility, and safe childbirth. Maidens who escaped these small torments were considered unattractive or undesired. As time passed, girls were just as likely as boys to be fiercely armed with water balloons and squirt guns. The event is called Dyngus Day (Śmigus-Dyngus in Polish), and began to be held on Easter Monday with the advent of Christianity.

The arrival of spring also marks the return of the *bocian* (the stork) in Poland. A Polish legend tells of how frogs, snakes, lizards, and other reptile and amphibian animals became so numerous and were causing so many problems that God gathered them all in a sack and tasked a human with throwing the whole sack into the sea.

As curious as always, this human snuck a peak and inadvertently let all the animals escape. Angered, God transformed the human into a stork and left him to find all of the creatures (Hodorowicz Knab 91). Many Polish folktales link humans with storks. It was believed that we have many similarities to the large birds. A stork brought great luck and prosperity to the family whose property a stork chose to nest on. Not to mention, farmers could mark the change of seasons by their coming and going.

Perhaps this spring you will mark the equinox by honoring the stork and reading fairy tales that feature it. This would be a good time to draw on our Slavic ancestors and say goodbye to Marzanna with a small ritual in her honor, while welcoming Devana with water and eggs. We're thankful that spring has returned and the earth is fertile again.

Bibliography

Asala, Joanne, ed. *Polish Folklore and Myth.* Iowa City: Penfield Press, 2001.

Dixon-Kennedy, Mike. *Encyclopedia of Russian & Slavic Myth and Legend.* Santa Barbara: ABC-CLIO INC., 1998.

Hodorowicz Knab, Sophie. *Polish Customs, Traditions, & Folklore.* New York: Hippocrene Books, Inc., 1993.

Montley, Patricia. *In Nature's Honor: Myths and Rituals Celebrating the Earth.* Boston: Skinner House Books, 2005.

Feasts and Treats

Linda Raedisch

OSTARA AGAIN ALREADY? WHAT to do differently this year? It can be a challenge to assert oneself at what sometimes seems to be a very unwitchy season, with all those bunnies and chicks and that alarmingly green Easter grass underfoot. So I've decided to get back to basics with a tribute to the birthplace of modern Wicca: a trio of English recipes. Pork with bay leaves, *bragget*, and Simnel cake were all once part of the mid-Lenten "Mothering Sunday" celebration, an observance which then evolved from the American Mother's Day.

Easy One Dish Chop Dinner

Here's another taste of One Dish Witchery. Actually, it's a pan, not a dish. The pork and bay leaves are relics of the old Mothering Sunday dinner, while the curry powder adds a contemporary note. I wasn't sure if I should call it "easy," because it does require some peeling, slicing, and coating, but it's certainly easy on the eyes. The following recipe serves 4 and requires a large skillet, but if it's just you and your mum, you can halve the amounts and cook it in an ordinary size frying pan.

Prep time: 30 minutes
Cook time: 21 minutes
Servings: 4

2 tablespoons olive oil
4 very small Yukon Gold potatoes, peeled and cut into wedges
6 baby carrots, cut in quarters
½ yellow onion, peeled and cut into wedges
4 bay leaves
Salt
½ cup bread crumbs
2 teaspoons curry powder
Dash pepper
4 boneless pork chops
1 egg, well beaten

Heat olive oil in a large skillet on low to medium heat. Add potatoes, carrots, onion, and bay leaves. Sprinkle with salt and mix until all ingredients are coated in oil. Cover and cook over medium heat for about 15 minutes, stirring up occasionally.

While vegetables are cooking, mix bread crumbs, curry powder, pepper, and a dash of salt in shallow bowl or tray. Dip pork chops in beaten egg and dredge in bread crumb mixture to coat both sides.

Push vegetables to edges of skillet. Add a little more oil if necessary and add pork chops. Fry uncovered 3 minutes on each side —longer if pork chops are very thick.

If possible, bring the skillet to the table, bay leaves and all, just because it looks so pretty.

Teatotaller's Bragget

No, that's not a misspelling; this recipe uses barley tea in place of the more usual ale—we wouldn't want to get tipsy in front of Mother on her special day! According to my *Webster's*, an "ale" in antiquated English could also refer to a "merry meeting," so I don't suppose it matters what we're drinking, so long as we're in good company and we're not reduced to drinking barley water, which is only for sick people.

Bragget is ale brewed with mead or fermented honey, sometimes brewed with spices or apples. No hops are added, perhaps because the drink is so old, dating back at least to the early thirteenth century. The name comes from Welsh *bragawd*, meaning "malt," which is barley that has sprouted, dried, and then fermented.

Prep time: 2 minutes
Brew time: 10 minutes
Chill time: at least 1 hour
Servings: 8

4 individual barley tea bags (found in your Asian grocery store)
1 tablespoon honey
Clothespin
4 cups water
1 quart sparkling nonalcoholic cider

Tie teabags together and use clothespin to clip their strings to edge of pot. Add water, bring to boil, and simmer for 5 minutes. Add honey and stir until honey is dissolved. Remove tea bags and chill tea for 1 hour. Fill each glass with half tea and half cider.

Simnel Cake

In western England, Simnel cake dates back at least to the early seventeenth century when it was baked in honor of Mothering Sunday halfway through the Lenten season. Today, Simnel cake is more commonly eaten at Easter. Traditional Simnel cake contains candied citron along with the currants and the raisins. In this recipe, I have replaced the citron with dried apricots because citron can be hard to find in the U.S. other than at Christmas time. You won't find the usual golden raisins either, for the simple reason that I despise golden raisins.

I have also deviated when it comes to the ring of marzipan balls on top: there are supposed to be 11 to stand for the 12 apostles, minus Judas Iscariot, but I have made it 13 to stand for a jolly coven of witches. After you've rolled and settled your marzipan balls on top of the cake, you will probably want to add a flock of marshmallow Peeps. Oh, come on, you know you will—it's springtime after all! Go ahead, but please don't put them on until AFTER the cake has come out from under the broiler. (And for the record, I had nothing to do with the Great Peep Roast of 2013. Yes, I provided the Peeps. And the candles. And the skewers. But I had no idea what my children were going to do with them!)

Prep time: best to start a day ahead

Bake time: 1 hour and then some for broiling

Servings: 13 small slices

½ cup black raisins

½ cup dried currents

⅓ cup dried apricots, diced

1 cup orange juice (or brandy if you prefer)

Butter for greasing

1 8-inch spring form or layer cake pan

Baking parchment

½ cup butter (1 stick)

½ cup white sugar

2 eggs

1 cup white flour

Zest of 1 small lemon

1 teaspoon cinnamon

1 7-ounce package marzipan (a. k. a. "almond candy dough")

Rolling pin

Wax paper

5 tablespoons apricot jam (approx.)

Pastry brush

1 egg yolk (for final step)

Place dried fruits in medium-sized bowl and cover them with orange juice. Set aside to soak. (For a moister cake, do this a day ahead of time.)

Grease pan and line with baking parchment. Preheat oven to 350 degrees F.

Cream butter and sugar together in large bowl. Beat in 2 eggs with electric mixer until thoroughly mixed. Sift in flour—you can sift it by pouring it into the bowl through a sieve. Mix again until blended.

Drain fruits well before folding into batter with wooden spoon and adding in lemon zest and cinnamon. Spread batter evenly in pan and bake for 1 hour or until golden brown on top and firm to the touch.

Cool for 10 minutes, then turn cake upside down onto a cookie sheet—yes, a cookie sheet—and cool for another 30 minutes. In the meantime, you can prepare the topping. Divide your marzipan in half and roll one half into a circle large enough to cover top of cake. Roll out on wax paper to prevent marzipan from sticking to table.

Spread top of cake with apricot jam—stirring it in a bowl first will make it easier to spread—then place marzipan circle over jam.

Preheat broiler. Slice remaining marzipan into 13 slices, roll each into a ball and place in a ring on top of cake. Use a little apricot jam to glue them in place. Paint marzipan with beaten egg yolk and place cake under broiler for...well, it depends on your broiler. Mine did the job in about 2 minutes, so keep an eye on it and take it out as soon as the marzipan turns golden brown.

Transfer to cake plate, address the Peeps question, and present proudly at table.

Crafty Crafts

Mickie Mueller

SEED BOMBS ARE A wonderful and colorful tool of guerilla gardening, perfect for the symbolic breaking of inertia that happens with the spring equinox. Seeds have slept beneath the earth all winter and buds are tightly wrapped on tree branches. Then Ostara arrives and it's like the alarm clock going off while the earth is snug under its blankets; the hardest part is just getting up and moving, so nature produces a lot of energy to get the season of growth started. Seed bombs are a great way to celebrate the season, bursting full of the power of rebirth as the sprouts, buds, and blossoms burst forth from the deep dark earth.

These easy eggs can be planted in pots, tossed into your garden, or cast into empty lots in your area to beautify and, more importantly, support local wildlife such as bees and butterflies. This project is made from recycled shredded paper mixed with water and wildflower seeds; dried flower petals can be added for color. These eggs are a lovely part of your Ostara décor, and they look beautiful on your altar or make a pretty gift. Fill them with your intentions for the future and plant them on or after Ostara. You can buy seed bombs, and some are egg shaped, but they're so darned easy and inexpensive to make!

Seed Bomb Eggs

Time to complete: about 1 hour (up to a couple days to dry)
Cost: $3 to $5 (depending on whether you use recycled paper or purchase colored paper)

Supplies

4 sheets of paper or equivalent amount from paper shredder
3 cups of water
Seeds (consider choosing mixed wildflowers native to your area)
Mesh strainer
Mixing bowl
Food processer or blender
Optional dried flower petals
Optional food coloring

If you're using four sheets of paper, tear them into small pieces. If you're using paper from the paper shredder, just grab about three sheets of papers worth—your shredding is already done. Drop your shredded paper pieces into your food processer or blender, and then pour in three cups of water. If you want to tint your seed bomb eggs, add several drops of food coloring in your water before adding it to the paper. Let it soak for about ten minutes. After the paper has soaked, turn on the blender or food processor and let those blades turn that wet paper and water into a nice mushy pulp. You might have to scrape the sides with a rubber spatula a couple times to make sure all the paper is finely blended.

Set the mesh strainer in a large mixing bowl so the mixing bowl can catch the extra water. Scoop the paper pulp from your blender or food processor and into the strainer and leave it for about five minutes to allow some of the water to drain out. Now add the seeds. About one pack of seeds is enough, and if you're adding flower petals, now would be the time to add them. With your hands, work the seeds and flower petals throughout the mixture, making sure that they're evenly dispersed.

Pick up a handful of the mixture. Squeeze the excess water out as you use your hands to roll it into a ball shape a little smaller than a golf ball. Roll the paper mixture gently on one end to taper the ball into an egg shape. If it crumbles, it means too much water was squeezed out. You can add a bit of water back in, squish it around in your hand, and reshape it. Repeat the process until you have a nice clutch of egg-shaped seed bombs. Set them on a plate and allow them to dry. Depending on your climate, it might take a day or two.

Optional: Here's a great way to add some petition magic to your seed bombs! On a tiny slip of paper, write a petition about something you would like to see grow and blossom in your life. Soak the paper petition in water and when you're ready to form your seed bomb, form it around the petition. Fill the seed bomb with your magical intention as you form it into an egg shape and visualize your goal already met and manifested in your life. When the seeds sprout, grow, and bloom, so shall your goal!

Bird's Nest

If you need a place for your seed bomb eggs to rest on your Ostara altar, mantle, or shelf until you're ready to cast them out into the world to grow, how about a lovely bird's nest! This nest is perfect for nurturing your seeds while they wait to be planted. It's really easy to make, lots of fun, and you can use materials from around the house or outside.

Time to complete: 20–45 minutes (more for drying)
Cost: $10 (or less if you're thrifty)

Supplies

A round cereal bowl
Round balloon
White glue
Nest materials (try raffia, dried grass, twine, paper shreds, string, small feathers, floral moss, yarn, or embroidery floss)

Blow up your balloon so that it fits snugly in the cereal bowl. Gather up your nest-making materials and cut the grass, twine, etc., into strips about six inches in length or less. Now mix your glue in a bowl with a little water; I used three parts glue to one part water.

Now start dipping your strings and things one by one into the glue, then run your fingers along the string to remove the excess glue, and lay it over the balloon. Keep adding more materials in a variety of directions one by one. Don't get too wrapped up in keeping it all even, the more free-form you make it, the more like a natural bird's nest it will look.

Mix up directions as you lay your materials and just keep on adding until you completely cover the balloon. You can build it up more and more with a variety of materials until it's about a half inch thick for a natural look, or you can leave it light and airy with just a single color of yarn or twine for a more contemporary artsy feel.

When you're happy with it, add a ring about three inches in diameter to the bottom of your nest. Use one of your thicker materials like a piece of heavy twine, yarn, or raffia. If you don't have heavy

enough materials, twist a few together after dipping them in glue. This base ring will help your nest sit nicely without rocking on the table. Leave it to dry completely for at least five hours to be sure.

Is it dry? Grab a pin and pop the balloon! Now you can lay a little thin layer of moss on the inside and maybe add a leaf or a little feather or two. Now your bird's nest looks amazing and you can place your pretty seed bomb eggs inside.

All One Family

Dallas Jennifer Cobb

ANY SABBAT THAT FOCUSES on feasting is one that welcomes the involvement of teenagers. Chocolate becoming an important part of the lesser sabbat Eostar certainly helps. Eostar is also known as Ostara and vernal (spring) equinox, from the Latin *aequus* "equal" and *nox* "night." This is a moment of balance when light and dark and day and night become equal again.

Easter has its origins in Eostar, and while it has shifted a bit on the Roman calendar, Easter maintains all the symbols tradition- ally associated with Eostar: eggs, rabbits, baby animals, lambs, and seeds. These symbols of Eostar are also symbols of fertility, spring, and rebirth. While Yule represented the rebirth of the sun, Eostar represents the rebirth of the earth.

In much of North America, the vernal equinox is a time of early planting. If you live in Canada like me, or the northern United States, then it is a time to start seeds indoors. These seedlings will grow strong, and will be ready to be transplanted outdoors when the threat of frost has passed.

Eostar is a time of celebration as the light gains. Life is growing and the quickened seeds stir deep beneath the soil, ready to sprout. The earth is awakening, slowly. This is a time of celebrating the young virgin Goddess and her energy of beauty, strength, and freedom that we now witness in the wildness of nature.

The word "virgin" didn't always have all the sexual connotations it has now. It actually once meant a woman who was not under the care and control of a father, brother, or husband; a woman who was autonomous, independent, and not required to answer to any man or child. The word has become subverted and is used in the modern era to denote a person who has never engaged in sexual intercourse. While historically the term was usually ascribed to female persons, specifically those who became priestesses of the Goddess and fulfilled the role of "vestal virgin," these days the word "virgin" applies to both male and female. And even though the use of the word "virgin" traditionally referred to power and autonomy, and solely to females, let's extend it to apply to both males and females for the sake of modern conversations about the word.

Leading up to Eostar, have some conversations with your teens about the word "virgin." Oh, I know, at first they will cringe and say: "No, Mom. No talking about sex." My daughter even stuck her fingers in her ears. But if you can be clear that you are really talking about the word's meaning, you may just hook them. My daughter loves to know things that her peers and even teachers don't. I think she feels quite powerful with the knowledge.

Introduce the ancient meaning of the word "virgin." Talk to your teens about autonomy. After all, the teen years are a time of exploring greater and greater autonomy and independence. Help to identify the areas that your teenager is becoming more autonomous in: Are they able to plan meals, shop, and cook? Do they do their own laundry and clothes shopping? Are they able to schedule time to get their homework and projects done on a timeline? Encourage your teenager to talk about how autonomy feels. Do they remember when they were young and could never be left alone? Compare it to now and how self-sufficient they are.

In some Pagan traditions, witches would make a list of injustices in the days leading up to Eostar: what others had done to them, and what they had done to others. With their list of negatives, the witches would set about doing positive acts to benefit those they harmed to attempt to right the injustice. The good they did helped to level out the scales of karma.

Practice: Burning Injustice

Gather a candle, matches, a fireproof bowl, a few slips of paper, and pens.

Sit with your teenager and recount the story of Persephone and Demeter. If you're like me, your teens are familiar with it from Samhain. Talk about Eostar being the time when Persephone begins her ascent, climbing back up to the earth's surface. She climbs back to Demeter, to love, and to the light.

Each take a slip of paper and a pen. List where and with whom you have experienced injustice.

Share your lists, and let your teen express how much injustice has hurt them.

On the other side of the same paper, each of you make a list of ways that you have been unfair to others. List the person and the injustice. It is not necessary to share this information. Then say:

It's time for us to begin the journey up, into the light, out of Hades.

Light the candle and let it illuminate you. Carefully light your slip of paper on fire, and set it in the fireproof bowl. Invite your teenager to do so as well. Then proclaim:

Now the light overcomes the dark.

With the candle still burning, each take another slip of paper. Write the antidote to your negative actions on the paper. Maybe it is doing a good deed for someone you have harmed or giving a small gift. Maybe the antidote is to draw closer to someone you have been apart from for a while, much like Persephone will be doing.

Using the candle, carefully burn the antidote lists, and release them into the light.

As you blow out the candle, implore your teenager to walk up and out and into the light. Now that they are autonomous and independent, teach them how to right their own wrongs.

Seal the deal with a sweet chocolate bunny or egg. As you hand the treat to your teenager, say:

Today we celebrate your autonomous journey, planting these seeds of wisdom and understanding. As the earth comes into balance, so do we. And as the light grows outside of us, let the goodness grow inside of us, becoming stronger than the dark.

Planting the Seeds of Spring

Michael Furie

IN MY PRACTICE, THE primary purpose of conducting a sabbat ritual is to send energy outward and to actually participate in the energy shift and help "turn the wheel," as some say. For this sabbat, a fantastic way to accomplish this while celebrating the growth and power of the season is through the use of a stang. A stang is a forked branch of wood that is cut at staff height and used as a magical implement. It can act as an antenna of sorts, a conduit for magical energy. In some traditions, there are specific methods for the creation of a stang, but for this rite, all that is needed is a forked branch about the size of a typical staff. If one cannot be obtained, a witch's broom or wand could be used as substitutes. Before the rite, make some decorations in honor of your chosen deities. These should be something small that you can hang on the forks of the stang during the ritual, such as bags of herbs or ornaments symbolic of the deities. This ritual is written as a solitary rite, but it could be modified for a group simply by assigning different people to various tasks and joining everyone together during the visualizations.

Items Needed

Flower pot filled with soil (large enough to support the stang)

Cauldron

Candles: green, black, and white

Incense (rose or preferred scent) and censer

Bowl of water

Chalice of water

Bowl of salt

Deity decorations

Flowers and/or ribbons to mark the circle's boundary

Four stones to mark the directions (or your preferred method)

Stang (or substitute)

Bowl of seeds from a plant you wish to grow

Place the flower pot filled with soil in the center of the circle area, and place the altar table just to the south of the pot that is facing north. On the altar, set the cauldron, which is holding the green candle (unlit), in the center with the black and white candles behind the cauldron: black on the left, white on the right, and the censer between them. The chalice and bowl of water go on the left and the bowl of salt can be placed to the right of the cauldron along with the deity decorations. Adorn the boundary of the circle with ribbons and flowers, preferably in festive pastels. Place the point stones at the cardinal directions. Instead of stones, you could use items tailored to the elements of those directions, such as a lump of moss agate or bowl of salt in the north for earth; a feather, lavender flowers, or a censer of incense in the east for air; a candle or lava rock in the south for fire; and a bowl of water or a moonstone in the west for water. Whatever your choice, place the objects just outside the boundary of the circle at the proper compass points. If you use a candle in the south, make sure it is lit before you do the circle casting, and light the black candle then the white candle at this time.

The next step is to cleanse and bless the water and salt. Hold both hands over the bowl of water and envision white light streaming from your hands into the water while saying:

I cleanse this water and banish anything not in harmony with me. As I will, so mote it be.

Then hold hands over the salt, envision the light, and say:

I bless this salt so that it may be in harmony with my rite. As I will, so mote it be.

Starting in the north, cast the circle by picking up the stang and pointing the forked end of the stang out and sending energy through it, moving in a clockwise motion to cast the circle. Walk the circle three times, ending in the north. Now, facing north, hold up the stang and invoke the element of earth, saying:

Power of earth, heed my call, join my circle and my rite.

Continuing clockwise, move around the circle and invoke the elements, substituting "power of air" in the east, "power of fire" in the south, and "power of water" in the west before ending in the north once more. After the elements have been called, pivot around and drive the single point of the stang into the flower pot so it is held in place like a small tree. As you place the stang, say:

In magic circle, here are joined, land, sea, and sky do merge; the three great realms of nature combine with sacred fire to seal the charge. The circle is made.

This draws the elements from the directions through the stang and into the circle's center point.

Pour the salt into the water bowl and sprinkle the saltwater around the circle, moving clockwise. Afterward, carry the incense around and then carry the black candle around so that each of the elements have further charged the atmosphere. It is then time to take the deity decorations and hang them on the branches of the stang while invoking them into the circle. For simplicity's sake, it is assumed that there are two deities being called on, a goddess and god, though whichever deities you choose to work with can be invoked with minimal adjustments. Your own words are best, but as you place the goddess token(s) on the stang, you could say:

Gracious maiden of the spring, I call you now into this ring. Channel your power through the stang to bring renewal back to this land.

As you place the god token(s) on the stang, you could say:

Bright new god on this blessed day, descend into my circle here. Send your energy through this stang to energize the atmosphere.

Once the gods have been invoked, it is time to charge the green candle. Pick up the candle in both hands, and in your mind's eye, conceptualize how you want the season to unfold. If you are working on specific projects or goals, they can be incorporated into this rite. It is very important to focus mainly on how you want to feel during this phase of the year and how you would like your personal environment to be—peaceful, busy, relaxed, etc. If weather is a concern where you live, it is fine to include the type of weather you would prefer to experience in your intent. This is not direct weather magic; it is implanting your desire into the seasonal and atmospheric shifts already taking place and sending it to the deities in a manner of making it known, versus an authoritative command. This isn't wordplay, but an important distinction. In weather magic, the goal is usually to change the already-formed weather patterns into something new. In this work, the goal should be to request that your preferred weather unfold through the season, creating versus altering. This has less potential for mishap since it connects to the deities. They have the power to override our influence if it would disrupt the balance too greatly.

Once the candle has been charged, set it back in the cauldron and light it with the words:

As Ostara brings the change, my vision I do now release: To Goddess and God I send this flame, charged with desire, balance, and peace. Without harm and blessed be, for good of all, so mote it be.

Since the stang is the conduit for the circle, elements, and deities, this chant will channel the energy of the candle into it as well. As the power is being released from the candle, it is time to take up the seeds, hold them in your hands over the candle (high enough so that you don't burn yourself), and envision that some of the magic is being absorbed into the seeds to charge them. When you feel ready, take the seeds and use your fingers to poke holes in the dirt, and plant the seeds in the flower pot in a circle around the stang. Return to the altar and pick up the chalice of water. Hold the cup in salute to the deities and say:

I charge this water with magical force, that it may nurture, bless, and heal. To encourage growth; a brave new course, sustain life, and turn the wheel.

Take a sip of the water and pour the rest over the seeds to begin the process of germination. As the seeds grow throughout the season, they'll be physical representations of your magical intentions, almost like living poppets. Care for them and your goals shall surely manifest.

To conclude the ritual, thank the deities in your own words and remove the tokens from the stang. Carefully pull the stang out of the flower pot and use it to release the elements from the circle, starting in the north. Point the stang at the north point and say:

Power of earth, I thank you for attending this rite. Blessed be and farewell.

Repeat at the east, south, and west, substituting the appropriate elements. Finally, open the circle by "cutting" through it with the stang, making one last walk around the circle, and saying:

This circle is open, the power set free; to turn the wheel, blessed be.

Extinguish the candles in reverse order of lighting: green, white, then black.

Notes

Beltane

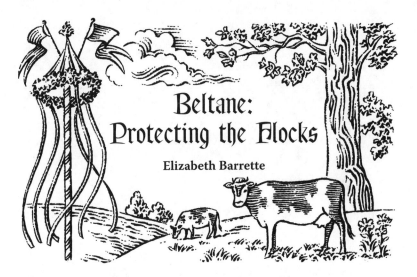

Beltane: Protecting the Flocks

Elizabeth Barrette

BELTANE IS A VERSATILE holiday spanning May Eve (April 30) and May Day (May 1). It is famous for having many different associations. These include bonfires, feasts, flowers, dancing, and, of course, the maypole. Activities may aim to convey fertility, purification, protection, or other desired benefits on people and livestock.

The Purposes of Beltane

A challenge in modern Paganism is that this holiday has been celebrated by multiple cultures over a long period of time. Naturally, each culture—even each village—developed its own favorite traditions. So when you look at the results from this end of the time stream, it makes quite a jumble. Therefore, designing a good Beltane celebration depends on picking a focus and choosing among the many options which support it best.

This time, we're going to concentrate on purification and protection. In ancient times, people had a lot to worry about: plagues, famines, invaders, violent weather, and so forth. Thus they developed ways to drive out malicious influences and keep them at bay. Today, some of those challenges remain, while others have changed to bring new and different threats. So we can still benefit from these traditional rites of cleansing and warding. Your "flocks" may be family, covenmates, pets, livestock, or whatever else you value.

Methods of Purification

Purification means cleaning away everything harmful—dirt, disease, negative energy, and so on. It also means making something spiritually clean. This creates a fresh, smooth base for whatever other magic you want to put on top of it. Think of it like washing a window before putting a sticker or decal on the glass.

A vital first step is to throw out old things and do some spring cleaning. At Beltane, people would empty the storehouses of any supplies that had gone bad. Tools in need of repair were set aside to be fixed; those that could not be repaired were discarded so that new ones could be made. Then houses, barns, and other buildings were scrubbed clean. Similar steps work today with housecleaning of any kind or tending to the covenstead and its landscape.

Water may provide the most common form of purification. Objects are washed. People bathe. In a ritual, an aspergillum or other artifact sprinkles holy water over people or items to be blessed. Other times, the water is presented in a basin where hands or objects may be dipped into it.

Fire is another form of cleansing. Heat and light destroy many germs. Smoke deters pests such as lice, fleas, and rats. Many celebrations involved driving livestock down a corridor of torches, between two bonfires, or some similar arrangement. People would customarily jump over a fire, which may have been done with a ramp above a bonfire, or with a row of coals scraped into a low trench for a safer version.

Plants also play an important part. It is traditional to gather flowers and insecticidal herbs for Beltane. Often the wood for the bonfire, or at least a symbolic bundle of it, consists of logs from specific trees chosen for their sacred or magical properties. Birching— gently tapping the skin with a bundle of twigs—is another method of purification usually performed in a dry sauna or steam bath. It removes sweat and dirt from the skin, a welcomed luxury after a long grubby winter. Despite the name birching, willow works as well as birch for this purpose.

Methods of Protection

Once everything has been cleansed, it must be guarded. Protection is the act of creating a powerful barrier to keep undesirable influences away. Different aspects of this appear in traditional Beltane activities, often combined with or following those for purification.

Walls are the most material way of blocking things out. For this holiday, people often created "fire walls," which could be a dotted line of torches, a tall sheet of flame, a long ditch full of coals, or the like. If you're working inside, you can substitute candles—or for a more modern flair, a rope light, as electricity is a form of fire. Another form of wall that was popular at Beltane is the wattle fence. Green withes are easy to cut and weave in the spring, typically taken from trees such as willow or hazel. Making these walls on the holiday imbues them with extra energy so they last longer and protect better.

Plants may be gathered for their protective abilities. This produces a slightly different collection than those for purification, although there is significant overlap between the two categories. Notably, trees with thorns and herbs with a "hot" flavor excel at guardian duties.

Defensive blessings may be conveyed in various ways. Singing and dancing are popular. Dancing has an additional use in frightening away evil, hence the use of noisemakers or fearsome masks. Another option is painting sacred symbols onto people or property. In this case, the paint itself may hold extra power. For instance, woad stands out as the mystical pigment in Celtic cultures, while some other European cultures prefer red ochre. For secret symbols, simply use transparent oil or even water.

Sacred Plants for Beltane

Beltane marks the beginning of the "light half" of the year in Celtic tradition, and in various others, the summer or growing season. For this reason, it has particularly strong associations with flowers, herbs, trees, and other plants. Some are sacred to gods and goddesses celebrated at this sabbat. Others have magical or practical applications. Bouquets, baskets, and garlands of flowers festoon revelers and the ritual site. Bonfires require a considerable amount of fuel, and using sacred woods for them can add a great deal of energy to the ritual for not much extra effort. Below are some of the numerous plants useful in a Beltane celebration for purification and protection.

Alyssum—These tiny flowers come in white to purple, useful for filling out spring bouquets. They convey protection and help minimize anger.

Ash—The wood of this tree lends power to spells and rituals. In addition to general protection, it is particularly good to guard against drowning and to promote invincibility. For this reason, it is favored in sacred tools and fires.

Blackberry—The leaves may be added to water for bathing or cleaning to give protection. Thorny branches made into a garland with ivy and rowan will protect against evil spirits, invite fairies, and attract the goddess Brigit. Berries are a traditional Beltane food.

Blue violet—This flower, associated with Beltane and the Goddess, can be white, blue, or purple. It protects against evil, bringing good fortune, love, and inspiration. It is a staple of May baskets, but should be picked and used immediately since it wilts quickly.

Camphor—Available as resin nodules or oil, this herb adds strength to any mixture. It is used for ritual cleaning in homes and covensteads. It also enhances persuasion and psychic awareness.

Cedar—Various small bushes and tall trees make up the cedar family. The wood burns with a sweet fragrance. The boughs may be used to sprinkle consecrated water. Cedar bestows purification, protection, power, and confidence. Hung in the home, it wards off lightning.

Club moss—Low-growing and humble, this herb provides protection and power. In the bath, it purifies. Burned as incense, it opens a line of communication with higher powers.

Copal—This spicy resin contributes to love and purification incenses. A nodule can also form the heart of a poppet, if you prefer to pass poppets over the fire to avoid people jumping it.

Dogwood—Growing as a large bush or small tree, it puts out white or pink flowers. It protects secrets, bestowing confidence and good health.

Eucalyptus—Available as resin or oil, this plant purifies and protects. It also has strong healing energy. It makes a good base for cleansing formulas.

Fern—Fluffy green leaves make terrific bundles for sprinkling blessed water. This plant purifies and cleanses. It aids mental focus and dispels negative energy. Burned with heather, it summons rain, so be careful not to combine them unless you want to work weather magic!

Frankincense—This famous resin forms the base of many sacred incense blends. It purifies, protects, and consecrates. It is a traditional offering on many occasions, including Beltane. It attracts divine attention. Mix with cumin for stronger protective properties.

Gorse—Thorns mark plants with protective powers. Springy and prickly, gorse provides a formidable barrier of protection against negativity or dark magic.

Gum arabic—As a resin, it makes a great base for incense aimed at protection, consecration, or meditation. It enhances both psychic and spiritual potential.

Heather—Low-growing plants cover themselves with tiny bells of white, pink, or purple. Heather brings protection, good fortune, and long life. It especially guards against sexual misconduct and other violence. This is an excellent herb for sprinkling blessed water. Burned with fern, it promotes rain, so don't combine them unless that's what you want.

Hickory—This sturdy tree has strong wood associated with protection, love, and justice.

Ivy—Its spiral growth makes this vine sacred in Celtic and other traditions. It conveys protection, fertility, and affection. Ivy growing outside repels unwanted guests and harmful energies.

Juniper—From creeping ground cover to vigorous tree, juniper banishes all manner of bad things and attracts the good. When burned, it gives magical protection. Hung over the threshold, juniper sprigs deter theft.

Lavender—Tiny purple flowers and gray-green leaves may be woven into wands of fragrant charm. It is also available as oil. Lavender promotes sleep, peace, purification, and protection. It is ideal for use in baths or wash water.

Oak—A vast spreading tree, oak produces holy wood ideal for both fires and toolmaking. It burns long and hot, but costs more than soft wood. The leaves may be burned for purification. Oak represents the God, especially Herne and Cernunnos.

Peony—Bushy dark-green plants produce enormous white or pink flowers in spring. The flowers protect against dark magic and attract good fortune.

Pine—Medium to large trees have long green needles. The wood burns with a sweet fragrance and much popping of resin and sparks. It's a cheap plentiful wood for bonfires, but stand back for safety. Pine is associated with grounding, growth, new beginnings, and the divine masculine. It cleanses and protects against hostile influences.

Rosemary—This small, dark-green herb resembles a miniature pine tree and smells similar. Rosemary is used in poppets for love or health, dream pillows for memory and protection against nightmares, and incense for purification and banishment of negative forces. Rosemary oil may be added to water for washing or bathing.

Sandalwood—Growing as a small tree, it usually arrives in the form of wood chips or incense, but sometimes you can find lovely fans made from sandalwood. It removes negativity and conveys protection. This makes a light, spicy base for incense blends.

Snapdragon—Spires of flowers come in all the hot colors plus white. Blooming spring to summer, they look gorgeous in a vase or basket. Snapdragons provide purification, protection, and exorcism.

Thyme—Like a miniature shrub, it grows dense and woody with tiny leaves. Thyme promotes affection, loyalty, and fellow-feeling. Burn it for purification and banishment. The leaves may also be steeped in cleansing baths prior to ritual.

Applications

Cleansing floor wash—a capful of camphor, eucalyptus, and rosemary oils in a bucket of water with a splash of vinegar.

Purifying bath—blackberry leaves, lavender, and thyme in a sachet.

Protection incense—Gum arabic, club moss, and sandalwood burnt over charcoal.

May basket—white alyssum, blue-and-white violets, pink peonies, and assorted pastel snapdragons.

Asperging bundle—green sprigs of cedar and fern, plus any color of heather in bloom.

Bonfire fuel (long-lasting, fewer sparks)—oak and ash logs, plus a big bag of cedar chips for fragrance.

Bonfire fuel (fast-burning, pretty sparks)—pine, cedar, and juniper branches plus a few hickory logs to keep the core going.

Cosmic Sway

April Elliott Kent

THIS BELTANE SEASON BEGINS with a very fertile combination of the Sun in stable, earthy Taurus and a waxing crescent Moon in nourishing Cancer. Whatever you wish can be brought to fruition during this season. There is a caveat, however: be sure you really want whatever you summon, because it's likely to change your life.

At Beltane, the Sun is always in Taurus, a sign of contentment, patience, and prosperity. But this season is also strongly colored by the position of Venus, Taurus's ruling planet. At this Beltane, Venus in Aries gives Taurus a boost of impulsiveness and dynamism. We generally move in a relaxed and contented way during this lush season, but this year there is a greater sense of urgency to act.

On May 18, Saturn and Uranus meet in the second of three exact trine aspects. The first was on December 24, 2016, and the last will fall during Samhain: November 11, 2017. Saturn and Uranus are planets with very different objectives. Saturn prefers structure, order, and rules; Uranus, to put it mildly, does not. But with the two of them coming together in a trine, the most harmonious of aspects, the time is right to bring their two worlds together. If you feel stuck, let Uranus break you out of your self-imposed prison. Invite Saturn to help you harness your chaotic brilliance into something inspiring, useful, and lasting.

Full Moon in Scorpio—May 11, 2017

You may be at a bit of a cross-roads, feeling as though greater forces are really in control of where you wind up. But with the Sun and Moon in powerful aspect to Pluto, you hold much more power than you may think.

The Sabian Symbol[1] for this Full Moon degree is, "Obeying his conscience, a soldier resists orders." This degree is about turning away from what goes against your beliefs and no longer seems right for you. That is how we empower ourselves: by living in integrity.

Scorpio is a sign characterized by release and the transformation that follows loss, so this is the best Full Moon all year for a "letting go" ritual. Here is one I learned from my friend, astrologer Dana Gerhardt, and I've used it many times with powerful results! It's a practice for getting unstuck or unburdened, which are the special purview of both Scorpio and the waning Moon.

Green Fire Ritual

Get a cast iron pot (I raid my kitchen for one of my good old cast iron skillets) and line it with heavy aluminum foil. Add two cups of Epsom salts, and cover the salt with rubbing alcohol.

Focus on what you'd like to release. It may be a specific grievance or a general wish to let go of whatever is blocking you. Be sure to write each item on a small individual piece of paper.

When you're ready, it's time to light the salts. Be very careful performing this ritual! I always set my skillet in my fireplace for extra caution. Using a long match, light the salts and stand back. You'll see a dancing green flame as the alcohol ignites. One at a time, toss in the pieces of paper on which you've written what you're releasing.

---

1. The Sabian symbols are a set of 360 unique word images, one for each degree of the zodiac. They were recorded in 1925 through a collaboration between the combined work of astrologer Marc Edmund Jones and psychic Elsie Wheeler.

Gemini New Moon—May 26, 2017

Gemini is the part of us that likes to be free and light. At this New Moon, however, there are complications. With Venus in a tight square to Pluto, it's common to feel tightly bound, even a bit obsessive about romantic ties in particular. And while the New Moon is generally the time each month when we affirm new hopes and initiate new actions, an opposition between Mars and Saturn makes it difficult to move forward.

The fundamental question is one of commitment. Gemini has a reputation for fickleness, but that's only when there is not a true meeting of the minds. However much an opportunity calls to you at this New Moon, whether it's for a relationship, a job, a place to live, a place to go to school, or anything else, you will not be happy there unless your mind can be fully engaged and you have room to breathe.

"Afformations" for the Gemini New Moon

Gemini is quick, mentally agile, and above all, questioning. In his book, *The Great Little Book of Afformations*, author Noah St. John recommends replacing affirmations with a simple questioning technique he calls "afformations." The idea is to ask yourself questions to allow the subconscious mind to find a suitable response.

Gemini describes the process of telling our story and understanding other people's stories as well. Try the afformation process at this New Moon to look at those stories in a new way.

Rewrite three difficult or negative stories that you tell about yourself. Begin by putting them in the form of questions, perhaps something like:

"Why do I always fall in love with the wrong people?" or
"Why doesn't anyone pay attention to anything that I say?"

Then turn them around in a magical, positive direction:
"Why do I always give my love to exactly the right person?"

"Why do I always find the most eloquent and compelling way of describing things?"

The point is less about the answer to the question than simply getting through the constant stream of negative chatter that keeps us trapped in old stories. This practice is a way to give your chattering, Gemini monkey mind some positive puzzles to solve!

Mars in Cancer—June 5–July 20, 2017

The energetic, assertive nature of Mars expresses itself better in some signs than in others. For instance, it's not at its best in the soulful, protective realm of Cancer. Imagine trying to light a match in a rainstorm, and you get the general idea of what Mars is up against here.

That said, Mars is still Mars, regardless of his sign, ready to help you get what you want and protect what is yours. In Cancer, Mars focuses on protecting the people you care about. Because Cancer rules home and hearth, this can also be a great transit for tackling home repairs or starting a home-based business.

If you've been trying to resolve family conflicts, this transit offers you the courage to confront and, if there is no hope of resolution, break off toxic ties. Mars is also related to work, and this is an appropriate time to examine the ways in which your need for security may be limiting your success and happiness in your career.

Full Moon in Sagittarius—June 9, 2017

At the Full Moon in Sagittarius, reflect on lofty questions such as what your life is really about, what you believe, and what you are capable of doing. With Jupiter, the planetary ruler of Sagittarius, turning direct the next day and in square aspect to Pluto, contemplate the ways in which you have grown, as well as the personal work that's left to do.

Six months from now is the last New Moon (on December 18) in Sagittarius conjunct Saturn for thirty years. This Full Moon sets the stage for some important life transitions around that time, particularly related to taking an important leap of faith. Think carefully now about how you would like your life to look by then.

The Sun and Moon are square Neptune in this Full Moon chart, so the changes that your mind thinks you need to make may be at odds with what your intuition is telling you. Both have about half the story right; it's up to you to listen to both.

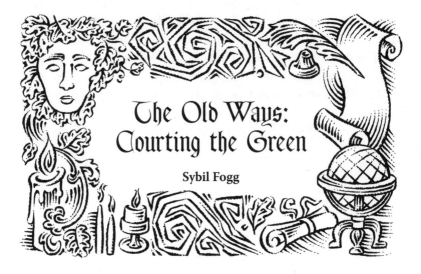

The Old Ways:
Courting the Green

Sybil Fogg

IN MANY PARTS OF the world, early May represents spring putting winter to rest. As the fields turn ripe and fertile and the color green is lush throughout the countryside, people rub the cold months from their eyes and shed layers of clothing to welcome the sun. They desire to celebrate in the jubilation that another winter has been conquered. Planting will start soon, and wildflowers are showing their many colors. May Day celebrations honored the growing part of the cycle of life, and many of the old traditions of this holiday are thus bound in fertility rites. Slavic representations of fertility were flowers, garlands, the maypole, dolls, and fire. Goddesses and gods of love were honored at this time, and youthful merriment was intertwined with courting and love rituals.

Dzydzilelya and Živa are the Polish goddesses of love, marriage, sexuality, and fertility invoked at this time of year; Milda is the Lithuanian goddess of love and protector against loneliness; Lada is the Slavic goddess of harmony, merriment, youth, love, and beauty. The gods that could be called upon were Siebog (husband to Živa), the Slavic god of love and marriage, and Jaryło, the Polish god of spring, fertility, and vegetation.

In Slavic countries, it was considered ill-fated to cut flowers before May Day, according to Roy. Due to this, flowers were a large part of May Day celebrations and were given as gifts, woven into hair, garlands, and used to decorate the maypole. During the Polish holiday, Zielone Świątki, homes and yards were decorated with flowers, branches, and greenery—mainly birch, yew, spruce, pine, cedar, and ash. Bringing in nature was done with the hope of ensuring an abundant harvest. Other rituals included cleansing the earth by sprinkling herbs and burning fires. Farm animals were purified with incense and decked out with wreaths and flowers.

On the eve of Zielone Świątki, a bonfire was built in a clearing and the people celebrated by leaping over the flames, feasting, and dancing. Beer flowed freely. Once the fires were raging, people ignited sticks that had been wrapped in straw and dipped in pine resin (or old brooms that had been saved for this purpose). They would walk through the fields of rye. The following night, they would repeat the ritual and consecrate the fields of wheat. This was all to ensure a good planting season (Hodorowicz Knab).

In the Kujawy region, focus was on the shepherds who were preparing to venture out for the summer months. Shepherds would wear the horns of the cows and oxen on their own heads and race. Whoever was able to drive his cattle to the pasturing grounds first was crowned king. The first shepherdess was crowned queen and presented with gifts and wreaths of flowers. A feast ensued and merriment was had. Afterward, an ox was decorated with flowers and ribbons, and the king and queen of the shepherds led a procession over a flower-strewn road, and the animal was eventually returned to its owner, but only handed over after it had been "purchased" with beer (Hodorowicz Knab).

The maypole rituals were popular in many Slavic countries in the old days and continue in some to modern times. In Poland, there were two methods of working the maypole tradition. One was a community effort and the other a more solo courting ritual.

Before the community could partake in the maypole dance, certain rituals were adhered to in preparing, selecting, and erecting the pole. All who were taking part in the gathering first decorated a wagon with greenery and flowers. Then they donned their finest clothing and headed out into the woods. Not just any tree would do, either. The maypole had to be the tallest evergreen, reaching high into the sky. Once the tree was felled and returned to the village, the lower branches were removed and the bark stripped. It was important to leave a bit of green at the top. The placing of the maypole varied. According to *Polish Customs, Traditions, & Folklore*, it could be erected in the village green, at a crossroads, or in the yard of a particularly revered member of the community. Over the years, it was customary to leave a pole up throughout the year and add a new evergreen top each May Day. This part of the maypole was decorated with flowers, ribbons, and whatever other trinkets people decided to add. In some areas of Poland, edible treats were left at the top, and young men would take turns attempting to climb up and retrieve the goodies.

In other parts of Poland, the maypole was used as a type of courting ritual. For this act, a young man would sneak into the woods at night and take down the tallest spruce he could find. After dragging it back to his home, he would remove all of the limbs and strip the bark. This pole was to be colorful, either in paint or paper. At the very top, a small fir tree was attached and decorated with flowers and ribbons. With help, the young man would erect the pole in the yard of his beloved, being sure to make enough fuss to awaken her. The maiden could show her affection in return by inviting everyone in for merrymaking.

Of course, there were times when a maiden would rise to find many maypoles going up in her yard. In this case, it was customary for her to choose the most becoming of them all. As one can imagine, fights often broke out amongst the young men and sabotage was not uncommon. A rejected suitor would often avenge his broken heart by vandalizing her yard with a *dziad*, a pole or worn-out broom on which a straw effigy was placed. It was common for the male members of a household to stay awake on Beltane eve to thwart such attempts (Hodorowicz Knab).

Today, the maypole is not as popular in Poland as it is in other countries in the region. Why not resurrect some of the old ways in your own Beltane celebrations? Consider calling on a Slavic god and goddess of love this year when you lay out your altar. Since it is probably not feasible to erect a maypole in the yard of your beloved, consider crafting a small one as a love token. This is a perfect way to honor this tradition. If you are part of a group that gathers, maybe this year the wreath at the top could be swapped out for a small fir tree in honor of the Polish pagans of the past. However you celebrate, revel and make merry in the month of May.

Bibliography

Dixon-Kennedy, Mike. *Encyclopedia of Russian & Slavic Myth and Legend.* Santa Barbara: ABC-CLIO INC., 1998.

Hodorowicz Knab, Sophie. *Polish Customs, Traditions, & Folklore.* New York: Hippocrene Books, Inc., 1993.

Ploetz, Karl Julius. *Epitome of Ancient, Medieval, and Modern History.* William H Tillinghast, trans. Boston: Houghton, Mifflin, & Co., 1887.

Roy, Christian. *Traditional Festivals: A Multicultural Encyclopedia,* Volume 2. Santa Barbara: ABC-CLIO INC, 2005.

"Zielone Świątki," *Wikipedia,* accessed September 9, 2015. https://pl.wikipedia.org/wiki/Zielone_Świątki.

Feasts and Treats

Linda Raedisch

BECAUSE OF THEIR COUNTRY'S hot, dry climate, the ancient Greek agricultural calendar was a little different from the one we are accustomed to. Crops were planted in the fall and reaped in the spring before the summer sun could singe the grain in the field. Springtime, therefore, was a heady time with both the harvest and the return of the wild lilies and asphodels to celebrate. The dead, too, were fêted during the early spring Festival of Pots, when offerings were left for the departed in clay dishes in the garden. Meanwhile, the radiant daughters of Pleione, the Pleiades, returned to their appointed places in the sky after an absence of forty days, to twinkle prettily and serve as a beacon to sailors.

Penne à la Circe

I like to think that this is the sort of dish the Greek witch Circe might have served to Odysseus had they both lived closer to our time, not in the Bronze Age before pasta and tomato sauce were available. Then again, who is to say that this witch, skilled in the use of herbs, does not still haunt the well-appointed island of Aeaea, wherever that might be? Circe is most infamous for transforming Odysseus's men into swine and distracting the hero from his quest to return home to his wife and family. This recipe calls for pancetta—thin-sliced Italian bacon. Best not ask where it came from!

Prep time: 15 minutes
Cook time: 30 minutes
Servings: 4–6

Salt
Water
Olive oil
3 cups penne pasta
¼ cup pancetta or lean bacon, chopped
1 clove garlic, minced
¼ yellow onion, chopped
1 tablespoon dried rosemary, crushed between two spoons
1½ cups tomato juice
Generous dash white wine
Dash black pepper
¼ teaspoon ground coriander
1 teaspoon dried thyme
1 bay leaf
½ cup light cream
½ cup pitted Kalamata olives, drained and halved lengthwise
Feta cheese crumbles for topping

Bring a large pot of salted water to a boil. Add a dash of olive oil and the penne pasta and cook according to directions on package. If you're in a rush, you can start the sauce in a smaller pot while the pasta is cooking. If not, wait until pasta is draining, and you can cook the sauce in the same pot.

Sauté pancetta or bacon with garlic, onions, and rosemary in your pot of choice until garlic is crispy and onions are glassy. Add tomato juice, wine, black pepper, coriander, thyme, and bay leaf and simmer for a few minutes until quite hot. Stir in cream.

Stir pasta into sauce (or vice versa), top with olives and feta cheese and serve.

Pramnian Wine

In the Indian version of Circe's story—yes, there is an Indian version—the witch attempts to transform the hero into a donkey by feeding him a porridge made from bewitched barley grains. Likewise, in "Book 10" of Homer's *Odyssey*, Circe stirs her magic potion into a brew of Pramnian wine mulled with barley, cheese, and honey. Polite guests that they are, Odysseus's men drink it down, and the next thing they know, they've dropped to all fours and sprouted bristles. Even without the magic potion, this sounds like an unpalatable concoction, but a similar mixture of cheese, barley, and Pramnian wine is also served in the *Iliad*—with no ill effects.

What is Pramnian wine? We know from writers who came after Homer that it was a dark-red late-harvest wine and therefore quite sweet. The best Pramnian wine seems to have come from the island of Lesbos. The ancient Greeks didn't shrink from adding other substances to their wine, perhaps because their wines were stored in a highly concentrated form and had to be mixed with water anyway. Once they'd gotten out their whisks and golden mixing bowls, they'd throw in whatever they had on hand: fenugreek, pine resin, and even seawater.

There are no rules here, but I would suggest leaving the cheese on the side!

Prep time: 2 minutes
Mull time: 5 minutes
Chill time: at least 1 hour
Servings: 4–6

1 bottle sweet red wine
1 single-serving bottle dark beer
2 tablespoons honey
Pinch of sea salt

Heat all ingredients together on very low heat until honey is dissolved. Pour into pitcher and chill well before serving. Wealthy

Greeks sent to the mountaintops for snow to chill their wine in summer, but Circe could have simply cast her own flurry on Aeaea.

Greek Farina Cake

I first ate farina cake at the home of my daughter's recorder teacher, an Israeli-born music librarian and Baroque musician. While conducting research for these recipes, I discovered that farina cake is also a Greek specialty. I imagine Circe and Odysseus sneaking into the kitchen late on a hot Mediterranean May Eve to enjoy this slightly sticky sweet dessert.

Prep time: 15 minutes
Bake time: 30 minutes
Servings: about 12 small pieces

For the cake:
8 tablespoons butter (1 stick), softened, plus a little for greasing
½ cup sugar
1 teaspoon vanilla extract
3 eggs
Electric mixer
1 8" × 10" rectangular baking pan (yes, you can use a round layer cake pan; it just won't be as Greek)
½ cup flour
½ teaspoon baking powder
½ cup farina
Zest of one small orange

For the syrup:
¼ cup white sugar
¼ cup honey
⅓ cup water
Juice of half a small orange

Cream butter, sugar, and vanilla together. Beat in eggs with electric mixer until well mixed and slightly frothy.

Preheat oven to 375 degrees F.

Sift flour and baking powder into butter mixture. Add farina and mix on low speed, scraping sides of bowl, until well blended. Stir in orange zest.

Grease pan and spread batter evenly in pan and bake for 30 minutes or until knife inserted in center comes out clean.

Now to make the syrup. Heat sugar, honey, and water in small pot on low heat until sugar and honey are dissolved. Remove pot from heat and stir in orange juice.

With sharp knife, cut hot cake into diamond-shaped pieces but do not remove from pan. Pour hot syrup over hot cake. Let cool completely before removing individual pieces to serve. I find the cake tastes best the next day when the farina has had time to absorb all the flavors. And because it's made with farina and orange juice, it's entirely appropriate for breakfast.

Crafty Crafts

Mickie Mueller

ALL OVER SCOTLAND, IRELAND, and the Celtic areas, sacred wells have special trees growing nearby where people tie colorful strips of cloth and ribbons called *clouties*. These are left as offerings to the spirits or as petitions for wishes. With this table-top version, you don't have to make a pilgrimage to partake in this lovely tradition.

Cloutie Tree Topiary

Time to Complete: about 1–2 hours
Cost: $11 to $15 (I recommend looking around the house first, and check your local dollar or discount store)

Supplies
A decorative flower pot
A small branch trimmed from a tree or bush (or from a craft store)
Floral moss
Small silk spring blossoms (dollar store ones work great)
Plaster of Paris (hardware store)
Paint stirring stick (free in the paint department)
Masking tape
Hot glue gun
Multicolored ribbons or torn strips of colorful fabric

If your pot has a hole in the bottom, cover it with duct tape. Place the branch in your pot, see how it fits, and trim as needed to make it look pleasing. You might need to group two branches together to make it evenly filled out. Once you're happy with your branch, it's time to prepare your plaster.

I recommend doing this part outside where you don't have to worry about any kind of mess in the house. Bring your branch, flower pot, dry plaster, measuring cup, and a water source; a hose or a large pitcher of water works. Before you begin, read over the instructions on the container of plaster and familiarize yourself with the process. Use a large bowl or bucket and mix two parts of plaster to one part water, stirring with the paint stick. Make enough to fill most of the pot you've chosen, leaving about two or three inches at the top. Work quickly—you want to use your plaster within six to ten minutes. Carefully pour it into your pot and put in your branch.

Make sure it's arranged how you want it. Run masking tape across the rim of the pot in several places to support the branch while the plaster sets.

DO NOT pour any leftover plaster down your sink! This might seem like common sense, but we've all done something silly and then immediately realized it was a bad idea, so let's just not go there. Dispose of any leftover mixed plaster in a disposable container and toss it. Clean out your bucket immediately and be sure to do it outside. Again, don't wash it in the house; we don't want plaster in your sink, bathtub, or going down your pipes, etc. Using a disposable container for mixing is also an alternative.

Once it's set, take your silk spring blossoms and cut them off their branches right at the base of the flower, making sure to keep them attached to the little green part that holds each blossom together. Now use hot glue to attach the little flowers along the branch to make it look like it's blooming. Continue until you're happy with it. Cover the top of the plaster with moss.

Now it's time to add your clouties! Hold the cloutie and focus on your intention. Once you have it set in your mind, tie it to the branch, thus sealing your intention with the knot. You can tie on many clouties yourself, or my favorite way is to tie on a couple for my wishes, and then I display clouties next to the topiary for family members, guests, or coven mates to make wishes and tie their own clouties on. Eventually, your cloutie tree will be dripping with colorful good wishes for Beltane. If you would like to, you can store it away and add to it every year.

Alternatively, you can make a cloutie tree out of fresh branches. If you have a lovely blooming tree or bush that needs to be pruned a bit, use those blooming branches! For woody branches that you want to keep fresh, carefully slit the bottoms of the branch before putting them in warm water. Prepare a tall vase by adding some lemon-lime soft drink (not diet, the sugar will feed the branches). You can add some marbles if you wish to help support your branches. Transfer the branches from the warm water into the vase. Now, you can tie your clouties onto the fresh flowering branches.

Fizzy Beltane Bath Bomb

Beltane is a time for beauty and love. During Beltane, I like to focus not just on romantic love but also on self-love. Pampering yourself is a nice way to celebrate, and magic for beauty is a Beltane tradition.

Bath bombs are usually pricey to buy, but they are inexpensive and super easy to make with simple grocery store ingredients and a few drops of essential oils. You can even add a pinch of herbs such as dried rose petals, lavender, or your favorite essential oils. Or why not use magical-purpose oils to create an enchanting bathtub brew? If you want to incorporate some traditional Beltane beauty magic, add a few drops of dew collected on Beltane morning into your water. Your bath bombs can be made into interesting shapes like hearts, stars, or flowers, or you using paper lined muffin tins.

Time to complete: 1 hour or less (at least 8 hours to dry)

Cost: $8 to $10 (if you already have household staples like baking soda, cornstarch, and food coloring)

Supplies

1 cup citric acid (or approximately 7.5 ounces, also called lemon salt, found by home canning supplies at the grocery store, health food stores, or a store that sells home brewing supplies)

1 cup baking soda

¾ cup cornstarch

¼ cup Epsom salt

Herbs or flower petals (optional)

10 drops or so of food coloring of your choice

6–8 drops of essential oil (use magical purpose oils if you like)

Spray bottle (dollar store or travel size section in health department)

Paper-lined muffin tins, ice cube trays, or fancy silicone muffin tins

Molds of your choice

Measure and mix together all your dry ingredients in a large bowl. I found that using a wire whisk or fork was really helpful to break up any clumps in the Epsom salt or cornstarch. If you're adding herbs or flower petals, toss them in now. Fill your little spray bottle with water and add the food coloring right into the spray bottle and shake a bit. This makes the color consistent when you mix it.

Add your essential oils to the dry mixture, and then spritz the top of the dry ingredients several times with your bottle of colored water. If you live where it's humid, you won't need much water. You don't want it too wet because then the finished product won't fizz, so your finished mixture will still be powdery. Test it by squeezing a handful—if it holds together, that's probably going to work.

Now press the mixture firmly into your molds. The tighter you pack it, the better they'll hold together. Let them sit undisturbed for at least eight hours before popping them out of their molds. When you drop one in the tub it fizzes up, like taking a bath in champagne!

All One Family

Dallas Jennifer Cobb

SITTING OPPOSITE SAMHAIN ON the Wheel of Life, Beltane is the second greatest sabbat of the eight sacred celebrations. It too is a time when the veils between the world are thin. Where Samhain celebrated death, the dead, and crossing over, Beltane celebrates life, the living, and the process of rebirth.

The Goddess becomes a lover at Beltane, and she is known as Aphrodite, Astarte, and Maeve the Fairy Queen. Beltane is a celebration of fertility, personified by the Green Man who mates with the Goddess, ensuring the fertility of the earth. Hand in hand, the couple jumps over the Beltane fires. Beltane festivities honor the plants, animals, and humans who are alive and have made it through the winter.

Traditional celebrations of Beltane included the rite of sacred sex, and babies born of Beltane unions were considered blessed. Of course, if you are like me, you don't want to encourage your teens to be too casual about sex, so why not introduce the concept of creativity as a powerful form of fertility. Let Beltane be a time to bring our creative babies into creation.

Beltane literally translates to "bright fire," and fire was honored because it had sustained us through the dark months. Fire meant survival, cooking food, and providing warmth and sustenance. In ancient times, the hearth fire was the heart of the home and held a sacred place in the cycle of continuation.

In fields where grains were grown, fire was set to clear the old chaff from the previous year, preparing the ground for new planting. Traditionally, animals being put out to pasture were driven between two fires, so that they too were blessed by the fire. People jumped over smaller fires at Beltane to ensure their blessing and fertility.

Practice: Creating Beauty and Joy

May Day is a great time to celebrate life, the living, fertility, creativity, and the process of rebirth. It's also a great time to get outdoors. Why not plan a hike with your teenager? Propose that you take a long walk together, enjoying the warming weather, greeting neighbors, visiting favorite places you haven't been to all winter, and consciously witnessing the beauty of the earth's rebirth. Marvel at the miracle of fertile creativity.

Take a bag with you so that you can collect grasses, flowers, sticks, and branches to make a vibrant spring bouquet. Not just collecting as you go, think of taking your warmth out with you and back to your neighborhood, your community, and your environment. So as you walk today, radiate blessings.

"Let's see how we can create happiness wherever we go."

Challenge your teen to think of small acts of kindness the two of you can commit to during your walk. Teenagers are tuned into Random Acts of Kindness Week, so tap into their culture and engage it to mark this sacred day. Simply stopping to chat with neighbors and reaching out to make social contact and exchange news is an act of kindness. Coax your teen to hold doors for people wherever you go today, and suggest that when people turn to thank them, they simply smile back.

"Shine your inner fire out into the world. Create kindness and joy."

If you live in a city, do not fret. Take a tour through your local park, wander by cemeteries with their wide open green space, and take note of "weeds" growing in abandoned lots. Spring is evident in all of these places, and if you look for signs of life, you will find them.

If you live in a rural area, visit the woods that are joyously erupting in flowers, wander by a stream alive with frogs, or take a stroll through the fields and see the wildflowers beginning to grow. Notice the way that the woods have filled in, buds and leaves bursting.

Wherever you walk, gather bits for your bouquet: a teasel from one of last year's dried coneflower plants, a tall spike from a mullein stalk, a few flowers. Gather some sticks and dried stalks of last year's growth. Maybe you will find some pussy willows. Be kind to the plants as you gather, never taking more than one branch from a tree or bush.

Gradually adding each small blessing that you encounter, make a gorgeous bouquet to take home to your house. If you know where there are any cherry or apple trees, make a visit to them and admire their boughs heavy with blossoms, and help yourself to a small branch.

When you get home with your bouquet of bounty, engage your teenager by enlisting them to arrange the flowers in a vase. Let their creativity and fertile energy be engaged. And as you work together to make something beautiful from your gathered treasures, talk about the day.

"How did it feel to do random acts of kindness?"

You might just find that your teenager received many blessings as a result of helping others and feels fertile and rich with the rewards of positive action. Help them to realize that when we do good deeds out there in the world, we are like the fires that prepare the fields. Our light makes new growth possible. Often the rewards of the process are so fertile that teens convert to regularly practicing random acts of kindness and employing their good manners.

Once you have creatively arranged your treasure so they are pleasing to the eye, use ribbons to decorate the vase full of flowers, red to honor the God and white to honor the Goddess. Place the symbols of fertility and creativity somewhere central in your home, and encourage your teen to take inspiration and weave fertile kindness into their daily life.

Beltane Ritual for Protection

Elizabeth Barrette

THIS RITUAL MAY BE adapted for indoor or outdoor use depending on your facilities and the size of your group. It helps to make a list of supplies beforehand so that you can check them off during setup. You may name specific deities in place of the Goddess and the God if you wish. It is advisable to keep a fire extinguisher and a bucket of wet sand handy when working with flames. If your group is very large, you can enlist all four quarter callers to lead the petitions for protection, and then to serve the cakes and ale. With each caller leading one quarter of the circle and serving people in that section, the whole process should finish in a reasonable amount of time.

Prior to May Eve, hand out sachets stuffed with blackberry leaves, lavender, and thyme so that everyone can take a purifying bath before the ritual. Do the spring cleaning for your covenstead with a floor wash using camphor, eucalyptus, and rosemary oils. If you wish to protect people who are not present, or animals such as pets or livestock, it is most practical to represent them with symbols such as poppets or photographs that may be carried by someone else during the ceremony. You will also need a drum or recorded music.

Outdoor setup: Place eight tiki torches in two rows of four, spaced widely enough for people to walk between the rows. Prepare the fire pit with wood for a bonfire. Decorate the altar table with May baskets or vases of spring flowers. Include a bowl of blessed water with an asperging bundle of cedar, fern, and heather. Set a bowl of protection incense made from gum arabic, club moss, and sandalwood next to the bundle. Cakes and ale should have their own dishes. Just before the ritual begins, light the bonfire and torches.

Indoor setup: Use two small tables, each set with a row of four candles, the rows placed widely enough for people to walk between. Decorate the room with May baskets or vases of spring flowers. Place a bowl of blessed water with an asperging bundle on the altar. Set a bowl of protection incense and a censer with charcoal next to the bundle. Cakes and ale should have their own dishes. Just before the ritual begins, light the candles and the charcoal.

Form the celebrants into a line and process between the lit rows. The first person through should take the bowl of blessed water and asperging bundle to sprinkle everyone else as they pass into sacred space. Then the last person sprinkles the first person, and returns the tools to the altar. Next, cast the circle.

Caller for the East: *I call to the East and the powers of Air. Spring winds, blow away all that would hurt us, and guard us against harmful storms. Hail and well met!*

All: *Hail and well met!*

Caller for the South: *I call to the South and the powers of Fire. Mighty sun, burn away all that would threaten us, and keep us safe against dangerous fires. Hail and well met!*

All: *Hail and well met!*

Caller for the West: *I call to the West and the powers of Water. Spring rains, wash away all that would stain us, and protect us from floods or drowning. Hail and well met!*

All: *Hail and well met!*

Caller for the North: *I call to the North and the powers of Earth. Stone and soil, swallow all that would undermine us, and hold us safe from being shaken or crushed. Hail and well met!*

All: *Hail and well met!*

High Priest/ess: *We gather here in this circle, purified by the elements, to raise protections for what we hold dear. Now let us call on the Goddess and the God to raise the power of Beltane to work our will.*

High Priest/ess reads the invocation:

Goddess, you bring forth the flowers of spring,
along with new life from the livestock and wild animals.
Join us in our ritual that you may help us to protect
the life and bounty which you have brought forth.

God, you nourish the plants and the animals
with your substance and your energy.
Join us in our ritual that you may stand guard
over us and all that we treasure.

All: *Hail and well met!*

Caller for the South: *We make our offering to the fire, that the smoke may grant protection to us and those we cherish.*

If outdoors, toss the incense into the bonfire. If indoors, sprinkle a pinch of incense onto the lit charcoal. Drum or play recorded music to raise energy.

Caller for the South continues: *Come forward, each in turn, and speak of what you would protect.*

Allow time for all the celebrants to name whatever they want protected.

Caller for the North: *Eat the cake of the God, and be protected.*

Take the cakes around to everyone in turn, then return the plate to the altar.

Caller for the West: *Drink from the chalice of the Goddess, and be pure.*

Take the chalice around to everyone in turn, then return the chalice to the altar.

High Priest/ess: *We have made ourselves clean. We have raised protections over what we hold dear. We have honored the holy day of Beltane with this work of magic. Now let us release those who have aided us.*

High Priest/ess reads the invocation:

Goddess, you came to our call
with the scent of flowers and spring.
Thank your for lending us your power
in our ritual. Hail and farewell!

God, you answered our invitation
with your strength and your support.
Thank you for helping us in
our ceremony. Hail and farewell!

All: *Hail and farewell!*

Caller for the North: *I give thanks to the North and the powers of Earth for supporting our protections in this ritual. Stone and soil, think of us fondly as you return to your rest. Hail and farewell!*

All: *Hail and farewell!*

Caller for the West: *I give thanks to the West and the powers of Water for the protection flowing through this ritual. Spring rains, run back from whence you came. Hail and farewell!*

All: *Hail and farewell!*

Caller for the South: *I give thanks to the South and the powers of Fire for lighting our protection in this ritual. Warm sun, shine on our path as you depart. Hail and farewell!*

All: *Hail and farewell!*

Caller for the East: *I give thanks to the East and the powers of Air for inspiring our protection in this ritual. Spring winds, blow back to whence you came. Hail and farewell!*

All: *Hail and farewell!*

High Priest/ess: *The circle is open, but unbroken...*

All: *Merry meet, merry part, and merry meet again!*

Take care to ensure that all fires are extinguished safely as you clean up after this ritual.

Notes

Notes

Litha

Litha

Suzanne Ress

WHAT WE CALL "LITHA," now more commonly known as Midsummer or the summer solstice, was the Saxon name for a period, roughly June and July, that marked the year's halfway point. The first part of it was called *Ærra Līþa* or "before Litha" and the second part *Æfterra Līþa or* "after Litha," so Litha itself must have fallen somewhere in the middle, although there was apparently never a designated holiday just called Litha.

The word *litha* means "gentle or navigable" and describes the breezes that make sailing and being outdoors near water during Midsummer a true pleasure.

Litha is both a fire and a water festival, and it is considered the optimal time to harvest herbs and other plants for magical and medicinal use, so it is an earth festival, too.

The Litha, or Summer Solstice, festival is ancient and has been handed down to us from pagan times, passing surprisingly unscathed through male-dominated, single-god religions and the Middle Ages.

The Christianized version of Midsummer, Saint John's Eve and Saint John's Day, June 23 and 24, celebrates the birth of Saint John the Baptist. John the Baptist was the forerunner of Jesus Christ, and it was just after John baptized Jesus by dunking him in the Jordan River that Jesus experienced his spiritual epiphany and became the Christ.

It is no accident that the birth of John is celebrated six months before the birth of Jesus: John, born at the summer solstice when days begin to shorten, could represent the Horned God, or Odin, who rules the darker half of the year. Jesus, born at winter solstice when days begin to lengthen, could represent the god of rebirth and resurrection, the return of light.

Festivities enjoyed by pre-Christian Pagans on the eve of the solstice included building giant bonfires at dusk to run around and jump through. These were left burning until midnight. Other activities included the harvesting of herbs at midday on the longest day, jumping into water (or dousing oneself) as a physical and spiritual cleansing ritual, and eating, drinking, and general merriment.

Surprisingly or not, modern Saint John's Eve celebrations are pretty much identical to the ancient Pagan ones.

Golowan is a festival celebrated in Cornwall, England, between Saint John's Day, June 24, and Saint Peter the Fisherman's Day, June 28. Great bonfires are lit on beaches, riverbanks, and lakeshores, and people enjoy boat rides, swimming, and fireworks displays.

Ivan Kupala Day, celebrated in Baltic countries, is named after John (Ivan), and bathing (Kupala). It is a holiday of fun and games—children pour buckets of water over each other, and people socialize around bonfires at sundown.

In Puerto Rico, San Juan Bautista is celebrated by traveling after sunset to a body of water and falling into it backward three, seven, or twelve times at midnight to cleanse the spirit and bring good fortune.

In Poland at Midsummer, single women gather flowers and herbs to make garland crowns. They wear these in the evening, dancing and frolicking around a great bonfire built on the shore of a lake, and then they toss the garlands into the lake at midnight. If a man has his sights on a particular woman, he will swim after her crown and bring it back to her in order to win her favor.

In numerous cultures, it is believed that the fern holds special magical powers at Midsummer. If you are able to gather fern seeds on this day, it will give you the ability to turn invisible.

Yarrow that is gathered during the day of Midsummer's Eve should be burnt to ash in the bonfire that night, and when the ash is cool, some should be collected and kept in a jar to use in healing spells.

Traditionally, Midsummer is celebrated on June 21, but the longest day can actually fall anywhere between the 20th and the 23rd of June. After this, the days begin to shorten ever so slightly. The 21st also marks the first day of summer, so the whole season stretches ahead with its adventures, joys, and surprises,

Knowing that I have many long, sunny days by the oceanside or in the cool woods ahead, I feel a great sensation of sweet relaxation taking me over at Litha. Warm, fragrant evenings with friends and family are before me, for the season has just begun.

⚜

One of my sisters got married some years back on the 24th of June on Cape Cod, where we've long spent our summer vacations.

I pulled the kids out of school a little early that year and, with my husband, flew across the Atlantic, from Italy to Boston.

The day after our arrival, June 21, we spent the afternoon on the long, white, ever-shifting sands of one of the gorgeous beaches of the Cape Cod National Seashore, with its soothing background sound of slow rhythmic waves, and seagull and tern cries.

The bright sun overhead warmed the gentle breeze, and it seemed I could feel the vitamin D soaking into my bones as I sat on an old towel next to my husband and watched my daughters chase waves. I helped them build a mansion for their beloved stuffed animals using pieces of found driftwood, shells, stones, and clumps of seaweed.

I took a walk with my younger daughter along the shoreline, and we picked up silver and golden jingle shells and carried them in the crown of my straw hat. On our way back to where we had left the towels and stuffed animals, there was an ice cream truck where before there had been none. It was parked at the edge of the parking lot, farther up the beach. My daughter was nursery school age at the time, and she gazed longingly at the truck, and said, "I wish I could have an ice cream!"

"I wish I had some money with me!" I said.

We walked on a few more yards. Then she put her little hand into my hat and ran her fingers through the jingle shells.

She said, "Maybe we could use mermaid money."

It was a magical idea, and there was no other way for me to respond but to take a leap of faith and say, "Okay. I bet they accept mermaid money here."

We made our way up the beach and got at the end of the short line in front of the ice cream truck's order window.

My daughter looked longingly at the glorified pictures on the side of the truck of frozen treats in all shapes, flavors, and colors.

When it was our turn, we stepped to the window, and I said to the young, nice-looking man inside,

"We only have mermaid money. Is that okay?"

I held up my hat full of jingle shells.

The man looked at the shells, then at me, then at my little girl, and he smiled.

"Yes, of course," he said. "What would you like?"

My daughter named her choice, and he gave it to her, and I put a handful of jingle shells on the window ledge.

"Thank you."

His eyes were twinkling.

❧

By late afternoon the air had turned cool, and we returned home to change into jeans and sweatshirts.

Back at the beach, my sister and her soon-to-be husband had built a bonfire high up in a sheltered place behind some dunes, but the echoing sound of the ocean's pounding waves was still very clear.

We gathered for libations around seven when the sun, still little more than halfway between the zenith and the horizon, made beautiful stark shadows of each rut, hillock, and ripple of sand. Its warm glow, ever more reddish as the evening wore on, created a flattering illumination.

My older daughter had brought along her new kite, and my husband was preparing to help her launch it when a gentle breeze swept it out of her hands and lifted it into the sky, like magic. Fortunately, she was holding tight to the end of the kite's string.

I took out my camera and got some beautiful photos of my daughter, her long hair flowing, lit with a rosy light, looking up at her kite in the deep blue sky.

The groom talked about his wonderful, long day of fishing with his friends out on the water. They had caught several striped bass and nearly caught a bluefin tuna, he reported. The bass had been cleaned and filleted, brushed with olive oil, and sprinkled with fresh herbs, ready to be put on the small portable grill set up near the bonfire.

It was my first taste of fresh ocean fish of the season. Perhaps I was especially hungry, or maybe the evocative surroundings added something, or it might have been just because the groom willed it to be so, but that grilled striped bass was one of the best things I have ever tasted.

The meal was rounded off with salads, brownies, and plenty of cold beer. By the end of it, the sun had finally set and we found ourselves sitting in the soft cool sand around the flickering fire, satiated, happy, and feeling magical.

My brother took out his mandolin and began to play, and some of us got up to dance, making long enchanting shadows on the sand. My younger daughter fell asleep on my husband's lap, while I danced with my older girl until we were both tired and we collapsed in the sand. My brother went on playing, and someone else joined in with a harmonica. Affected with jet lag, I could barely keep my eyes open.

Around midnight, we smothered the last embers of the fire and trudged shivering back along the dark beach, as we saw here and there the strange moving light, like a fairy light, of a glow stick carried by someone walking at a distance.

As we neared home, fireflies twinkled surreally near the ground by the hedges. It was the perfect ending to the longest day of the year, I thought, as I drifted off to sleep listening to the croaking of mating frogs in the pond across the street.

⚶

Many recreational fisher people say that the day of the summer solstice is the best day of the year to go fishing because it is the longest day.

In most places there are limited fishing seasons for all or some breeds of fish. The dates and rules are extremely variable from place to place, even between counties sharing a border, but in general, the season is closed when fish are spawning. Most places also require that recreational fisher people obtain a license and know and follow the rules for permissible equipment and daily catch quotas.

Many of us have questioned the ethics of fishing and sometimes even equate it with hunting. My personal view is that it is not wrong for a recreational fisherman to catch and keep what he can eat. Often inland waterways, lakes, and ponds are stocked with hatchery born fish, and even ocean shellfish in popular fishing areas are frequently planted by hatcheries.

Catching a few wild fish for personal consumption during open season is certainly no worse, and also much less environmentally harmful, than purchasing fresh, frozen, or canned commercially caught fish. If you are not a dedicated vegetarian or vegan, and wish to occasionally eat the flesh of another creature, probably catching your own fish is one of the most ethical ways to do this.

Recreational fishing has been compared to "playing tennis with God." The solitary fisherwoman, alone with her thoughts and the beauty of the scenery, is spiritually and physically connected to the mystery of nature. It brings together the elements of earth and water, and if you grill your fish there's fire, too. Perfect for Litha!

Cosmic Sway

April Elliott Kent

I WAS LUCKY ENOUGH to visit Stonehenge during one remarkable Midsummer season. Initially, I was disappointed; it seemed so small. But the longer I was there and the more times I walked around the monument, the more mesmerizing it seemed. There was a kind of low-level buzz about it, like a radio that's caught between the frequencies of two stations, like something very old that was sending out a homing signal.

When we're young, that's how we feel about ancestors. They are a bunch of grim-looking people in washed-out photos that our mothers periodically pulled out of an old trunk. They don't look very impressive, and we can't imagine what in the world they have to do with us. But then we get older and make more and more trips around the Sun, and before you know it, we find the ancestors fascinating. We feel our connection to them. We wonder what they could tell us about the world and about ourselves, if only we had the chance to listen to them.

Midsummer, when the Sun reaches the familial sign of Cancer, is the time to pause in our tracks and get in touch with the ancestors. Some of them shared your family name, your Roman nose, your father's profession. But if you trace your roots back far enough, you eventually find a little bit of yourself in everyone.

We're all related. We're all family. And if you're estranged from the family who brought you here, or have lost a lot of those people, there is enormous comfort in the idea that you're related to everyone. Just as every kooky member of a family has his or her place, so does each of us in the larger family of man.

Cancer New Moon—June 23, 2017

This New Moon—with a powerful stellium of the Sun, Moon, Mercury, and Mars in Cancer—encourages you to find the place that feels like home and the people who feel like family. Cancer is an extremely protective sign and symbolizes the part of us that holds on to old hurts and grudges. With all these Cancer planets in a challenging aspect to Jupiter in Libra, perhaps it's time to get beyond raw emotion and apply intellectual adjustment to the situation.

If you harbor grievances, ask yourself what would happen if you let go of them. And—this is a very tough one—are you being fair toward the people closest to you?

You can protect yourself from harmful people without carrying anger in your heart. (Try the protection practice below.) And as for those whose chief offense has been hurting your feelings, consider whether the punishment you're giving them is appropriate for their crime.

Protection Practice

Sit alone in a room and relax completely, becoming aware of each part of your body. Project your consciousness outside of your body and into your auric sphere. (You'll know you're there when you experience a kind of mental tingling.)

Now surround yourself with a clear shield that extends a couple of feet above your body. Gather all your emotions inside the shield; hold them there as long as possible, with intense focus, then relax and begin again. Imagine that the shield is able to dispel all unwanted thoughts and emotions and protect you from absorbing negativity from others.

Practice this exercise every day until you feel you're able to summon the feeling of protection upon command. Now you're able to surround yourself with this shield whenever you feel vulnerable.

Full Moon in Capricorn—July 8, 2017

If you're still having trouble letting go and forgiving, this Full Moon will force the issue. Carrying anger toward someone keeps you connected to them and ensures that you are not in full control of your life. This Full Moon in tough Capricorn is conjoined Pluto; you have the strength you need to draw strong boundaries to keep yourself safe. Don't give your power to those who have hurt you.

Forgiveness Ritual

The Sun is still in Cancer at this Full Moon, a sign with a great affinity for bowls. These womb-like containers hold everything from the food that nourishes us to the collection of remote controls on the coffee table. Cancer's love of bowls makes the Burning Bowl ceremony a perfect ritual for forgiveness and release at this New Moon. It is simple but powerful.

All you'll need is a fire-safe bowl or cauldron, a small piece of paper, pencil or pen, and a match. First, write down on paper the names of no more than three people whom you feel the need to forgive. As you write each name, picture the person and relive the incident or incidents that hurt or angered you. Take your time, and don't hesitate to summon every wound in vivid detail.

Next comes the hard part: Commit yourself to change. Spend a few minutes in meditation. Commune with the highest and wisest part of yourself and ask for wisdom and surrender.

Fold or roll up the piece of paper, place it in the bowl, and set it on fire. As it burns, bless and forgive each person on the list, saying something like, "I fully forgive you, so that we both can be free."

When the paper has burned, carry the ashes to a source of moving water and sprinkle them in.

Mars in Leo—July 20–September 5, 2017

Mars is not at its happiest in Cancer, where it's been since June 5, 2017. That's especially true this summer, with Mars making an opposition to Pluto (July 2) and a square to Uranus (July 17), aspects that can symbolize intractable power struggles and rash behavior, respectively.

On July 20, Mars enters Leo, a somewhat happier environment for its assertive, ambitious energy. This will be an especially energizing period for those with planets in Aries (especially creatively), Leo (putting yourself forward), or Sagittarius (taking a chance of some kind). It's a time of opportunity for Gemini (learn something new) and Libra (work with others toward a shared goal), and a motivating but challenging period for Taurus (hard work at home), Scorpio (pressure in career), and Aquarius (conflicts with partners and close friends need to be resolved). Cancer can put some energy into increasing earnings, Virgo may have trouble resting because you need to confront inner conflicts, Capricorn can be creatively frustrated, and Pisces will have to make adjustments in health routines or in the workplace.

New Moon in Leo—July 23, 2017

The Sabian Symbol for this New Moon point is, "Under emotional stress, blood rushes to a man's head." It's appropriate given the Sun and Moon are in a close conjunction with Mars at this New Moon, all in hot-blooded and fiery Leo.

The source of stress during Leo times is one of these: You're not receiving sufficient attention and appreciation. You're carrying too heavy a load. You're trying to resist chaos and inevitable change. To some degree, you may experience all three, and more so if you have planets in the first few degrees of the fixed signs: Taurus, Leo, Scorpio, or Aquarius.

The job of a fixed sign like Leo is to hold things together. The cardinal signs (Aries, Cancer, Libra, Capricorn) initiate things, and the mutable signs (Gemini, Virgo, Sagittarius, Pisces) share and disperse the results. But in the middle of the process, it's the fixed signs that organize, create systems and structures, and make sure things keep going. So when carefully laid plans are thrown into chaos, as they are likely to be during this New Moon period, we are all called upon to follow Leo's lead. With enough heart-centered warmth, joy, and courage, we can create a sort of gravitational pull that holds everything together.

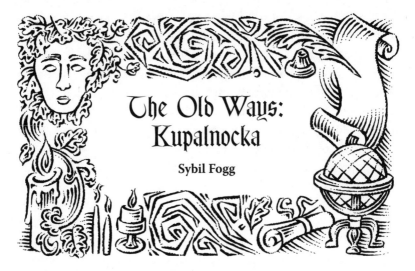

The Old Ways: Kupalnocka

Sybil Fogg

CLOSE YOUR EYES FOR a moment and call up an image of Midsummer's night. If you are anything like me, swirling colors of green, gold, brown, and shimmery glitter cascade down over a scene straight out of Shakespeare's play of foolish lovers and merrymaking in the forest. There is music, dancing, bonfires, and freely flowing honey wine, all in a flutter of fairy wings. If you reach your hand out, it will be clasped and in you will be pulled, leaping over fires, tasting ripe fruit, and filled up with revelry. Many Pagans celebrate Midsummer by honoring the sun god's strength as he fills the day with light. But in Slavic countries, particularly Poland, where the holiday is called Wianki or Kupalnocka, and Lithuania, where the holiday is known as Kupolinėmis or Rasos, Midsummer is a time to honor the God *and* Goddess, Sun *and* Moon. Midsummer is also akin to the West's Valentine's Day.

In old Lithuania, there is a song that tells the story of how the Moon was once married to the Sun. The Moon was the god aspect and the Sun was the Goddess. They married at spring and by the summer solstice, Moon had betrayed Sun and left with Dawn, or the Morning Star. Sun's father was the thunder god, Perkurnas, and he avenged his daughter by splitting their union in half, and Moon fled into the night. They forever reflect each other even if they are no longer together. Sun and Dawn continue their battle, tempers fueling even stronger on the summer solstice as the longest day and shortest night. So when the sun sets, the night is lit up in flame with bonfires and paper lanterns. In this way, Sun reminds Moon that she is still here, still angry, but still longing for him.

The Polish holiday Kupalnocka means "Kupala Night," and it was a time to honor the goddess Kupala, who governed herbs, water, love, magic, and sex. If one bathed in the waters of Kupala, he or she would find their illnesses cured and their strength restored. The herb most sacred to Kupala was purple loosestrife. It was believed the roots had the power to banish demons if gathered on the summer solstice. In Lithuania, nine herbs were collected, specifically wormwood, mugwort, heartsease, chamomile, lavender, purple centaury, cinquefoil, flathead, and arnica. They were gathered into bouquets called *kupolémis* that were believed to hold magical properties. Tradition dictated that all herbs must be collected before midnight, as they would lose their magical potency after that. One of the most important rituals of the solstice was to look for the magical fern flower that bloomed only at midnight on Kupalnocka. To gaze upon the fern flower would bring great fortune, power, and wisdom. In some Slavic countries, couples would head forth into the forest to search for the sacred fern. There are some who believe that the "fern flower" was euphemism for coupling, another aspect of the goddess Kupala.

Similar to Shakespeare's *A Midsummer Night's Dream*, the Kupalnocka has been considered a night full of magic and mischief, when fairies, imps, and other mystical creatures roam freely, looking to delight or fright those celebrating. Due to this, it was integral to pay homage to all the sprites, dryads, and sylphs lest they be angered and the harvest season run afoul.

Another way to show honor to Kupala was by making wreaths of the nine sacred herbs and throwing them over the "heads" of apple, birch, or willow trees. The amount of times one made the throw would determine how much longer they had to wait until marriage. There are more Lithuanian traditions of wreaths and water in *Llewellyn's 2015 Sabbats Almanac* for further study.

Not to be left out, the Polish have their own wreath traditions. Another name for Kupalnocka is Wianki, which translates to "wreath." It was common for young girls to wear wreaths made of flowers and herbs throughout the summer solstice rituals. At riverbeds, they would attach candles to the wreaths and set them afloat. As flowers and herbs are sacred to many summer spirits, it was customary to toss them into the rivers and creeks to gain the good graces of the water spirits.

Honoring Kupala's water incarnation was even more significant along the Polish seashore. Here, people made their living off of the ocean and it was imperative to gain the blessings of the water goddess before the summer season set in. Polish fishermen and fisherwomen would weave the sacred herbs through their nets and strew them across their boats in the hope that the Goddess would give them calm seas for fishing.

Like Moon has Sun, water has fire, and many other countries across Europe celebrated the solstice holiday chiefly with fire. Bonfires burned on hills and in clearings as the sun set and night waltzed in. There was much merrymaking, feasting, singing, and dancing to be had. People had fun teasing one another with riddles and calling out improbable love matches, according to Hodorowicz Knab. Of course, they also suggested couples that were known to fancy each other. It was believed if these couples clasped hands and leapt over the bonfire still holding hands, they would soon be married.

Kupala made her appearance here too. Men and women would leap over the bonfire dragging with them a straw effigy in honor of the goddess. The following day, the figure was dressed in a white gown with herbs and flowers woven through the straw and fabric. She was hung from a tree to form a kind of wood nymph or spirit of the forest. Charged with three of the four elements, she was then released into a river to float downstream taking all of the evils away from the community.

The bonfires also held a practical purpose. They appeased the sun and fire gods and goddesses and ensured a good harvest. It was believed that the fields would be protected as far as the smoke from the fires traveled. Garlands of flowers and herbs were thrown into the fires to protect the bearers from ill fortune for the upcoming twelve months.

Consider bringing some of Kupalnocka into your Midsummer celebration. Plan a date with your significant other and honor romance on this Slavic Valentine's Day. Together or on your own, consider building a small fire and effigy of Kupala that is complete with a mini-wreath made of the nine herbs. Pass her through the flames and smoke and then press her into the ground. Whisper in her ear all that you would like to release from your life. Complete the honoring of the elements by releasing the effigy into water. And then return to your Midsummer revelries. Dance and make merry!

Bibliography

Dixon-Kennedy, Mike. *Encyclopedia of Russian & Slavic Myth and Legend.* Santa Barbara: ABC-CLIO INC., 1998.

Hodorowicz Knab, Sophie. *Polish Customs, Traditions, & Folklore.* New York: Hippocrene Books, Inc., 1993.

Monaghan, Patricia. *Encyclopedia of Goddesses and Heroines, Revised.* San Francisco: New World Library, 2014.

"Old Lithuanian Songs," *Majzooban-e Noor,* accessed Sept. 18, 2015. http://www.majzooban.org/en/articles/28-old-lithuanian-songs.html.

Feasts and Treats

Linda Raedisch

IN THE NORTHERNMOST REACHES of Europe, the sun never sets on Midsummer Eve. What better time to keep an eye peeled for fairies? Nordic fairies, or "hidden folk" as they are known in Scandinavia, engage in most of the same activities that fairies of other regions do: they dance in rings, avoid baptism at all costs, and steal human babies, leaving their own offspring behind in the cradle. They also abduct older children and even adults, carrying them off into their mountain halls. While Scandinavian fairies can be devastatingly attractive, they never look as good from behind as they do from the front. Even the most handsome fairy prince is likely to have a tail, shaggy bark growing on his back, or a hollowed-out back like a trough.

Whenever the weather permits, northern Europeans prefer to dine outside. Lingering over a delicious meal in the garden while the Midsummer sun flirts with the western horizon is perhaps the best way to catch at least a glimpse of the fairies.

Nordic Hot Dogs

In Sweden, they're called Swedish hot dogs. In Denmark, they're called Danish hot dogs. You can get Danish hot dogs in Germany, but my German cousin insists on driving over the border for the real thing. They really ought to be pork, but they have so many good things piled on top of them that if you must use vegetarian hot dogs, they just might not taste too awful. As far as I'm concerned, the hot dogs are really just a vehicle for the remoulade sauce and curry ketchup. No, I haven't made this one into a casserole: one has to draw the line somewhere!

Prep time: 15 minutes (longer if you fry the onions)
Cook time: 10 minutes
Servings: 8

8 high quality hot dogs
8 submarine rolls
For the remoulade sauce:
2 tablespoons yellow mustard
1 tablespoon mayonnaise
¼ teaspoon dried tarragon
¼ teaspoon dried cilantro
1 teaspoon chopped capers
For the ketchup:
½ cup ketchup
½ teaspoon curry powder
Other toppings:
1 large yellow onion or 1 cup dried fried onions
4 baby dill whole pickles
Mayonnaise (optional)

For the hot dogs, the longer the better. For authenticity, I recommend a good pork hot dog like Thumann's or Schaller & Weber, but if you have another favorite hot dog, that's fine. Why sub rolls? Because they're sturdier than hot dog buns and capable of supporting all those toppings. Besides, leftover bits of roll can be soaked in milk and deposited in the corners of the garden as offerings to the fairies.

The sauces and toppings can all be prepared ahead of time, but let's assume that it's already Midsummer Eve and a party of hungry Witches and fairies is soon to descend on your garden.

First, the remoulade sauce. In a small bowl, stir the mustard and mayonnaise together vigorously until there are almost no lumps. Stir in the herbs and chopped capers. Set aside.

For the curry ketchup, simply stir curry powder into the ketchup. Set aside.

Now for the toppings. If you are making your own fried onions, start by halving your onion, then slicing it very, very thin. Fry them in a nonstick frying pan WITHOUT any butter or oil until they are brown and decidedly shrunken. They will crisp up as they cool. The pickles should also be sliced very thin. Why not just buy sliced pickles? Because they won't be thin enough! We want ours to be paper thin. Authentic Nordic hot dogs also have a line of mayonnaise piped onto them. This seems a bit much to me, but I'll leave that up to you.

As soon as all of your toppings and sauces have been ensconced in their own attractive serving dishes, each with a little serving spoon, it's time to cook the hot dogs.

Boil hot dogs according to package directions. Cut the sub rolls lengthwise, but only cut halfway through. You want them to cradle the hot dogs without them falling through. Warm the sub rolls in the oven or toast lightly in a toaster oven.

At the table, demonstrate proper assembly to your guests: Put a little remoulade in the crevice of the bun, followed by the hot dog. Top with another line of remoulade, a drizzle of curry ketchup, and mayonnaise, if desired. Place fried onions and overlapping slices of pickle, as many as you like, on top. Now all you have to do is figure out how to bite into it!

Black Iced Tea Punch

Many magical things are supposed to happen at the stroke of midnight on Midsummer Eve, including rivers turning to wine, but all you really need is a glass of my Black Iced Tea Punch. This is actually a version of a fruity iced tea my cousin Astrid made one summer to accompany our *Currywurst*—yet another Germanic hot dog tradition. Astrid used herbal tea for her punch, but I figured we could use a hit of caffeine tonight while we're out gathering fern seed and watching for hidden treasures to reveal themselves. (Because she is an altogether better person than I am, Astrid also used agave syrup instead of sugar.)

If you don't have a lemon balm plant, you must get one! They're easy to grow from seed, and if you plant one in the ground, it will come back twice as a big in the spring. You can also grow them indoors: not only is it not poisonous to cats, my cat hasn't had a hair ball since she started herself on a daily regimen of fresh lemon balm leaves.

Astrid also recommends the addition of dried sweet woodruff to any iced tea punch. In Germany, you can find it in syrup form, but in the United States, you might have to grow and dry your own.

Prep time: 5 minutes
Brew time: A few hours
Servings: 8

4 bags black tea
4 cups water
4 teaspoons sugar
2 cups blackberry, black currant, or other dark berry juice
1 orange cut into thin slices
1 tray ice cubes
Fresh lemon balm leaves

Early in the day, put the tea bags and water out in the sunshine in a glass pitcher or large jar to brew. (It's the longest day of the year, after all!) When the tea is nice and dark, bring it inside and add sugar, berry juice, and orange slices. Add ice cubes and lemon balm leaves just before serving.

Cold Rice Pudding with Raspberries

According to Swedish folk wisdom, rain falling from a sunny sky means the Witches are baking cakes. So, if you want fine weather for your Midsummer merrymaking, make this cold rice pudding instead. On Christmas Eve, I make a warm, sweet rice porridge for the nisse or Nordic house elf. This rice pudding, which is served chilled, is strictly for human consumption, though you never know who might be joining you for dessert on Midsummer Eve!

No time to make the raspberry sauce? Top with mandarin orange segments instead.

Prep time: 5 minutes
Cook time: 30 minutes for pudding; 10 for raspberry sauce
Chill time: 2½ hours
Servings: 6–8

For the pudding:
¼ cup water
2½ cups 2% milk
1 teaspoon vanilla extract
⅓ cup short grain rice (actually a little bit more)
1 envelope Knox unflavored gelatine
⅓ cup sugar (added first)
½ cup heavy cream
2 tablespoons sugar (added later)

For the raspberry sauce:
2 cups frozen raspberries
Sieve
2 tablespoons white sugar

Garnish:
Raspberries, blackberries, strawberries or fresh seasonal berries
Fresh lemon balm leaves

Pour ¼ cup cold water in a small bowl. Stir gelatin into it and let sit.

In a medium-sized pot, heat milk and vanilla until bubbly. Stir in the rice and simmer uncovered for around 30 minutes, stirring occasionally and smooshing any lumps with a wooden spoon. Don't let it boil over!

Turn off heat and add your clear blob of gelatin to the rice, and stir for a few seconds until gelatin disappears. Stir in ⅓ cup sugar and pour rice into a large bowl. Chill for 90 minutes. In the meantime, you can make the raspberry sauce or catch up on all those shows you missed during the week.

Whip the heavy cream with 2 tablespoons sugar until stiff. Take the now-gelled rice out of the refrigerator and gently fold in the whipped cream. Cover with plastic wrap and chill for another hour or until ready to serve.

Still haven't made the raspberry sauce? Now is the time!

In a small pot, heat frozen raspberries over low heat until berries are thawed and mushy. Strain into a bowl, stirring the seeds round and round with a wooden spoon or pestle to separate as much juice and pulp as you can. When there's not much more than a clump of seeds in the sieve, give up, discard seeds, and stir 2 tablespoons of sugar into the sauce. Pour sauce into a small pitcher.

Just before serving, spoon rice pudding into glass dishes, top with sauce, and garnish with fresh berries and lemon balm leaves.

Crafty Crafts

Mickie Mueller

THE TIME WHEN THE sun is at its zenith is a great time to make an empowered crystal grid. This one is permanent and allows you to draw upon that sun energy anytime you want. You can make this cool craft on your back porch, in the sandbox, or even at the beach.

Sand Cast Crystal Grid Candleholder

Time to complete: 30–45 minutes (plus 30 for plaster to set)
Cost: $8 to $16 (depending on what you have on hand, like plaster from Beltane craft)

Supplies

Sand: playground sand can be purchased at your local garden center (craft sand from the craft store works great)
Plaster of Paris
Paint stirring stick
Water
Crystals: tumbled stones, quartz, citrine, or stones of your choice. I found a string of wand shaped crystal beads with holes in one end at my local craft store for about eight dollars.

An empty tea light cup (Plastic ones are a little bigger than the metal
  ones, so they work great.)
Cooking spray
Sticky felt
Bowl or bucket
Optional: A disposable container to mix your plaster in; you can re-
  use a plastic ice cream tub, large butter tub, or something similar

If you're lucky enough to have a beach nearby, some people do sand
casting right on the beach. If you're not at the beach, you'll need
a container for your sand, such as a shallow box or a flat that soft
drinks comes in. You can also use a disposable pie or cake pan. Once
you begin, you should not move the project until it sets and you remove it from the sand, so find a good place to work undisturbed.

Mix your sand with enough water so it's damp but not dripping
wet. Dump the wet sand into the box and then push the pile of sand
down using a shallow dish with a flat bottom. Press down into the
sand about an inch deep. You may need to work the sand around to
get the shape of the bottom of the dish with a good edge. Lay out
your crystals and stones on the table next to your box of sand. Place
the tea light cup in the middle with the crystals arranged around.
Keep in mind that you can push shapes into the sand that will become part of the crystal grid: a spiral, sun rays, whatever you like.
Decide if you want to add shapes to the sand, and if you do, arrange
your crystals and stones accordingly.

Now that you've planned it out, you can start to work on your
sand creation. Add the designs you planned in the sand first. You
can press seashells, amulets, or other objects to leave an impression
in the sand, or you can trace shapes with your finger. Keep in mind
that you're creating a mold so whatever you press into the sand will
actually be raised in the finished item.

Next, lay out your crystals and stones as you wish. You can lay
them flat as you would with a traditional crystal grid, or if you want,
you can have them pointing up because they will be embedded in
the plaster. If you want them lying flat, be sure to push them down

into the sand. Keep in mind that the part facing down in the sand is what you will actually see when it's finished. The part you can see while you're arranging it will actually be covered in plaster. If you want the crystals standing up and pointing out of the top of the plaster, you'll want to push them point first into the sand so the bottoms are all that you see. Keep about a quarter of an inch of the crystal bottom showing so the plaster has something to hold on to.

Once your stones are all set the way you want them, it's time to place the cup for your candle holder. Spray the outside of the tea light cup with cooking spray; the spray will keep the plaster from sticking to it. Set the tea light cup upside down in the center of your arrangement, and push the rim of the cup just about a quarter of an inch into the sand. Once you have your sand mold exactly how you want it, prepare the plaster.

Use a large bowl or bucket and mix two parts of plaster to one part water, stirring with the paint stick and making sure it's nice and smooth. Being careful not to disturb any of the details you've added to your cast, very slowly pour the plaster into your mold. Be sure to fill up your cast to cover the tea light cup. Now the hardest part—you have to wait. Oh yes, but you can do it, it's only thirty minutes or so. Or, if you're in a really humid environment, forty-five minutes to be safe. While you wait for the plaster to set, clean up your plaster mess and dispose of any extra plaster in the trash. If you're on the beach or working in a sandbox, another option is to use up the rest of the plaster making cool casts of shells, leaves, or other interesting things. Otherwise, pour any leftover mixed plaster into a disposable container, and throw it away. If you're using a disposable container for mixing, you can toss the whole thing. NEVER pour any plaster down your sink! Clean out your bucket immediately and be sure to do it outside. Again, don't wash it in the house or it might clog your pipes!

Now that your plaster casting has set, you can wiggle your fingers under the sides of the casting and gently lift it out of the sand. Gently blow the extra sand off of the top of the crystal grid. Turn the tea light cup to loosen it until it lifts out of the center. The hole left behind is where you can put a tea light; you'll find that the kind with a metal cup will fit perfectly in the hole left by the slightly larger plastic one you used. Allow the cast to cure overnight. The next day, you can use a soft toothbrush and a little water to clean it up. Apply a few dots of sticky felt to the bottom to protect your table tops, and now you're ready to use your candle crystal grid anytime you want.

All One Family

Dallas Jennifer Cobb

THE LONGEST DAY OF the year, the lesser sabbat of Litha, is traditionally a time to celebrate the light. Known as the summer solstice, Litha's long day combines with the shortest night of the year. Moving into the northern hemisphere, the sun has traveled as far north as it will. While we enjoy the long days of light, we know that now the length of the days will diminish and we will slide back, eventually toward darkness.

Represented by the sun, which is at its highest point overhead, the God is in his glory. He has grown strong and tall and reached the zenith of his life. He has conquered darkness and brought fertility and abundance, and he sees this in the abundant crops of the season. But from this height he sees what lays ahead, and the God knows that now it is all downhill: aging, diminishing, failing, and eventually death. Introspective and thoughtful, the God accepts that his sacrifice is necessary and will lead to rebirth. Quietly, the God gives thanks for all that he has enjoyed in his life, and he gives thanks for his strength, fertility, and power in the moment. The God is mindful of his blessings.

In this bright light, the Goddess also looks ahead, knowing that croning approaches. Both God and Goddess must come to terms with change and transformation. They celebrate their fertility, virility, and glory, realizing that the harvest is soon to come, and after that, the dark.

While the summer is a carefree time for teens, with school out, they are aware of the transitory nature of summer. Too quickly summer will end, and it will be time to return to school. So while the days are long, encourage your teens to rejoice in the warm sun and celebrate youthful energy, strength, and beauty, and encourage them to celebrate themselves. We know what lies ahead for them (aging, weakness, infirmity, and eventually death).

Too soon the days will grow shorter and darker. Too soon summer will end. And too soon our teenagers will grow into adults and move out into the world.

When we're young, it feels as though we are invincible. Our strength, energy, and beauty is complete. We think we shall live like this forever. But like summer, youth is fleeting. Without the proper attention paid, many young adults find themselves saddled with responsibility, debt, mortgages, and families without having fully enjoyed their youth. As adults, we know that we are all mortal. The carefree days are limited.

Litha is a great time to introduce mindfulness. Not a big fan of sitting still or meditating, my daughter easily grabbed onto this simple practice. It helped her to look at her bounty and take stock of where she was. And it enabled her to do that without focusing on what was not done, what was lacking, or still in need.

In life I have learned that we are wired to always look for the negative. Maybe it is the old, reptilian part of our brain that is always on the look out for danger, but it is easy for us to slide into patterns of negative anticipation. And if you remember the basics of the Law of Attraction (like attracts like), guess what that will bring?

Practice: Count Your Blessings

A simple mindfulness practice that cultivates a positive outlook and also helps to take inventory of everything that is going well in life is a gratitude list. I know, it sounds so simple, but it can actually take a bit of mindful focus to get yourself or your kids into the habit.

Each night before bed, urge your teenagers to take a notebook and pen and create some quiet time without distractions. Suggest a structure they can consistently complete for the first week, like writing one full page of gratitude. They might find it hard to fill a full page, but ask them to commit to trying for the whole week.

I got my daughter a special notebook to keep by her bedside. It wasn't to be used for anything else, just her "thanksgiving." I also purchased a Pilot Hi-Tecpoint pen in purple, her favorite color. While these little details seem petty, they communicate care to our teens. Our gifts help them to know that we love and support them.

On the first night, sit together and go through the exercise. Suggest phrases to start out the list like "Thank you for...," "I am grateful for...," "I am thankful for...," "With all my heart, thank you for...," and "Thank you, thank you, thank you for..." Either start with these or make up some of your own.

The point is to get your teens to start identifying the bounty in their lives, everything from the smallest achievement—"Thank you for the loud alarm clock that doesn't let me go back to sleep"—to the largest—"I am grateful that the school year is coming to an end, and I have the summer ahead of me to look forward to." Even on a really hard, stressful day, it is possible to find something to be grateful for in the ordinary things we usually take for granted: I am thankful to wake up to the light. It beats waking up in the dark of winter. And it's easier to get going.

Writing gratitude lists before bed not only helps your teens to inventory the good stuff in their lives, but it provides positive feeling endorphins, calms their worries, and prepares them for a restful sleep. As they write their gratitude lists, it is as if they are gathering nuts, berries, and fruits of the vine. These little treasures that they can value and conserve will be there when they need them most. Gratitude lists are sustenance for the soul, growing the light inside and out.

Litha Ritual

Suzanne Ress

THE PURPOSE OF THIS ritual is to celebrate the union of the Sun King with the Moon Goddess around a traditional bonfire, and to fill our hearts and spirits with limitless compassion, intuition, and healing power.

Items Needed

A flask or bottle of fresh water previously charged in the moonlight
A safe location (a permit for a bonfire if necessary)
Wood
Fern fronds picked at midday—one for each participant
Five red candles in safe portable lanterns
A silver or blue chalice
Wand or athame
Refreshments and musical instruments for post-ritual

For this simple ritual to be successful, you will need to do some preparation ahead of time. The fresh water is best collected from a natural spring, but tap water or even bottled water in glass (not plastic) will do. Take this outside when the moon is bright, on some evening before Midsummer, and leave it one full hour under the moon's light. Store in the refrigerator until needed.

Prepare a safe place for a bonfire, preferably on a riverbank, lakeshore, or oceanside. Clear away anything that can burn—sticks, dried plant matter, etc. Make a circle that is three or four feet in diameter using a double row of large stones, rocks, or bricks. Make certain there are no low-lying tree branches nearby. Be sure to obtain the necessary permit, if required. Gather plenty of split wood that is dry and ready to burn.

At noon on the longest day of the year, go into a shady wood and pick enough green bracken fern fronds so that every participant will have one.

The bonfire should be started a little before sunset. The ritual will commence at sunset.

Place the five red candles in their lanterns around the bonfire, about four feet away from it. This forms a circular pathway around the bonfire wide enough for participants to move safely around in. One lantern shall be placed at the northeast point of the circle, one at the northwestern point, one at the northernmost point, and the remaining two in the southeast and southwest points. These form the points of a pentacle with the fire as the center.

Put the silver or blue chalice and the container of moon water (holding the fern fronds) on a rock, tree stump, or small table. Make sure this is far enough away in an easterly direction so they will not be accidentally knocked over.

Participants can be skyclad if possible and desirable, or merely barefoot, as they wish. They should gather in a circle around the bonfire and hold hands.

Using a wand or athame, the speaker should draw all attention to the southeast lantern, and announce:

We are gathered here to celebrate the union of masculine fire—

Now the speaker turns and points her wand to the northeast lantern, and says:

With feminine water.

Facing north, she says:

This is spirit,

Facing northwest, she says:

And air.

And facing southwest, she says:

And earth.
Let us dance.

Participants will drop hands and begin to move clockwise, slowly at first, then gradually faster—skipping, leaping, or jigging merrily in whatever way they choose. They may also sing, chant, play drums, horns, flutes, or mouth harps. This joyful celebration shall go on for some time until all present feel the relaxation that comes with prolonged uninhibited and joyful movement.

The movement gradually winds down until everyone is again standing still around the bonfire.

The speaker says:

Let us now all focus on our heart chakra, anahata.

She touches the center of her chest with her wand or athame and breathes in slowly and deeply, opening up the chakra.

All participants stand straight, breathe deeply, and place both hands on their neighbor's heart chakra for a moment before opening the hands outward. Participants should turn toward the neighbor on their other side and do the same thing.

The speaker says:

Our hearts are open to allow the sacred fire of universal compassion to enter into them. Let it now enter into us all.

Silence will reign for a few minutes as compassion enters and fills everyone's hearts.

Now the person standing nearest the space between the lanterns that represent water (to the northeast) and fire (to the southeast) shall leave the circle and walk between these two lanterns, and everyone else shall follow him.

The leader will proceed to the rock, stump, or table that holds the moon water, ferns, and chalice, and the leader will distribute the fern fronds, one to each person.

The ferns are to be held in your left hand.

The leader will pour some of the moon water into the chalice, and say:

With this water, charged by Lady Moon, we take the powers of healing and intuition into our bodies and spirits, and manifest the magic of this special evening.

He takes a sip of the water and passes the chalice around so that everyone may have a sip.

A moment of silence ensues as the feminine powers of healing and intuition join masculine universal compassion in our hearts.

The leader says:

The Sun and Moon are united!

And everyone may laugh and cheer joyously. The leader says:

And now for some magic!

Each person shall scrape some fern seed (which are actually spores) from the back of their frond and swallow it and then dance off into the darkness to become temporarily invisible.

During this period of invisibility, anything can happen, and no one will ever know or speak of it!

After the frolicking winds down, refreshments or even a full meal are to be offered. This can be as simple or as elaborate as you like, but make sure to include some form of sea, lake, or river food, such as fish, shellfish, or seaweed. Include plenty of golden ale or mead.

Refreshments can be followed by music making and more dancing and frolicking, and if the place and weather are appropriate, a swim or skinny dip. The celebration should go on at least until midnight, but could continue until dawn.

Notes

Lammas

Lammas & Lughnasadh

JD Hortwort

AUGUST FIRST MARKS THE start of the harvest season at Lughnasadh in the northern hemisphere. The name of the ritual varies depending on the source. Some call it Lammas or loaf mass. It can also be spelled Lunasa or Lunasda.

However you spell it, Lughnasadh is associated with Lugh, a sun god and warrior who led the Tuatha De Danann in battle against the Formorians. It's interesting to note that, while we call it Lughnasadh after the god, legend tells us this time was not set aside to honor Lugh's achievements. Lugh set this time aside to honor his foster mother, Tailtiu, for her sacrifice for her tribe.

This is the first harvest. For many Pagans, it is the grain harvest, soon to be followed by the fruit harvest at the fall equinox and last, by the blood sacrifice at Samhain.

For me and fellow members of the House of Akasha in North Carolina, this is a time to get back to our agrarian roots. Whatever the Gregorian calendar says, summer is over. The plants are tired and seem to be looking forward to rest—whether that means a final death in the compost heap or a respite from the chore of producing fruit until next season.

When the House was first forming about eight years ago, we wondered how to honor this season. Somehow, Lughnasadh feels like the red-haired stepchild of Pagan holidays. It doesn't seem to have the high energy of the summer solstice. But it's not quite as festive as Mabon, with its anticipation of all those wonderful fall activities.

We came up with the idea to have our own version of the Tailteann games. We lightheartedly called them the Low Country Games, which, if you know much about North Carolina, was a poke at the Highland Games held at Grandfather Mountain.

We could have played pickup basketball or soccer or volleyball. But instead, we decided to try to emulate older games. That meant doing a caber toss, a boulder toss, and a spear toss. Mind you, at the time, we didn't really take into account that we were Irish Celtic reconstructionists putting on Scottish-style games.

The problem was we were a motley crew with limited funds, and we didn't have any bits of Scottish gaming equipment. What do good Pagans do? We improvised.

I cut a length of oak for the caber toss. It wasn't the standard nineteen feet six inches long and it wasn't made of larch. It was about five feet long and six inches in diameter and weighed a ton since it was cut from green wood! But it was a length of wood that most of us could at least manage to pick up, if not toss end over end.

For the boulder toss, no one really wanted to try to heave a huge boulder. One of our members came up with the idea of using an old bowling ball. Fortunately, it was an eight-pounder and relatively easy to grasp. Plus, the owner didn't care that we would be chucking it around in a gravel driveway, guaranteeing it would be nicked and dented when we were done with it.

For our spear, a more enterprising member resurrected his Boy Scout skills, found an old spear point in a storage trunk, and scrounged a relatively straight branch from the nearby woods. It might have earned him points with his old Scout troop, but it certainly wasn't going to challenge one of the four treasures of the Tuatha De Danann.

On the day of the first Low Country Games, we all gathered in the late day heat of summer to try our hand. It was a pitiful sight and nothing that would get any of us inside the gates of Tara.

The majority of us wrestled the caber up about hip high. A couple did manage to get the log to fly end over end. Most found they could at least toss it away from their bodies with an "umph," a groan, and a sigh.

The bowling ball toss wasn't much better. The average distance tossed was probably six feet. One "athlete" scored a good eleven-foot toss. There were cheers and hurrahs all around until the bowling ball rolled back toward the group. We forgot to take into account the slight incline in the driveway.

For the spear toss, the incline wasn't a real problem. We set up a hay bale roughly fifteen feet away from the toss area. This game turned out to be the most thrilling, mainly because we discovered the bend in the spear shaft and its unfortunate lack of balance made our spear a primitive ballistic missile without much of a guidance system. After about the third warrior, someone figured out that the best way to hit the hay bale was to aim for the nearby ditch.

We didn't set any Olympic records, but as the light of the day ended and we headed to ritual, there were definitely winners to be honored. More importantly, we had stories to tell over the balefire. Heroes were humbled and losers were heckled like family.

Since those first games, we have gradually acquired a proper spear, a bow and arrow set, and some shot puts and discus. We have added some games and given up others. The idea to have a hatchet toss was probably the least well-advised. Possible future additions might be games of mental dexterity for those of us who are less athletically inclined. After all, we all can't be warriors and jocks.

The entire concept of attempting ancient games may be a bit silly. We have found a number of benefits. Some of our members are natural coaches with infinite patience to school other members in the mysterious ways of the discus or the bow.

Those of us who cringed in middle school or high school at the humiliation of being clumsy at sports have a safe haven to try the things we always secretly wanted to try.

However, the most important outcome of our Lughnasadh Low Country Games is the bonding agent they create in the stories that we can share from year to year. We have stories of triumph. We have stories of valiant effort. We have brave challenges to carry us into the winter and taunts of "Wait until next year!"

That is what Lughnasadh has come to mean for the House. It is a time of revelry. It is a connection to a not too distant past when our great-grandparents came together at first harvest to help each other bring in the corn or cotton. They didn't call it Lughnasadh, but it was a celebration of the season as surely as our festival today.

Because after the hard work was done, families that had gathered together for the grain harvest then stayed a few days more. They feasted. They sang and danced. They told stories. They enjoyed games of strength and games of chance, with all the bragging and ribbing those activities entail.

This is our Lughnasadh, our honoring of our Celtic deities and the bonds that hold us together as a group.

Cosmic Sway

April Elliott Kent

THIS LAMMAS HARVEST FESTIVAL begins on a bright, first quarter Moon. But this Moon in Scorpio has finished all its aspects in its current sign; this will be a Lammas season that is best experienced without a lot of expectation. If you have a fixed agenda in your head, things are not likely to go exactly as you had hoped, and you will be disappointed. But if you are willing to make room in your life for things to be what they want to be, truly magical surprises can come your way.

What are you harvesting during this Lammas season? For most of us, it has something to do with increased personal freedom and a true appreciation of ourselves. It's not that any one of us is more important than anyone else, but all too often we are apt to make ourselves less important, and that's not right either. Constantly giving in to others to avoid conflict is a common mistake that most of us have made at one time or another. And every time we do, we tell ourselves that we matter a little bit less than other people.

But this season, with its powerful eclipses and other strong celestial events, sends the message that relationships purchased at the expense of your self-respect can never bring real happiness.

Uranus turns retrograde on August 2, and the period between August 1 and 3 is when exasperation with the status quo reaches its peak. It's always worth noting major aspects between the outer planets, and Jupiter's square to Pluto on August 4 brings a moment of critical decision involving laws, power, and possibly relations among nations. This is an aspect that happens at least twice each year, however, so it will likely be an important catalyst for long-standing issues.

Full Moon/Lunar Eclipse in Aquarius—August 7, 2017

This Aquarius Full Moon brings a lunar eclipse, and eclipses always signal the need to make a change. That is doubly true of eclipses in the sign of Aquarius, a sign that has refined the art of getting unstuck. The chart for the Full Moon features a bright conjunction of the Sun and Mars in prideful Leo, reflecting the struggle to gain the appreciation and recognition we feel we deserve. Before you take up the battle, however, let this cool Aquarius eclipse give you a dispassionate perspective. Stand back and try to see yourself as others do. More importantly, try to get a clear picture of how you'd like to see yourself. Sometimes when we crave recognition from others, it's because we lack appreciation for ourselves.

To fully appreciate what this eclipse will bring to your life, look back to previous years when eclipses fell near this point: Feb. 1981, Aug. 1990, Aug. 1998, Feb. 2000, Feb. 2008, and Aug. 2009.

Eclipse Wisdom Ritual: Getting Unstuck

The energy of eclipses is energy of change. Like sudden summer storms that erupt from still, inky skies and leave the landscape bright and freshly washed in their wake, eclipses in Aquarius bring forth a sense of personal revolution. But before you can change, you have to let yourself get unstuck from your current circumstances.

If you're lucky enough to live in a place where summer lightning storms are common, use them by performing your ritual during one! Otherwise, an image of lightning propped up on your altar, or simply a good imagination, will do the trick.

For your altar, assemble tools of Aquarius: candles, stones, metals of purple or silver, a sheet of heavy aluminum foil, salt, something mechanical or electronic—a radio, cellphone, tiny model airplane made of metal, or similar gadget will work fine—and any of these herbs: dragonwort, frankincense, rue, china berry, or sage.

Use the aluminum foil to cover your altar. Scatter your salt and herbs, place stones and gadget, and light your candle while saying something like:

> *As lightning and electricity,*
> *Change has the power*
> *To animate me*
> *Let me move toward the change that's right,*
> *With knowledge to improve my sight.*

Mercury Retrograde—Aug. 12–Sep. 5, 2017

Mercury is especially strong in Virgo, so this retrograde is liable to be more aggravating than usual if you insist on pushing forward with new plans and projects. Instead, use this harvest season Mercury retrograde to gather together valuable insights and skills that may be languishing from disuse. In business, writing, or the arts, now is the time to rediscover half-finished projects or ideas and bring them to completion.

With Venus's opposition aspect to Pluto on the fifteenth, old conflicts within relationships are apt to flare up. Instead of feeling a sense of failure because you have not overcome them, approach the other person with patience. See if you can talk things over, come to a better understanding, and bring new insights to old disagreements.

Leo New Moon/Solar Eclipse—August 21, 2017

This New Moon is a solar eclipse, with the Sun and Moon united with Mars and the Moon's North Node, all in harmonious aspect with Jupiter, Saturn, and Uranus. It is a hard New Moon chart for relationships, at least for the sorts of relationships that have been living on borrowed time. The awareness of the need for freedom that was awakened at the August 7 lunar eclipse in Aquarius is now realized—particularly around August 24, when Venus makes an exact square to freedom-loving Uranus. If you feel you aren't being appreciated, this solar eclipse will give you the courage you need to move on to greener pastures.

You can often gain more personal insight into an eclipse by reviewing years when other eclipses fell near the degree (28.52 Leo) of this one. Many of the same issues that were important in your life around Feb. 1989, Aug. 1998, Feb. 1999, and Feb. 2008, could be awakened now.

Affirmations for the New Moon/Solar Eclipse in Leo

Writing affirmations at the New Moon focuses your mind toward a positive outcome. At the Leo New Moon, it's appropriate to celebrate your unique qualities and joyful engagement in the world. Here are a few examples. Try writing them (or adapting them) and using them as part of your New Moon observance.

- I appreciate my talents, gifts, and contributions.
- I express myself with creativity and boldness for the sheer delight of sharing and connecting with others.
- I celebrate each day with joy, always looking for opportunities to laugh and open my heart.

Virgo Is for Lovers!

Mars (Sep. 5) and Venus (Sep. 19), which together symbolize romantic lovers, both enter Virgo during this Lammas season. Virgo is symbolized by a maiden, but don't limit your interpretation of this sign's "virginity" to the modern sense of having abstained from sexual activity. Rather, Virgo symbolizes virginity in the sense of being independent, self-sufficient, and complete to oneself. This is actually the best state for finding happiness in a relationship, because if you are satisfied with yourself and your life, you can happily and confidently share both with deserving others. (Not to mention Virgo is an earth sign, and earth signs are pretty darn sexy!)

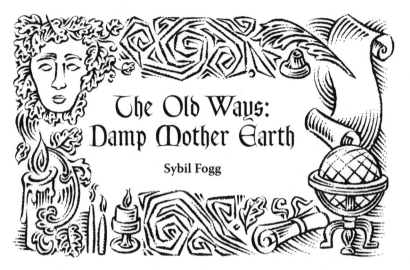

The Old Ways: Damp Mother Earth

Sybil Fogg

THE BEGINNING OF AUGUST is the home of Lughnasadh or Lammas, which derives its name from "hlåf-mæsse," or loaf-mass, and is often celebrated as a festival of bread, beer, and other grain-centered edible treats. This is the first of three harvest festivals, and it is also the moment farmers are about to partake in the backbreaking work of harvesting their crops. It is not surprising that the beginning of the harvest was viewed with trepidation in ancient times.

In Poland, a set of rituals was placed down to ensure a good harvest. Scythes used for reaping were blessed before entering the field. Harvesting generally began on a Saturday, a day sacred to the Great Mother. The Polish people originally worshiped a snake, bird, and bee goddess, but this changed to an earth goddess with the influence of Indo-European peoples. They knew her as Matka Syra Zemlya, also known as Matka Syra Ziemia, literally "Damp Mother Earth." As a goddess of the soil and all that inhabit it, if she takes human form, she will appear as the color of dirt. This is rare, however, since the ancient Slavs viewed Matka Syra Zemlya as the earth itself without a body or human form. Each spring, bread was buried for her to eat, and beer and wine were poured into holes for her to drink, according to the *Encyclopedia of Russian & Slavic Myth and*

Legend. Her sacred day is August 1, and bread and beer would be left in the fields for her to ensure a healthy harvest. Before beginning the harvest, reapers would bless themselves as well as the field. Reapers would don their most formal clothing. Often girls were sent into the field first to dance with their hair decorated with flowers and ribbons, their joy consecrating the crop.

Upon beginning the harvest, the initial stalks of grain were gathered and formed into the shape of a cross. Other traditions that ensured good luck or strong future harvests included tucking stalks behind a mirror, placing stalks in the corner of a room, or tying them around the waist of reapers (Hodorowicz Knab). It was a hard day, and the people worked from dawn to dusk, careful to leave a sheaf of wheat standing in the field as an offering. After all this work, the celebrations began.

It was traditional for the landowner to either wear a wreath or crown, or the landowner would bestow this honor on one of the peasants, who would wear the wreath for some of the festivities, and then they would ritualistically return it to the landowner's head. This presentation of the wreath was the hallmark of the festivities. It was made of the most appealing stalks of grain harvested and then decorated with ribbons, flowers, and herbs. As might be expected, much of the celebration included bread and ale in honor of the grain gods.

In Lithuania, the first harvest was traditionally celebrated on August 15, a day sacred to Žemyna, an earth goddess who, like many of her grain and harvest counterparts, governed birth, fertility, and nature. It was common to bestow beer and bread along with flowers, corn, and herbs upon altars in honor of Žemyna at this time of year. Another fascinating tradition in Lithuanian is that of *keptinis*, which is ale made from hops and malts and baked in a bread form and added to the beer. There are a few brewers in Lithuania today who are revisiting this old method of beer craft.

Another beer tradition in Lithuania is that of the feast of the goddess Gabjauja (also known as Gabija, Gabieta, or Gabeta). For this feast, women made beer and bread to honor this goddess of the hearth, fire, and grain. Only family was allowed to attend the celebration. It was the task of the head of the household to spill beer onto the ground and begin the prayer to Gabjauja.

The Latvians honored Cerklicing, the god of corn and fertility, by leaving corn and beer in the fields to ensure crop abundance. According to the Jesuit Joannis Stribingius, Latvian farmers gave the "first bite of any food, and the first drop of any drink" to Cerklicing when he visited eastern Latvia in 1606 (Putelis). Another god that the Latvians called on to ensure a strong harvest was Jumis. It was believed he lived in the fields.

The ancient Russians worshiped the sky and thunder god Perun until Christian times when he was merged with the prophet Elijah. Together Elijah-Perun were given the unofficial title of "Lord of the Harvest" (Gilchrist). Elijah-Perun is honored on August 2. This is a day when no labor is to be performed. It was believed if rest was not taken in honor of the god, then those being active might be struck down by lightning or be unfortunately punished with the destruction of their crops by fire or hail.

Matka Syra Zemlya was not the only Slavic goddess honored at the first harvest. The Baba Yaga, a Russian goddess figure featured in many fairy tales, is represented at the harvest time as a repulsive, frightening old woman who flies around in a pestle and mortar and lives in the middle of the woods in a hut that stands on chicken feet. A representation of death and decay in old traditions, a straw figure of the Baba Yaga was fashioned and then destroyed as a reminder that the great reaping will come to all.

As Lughnasadh comes closer, perhaps it is time to honor the great reaping and first harvest by donning fancy clothing and weaving flowers and ribbons through our hair and taking a walk through a field (if one is readily available). For those who are more introverted, try baking bread and celebrating the grain holiday with a few close friends or family in honor of Gabjauja. Perhaps organizing a party at a friend's farm to celebrate the first harvest would be a better choice for those more social. Don't forget to bring beer and bread out into the field to honor the gods and ask for a successful crop yield. Try your hand at the hard work of harvest to take you back to ancient rites. Craft a wreath crown of wheat and flowers to take turns wearing when the hard work is over and the celebrations have begun. End your day by burning an effigy of the Baba Yaga as a reminder that the harvest will come to a close. But don't forget to rest on August 2 to honor the harvest deities of the Slavic states. Summer is drawing to a close. Blessed Be.

Bibliography

Dixon-Kennedy, Mike. *Encyclopedia of Russian & Slavic Myth and Legend*. Santa Barbara: ABC-CLIO INC., 1998.

Gilchrist, Cherry. *Russian Magic: Living Folk Traditions of an Enchanted Landscape*. Wheaton: Quest Books, 2009.

"Harvest Holiday, Aug. 15 (Dozynki)," *Polish Genealogical Society of America*, accessed Aug. 3, 2015. http://pgsa.org/polish-traditions/.

Hodorowicz Knab, Sophie. *Polish Customs, Traditions, & Folklore*. New York: Hippocrene Books, Inc., 1993.

"Introduction to Lithuanian Paganism," *Romuva*, accessed August 4, 2015. http://www.romuva.lt/new/?page=en.

Lars Marius Garshol, "Lithuanian beer, again," *Larsblog* (blog), Nov. 18, 2012, http://www.garshol.priv.no/blog/239.html.

Putelis, Aldis. "Cerklicing," *Encyclopedia Mythica,* accessed August 6, 2015, http://www.pantheon.org/articles/c/cerklicing.html.

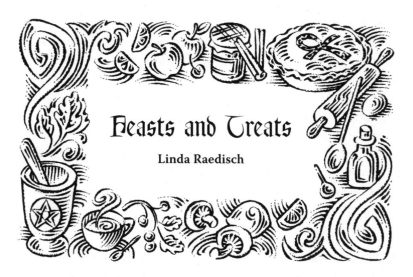

Feasts and Treats

Linda Raedisch

LIKE HALLOWEEN AND THE German *Walpurgisnacht,* Lammas Eve used to be one of those dangerous nights when witches were about. Is it irony, then, that the Witches are the only ones still keeping the festival of Lammas these days? I'm not sure. It is probable that the mysterious feast of Lammas was originally a Germanic observance, so we're observing it this year in Germanic fashion—by eating dessert first.

Serve the *Pflaumenkuchen* around three or four o'clock in the afternoon—that's the coffee hour in Germany. In August, coffee and cake is best consumed on the terrace, so as not to miss a minute of this last full month of summer. When evening comes and everyone is hungry again, it's time for *Zwiebelkuchen,* which busy Lammas-keeping Witches can bake a day or two ahead of time and quickly warm up in the oven.

Little Witch's Friday Cake

No, I don't know for certain what kind of cake Otfried Preußler's titular children's book heroine bakes on Fridays, only that she does always bake one in the hope that visitors might drop by. Pflaumenkuchen, meaning "plum cake," figures into the plot of another

Preußler novel, *The Robber Hotzenplotz*, so I would not be at all surprised if the Little Witch favored plum cake at Lammastide when *Zwetshgen* (Italian prune plums) come into season.

Here follows my German mother's recipe for Pflaumenkuchen, which she serves with *Schlagsahne*—lightly sweetened whipped cream. Just to be different, I have provided a recipe for vanilla sauce that can be poured over the individual cake slices. One of the wonderful things about Pflaumenkuchen is that it makes a lot—enough to have some left over for breakfast the next morning.

Prep time: 30 minutes, if you don't have help pitting the plums
Bake time: 40 minutes
Servings: 10–12

¼ cup butter (½ a stick) plus butter for greasing pan
¼ cup white sugar plus some for sprinkling
1 egg
½ teaspoon vanilla extract
1½ cups white flour
1 teaspoon baking powder
½ cup low fat milk
25–30 Italian prune plums or president's plums, cut in half lengthwise and pitted
10-inch spring form or similar size square or rectangular baking pan

Cream butter and sugar together. Beat in egg and vanilla until well mixed. Sift in flour and baking powder a little at a time, alternating with milk. Dough will be stiff. Preheat oven to 375 degrees F.

Spread dough evenly in pan. Press plum halves cut-side-up into the dough in neat rows. Sprinkle lightly with sugar and bake for about 40 minutes. While cake is baking, you can prepare the vanilla sauce.

Vanilla Sauce

Prep time: 5 minutes
Cook time: 15 minutes
Servings: 10–12

1 vanilla bean
1 cup whole milk
2 tablespoons white sugar
½ teaspoon cornstarch
Water
3 egg yolks, beaten

With a sharp knife, slit the vanilla bean lengthwise and scrape out the "mark," as the soft insides are called, into a small pot. (You can store the empty bean, which is still full of flavor, in a jar of sugar to make vanilla sugar, which is the kind of sugar my mother prefers for sprinkling over plum cake.) Add milk and sugar and stir until very warm but not boiling.

In a cup, mix the cornstarch with a tiny bit of water—just enough to dissolve it. Whisk egg yolks and cornstarch into vanilla mixture and continue whisking over low heat until sauce thickens. Pour into pitcher or gravy boat, straining out any lumps, cover with plastic wrap and chill. Pour over plum cake before serving.

Zwiebelkuchen

Zwiebelkuchen translates literally as "onion cake," but it's obviously a pie. The Germans have two words for cake, two words for cookie, but no word for pie. Go figure.

Prep time: 20 minutes
Bake time: 35 minutes
Servings: 8

2 tablespoons olive oil
2 medium yellow onions coarsely chopped (or Vidalia, red, a bunch of scallions, or a mixture thereof. There are no rules!)

1 egg
½ cup sour cream
1 tablespoon white flour
Generous dash white wine
½ cup grated Gouda cheese
Deep dish frozen pie crust, thawed

Heat olive oil in pan, add chopped onions, and cook until onions are glassy to golden.

Preheat oven to 350 degrees F.

Whisk the egg in a large bowl and then stir in sour cream, flour, wine, and cheese. Stir in fried onions and spread in pie crust.

Bake for about 35 minutes or until firm and golden. Cool just a few minutes before serving.

Radler

A *Radler* is a cyclist. The kind of Radler you drink is called a shandy in English: half beer and half soft drink or fruit juice. The Radler is the favorite drink of Germans in the summertime, and it comes in many flavors: apple, orange, lemon, raspberry, ginger, or even *Waldmeistersirup* (sweet woodruff syrup). Drink enough of these "cyclists" and you might just see Margaret Hamilton cycling furiously by through the golden dusk of a Lammas Eve.

Prep time: 5 minutes
Servings: 4

¼ cup sugar
½ cup warm water
¼ cup lemon juice
1½ cups seltzer
2 cups "white" or light-colored beer

In the bottom of a pitcher, mix sugar and warm water until sugar is dissolved. Add lemon juice and seltzer. (Fizz!) Fill each glass half full with lemonade, then fill the rest of the glass with beer.

Crafty Crafts

Mickie Mueller

WHEAT WEAVING ORNAMENTS ARE perfect for Lammas because it's the season of the grain harvest, so these projects tie back to the mysteries of the sacred land and traditional celebrations. There is usually a learning curve for wheat weaving projects, and some of the weaves can be pretty complex. I had never attempted wheat weaving in my life when I tried these two projects, and I must say these ones were super easy, but really looked great when complete. They are beautiful in their simplicity. If you love making these easy projects, you may want to go online and look up directions for more complex wheat weaving projects in the future.

Harvest Abundance Braid

Time to complete: 30 minutes
Cost: $10 to $14

Supplies
9 stalks of wheat (from the craft store, or wild grass stalks for free)
A bit of raffia or twine
Ribbon (optional)

Carefully remove any remaining leaves and loose-hanging pieces from the wheat stalks. Soak nine wheat stalks in the bathtub in about an inch of hot water for thirty minutes. Lay two shampoo bottles over the stalks to keep them from floating. Don't soak them for more than an hour—if you over-soak them, they can become too soft to handle.

Bundle the seed heads together so that the bases of all the seed heads are pretty close to even. Tie a piece of raffia to bind the stalks together right beneath the seed head. Now lay the bundle on a table and carefully divide the stems into three sections that each have three stalks. Now you simply begin to braid them. As you braid, keep each section of wheat flat; this will make it look nice and neat. To do a braid, basically bring the right section in between the other two. Holding them in place, bring the left section between the other two, proceeding in this way back and forth. If you're not familiar with braiding, watch a video online to see how it's done. It's really not hard at all.

Keep braiding until the thicker parts of the stalks become too hard to bend, and then tie off the braid tightly with another piece of raffia. Now take a sharp pair of scissors and cut the stalks off evenly, leaving about two inches below the knot.

Take the ends of the raffia you just used to tie the stem bottoms together and make a knot to form a loop; this is how you'll hang your harvest braid. The raffia used to tie the seed-head end together can be trimmed close to the knot.

You can then gently press and twist slightly if needed to neaten up the braid. Tie a pretty piece of fall-color ribbon or ribbon that matches your décor to cover the raffia knots, if you wish. Hang it in your home with the seed heads downward to pour blessings of abundance into your home.

Wheat Pentagram Wall Hanging

Time to complete: 30 minutes
Cost: $10 to $14

Supplies
6-inch steel hoop used for macramé
10 stalks of wheat (craft store) or wild grass stalks
Raffia

Tie the end of a piece of raffia to the hoop using a simple double knot. Hold the short end of the raffia against the hoop and wrap the long end of the raffia around the hoop and over the top of the short end of raffia to keep it down. Continue to wrap around the hoop, keeping the raffia wrapped tightly on it and without leaving any metal showing as you go. If your piece of raffia runs short, you can tie it to another piece, wrapping as you were and covering the knot. Continue in this manner adding strips of raffia until the whole hoop is covered. Before you stop, you may wish to push the coils together closely to make sure that metal does not show, wrapping your final section a few more times to complete it. Once you're happy with your hoop, split the end of the raffia into two. Wrap one end firmly around the hoop a few more times and tie the two pieces of raffia in a simple double knot. Then tie the two ends together to form a loop so it can be hung later.

Now that you've created the raffia-covered hoop, let's make the star in the middle that will turn it into a wheat pentagram. Start by cutting five pieces of raffia that are eight inches each.

Then line up each wheat stalk across the widest part of the hoop so that the base of the seed head is resting on the hoop. Cut the stem about an inch longer than the widest part of the hoop (i.e., if your hoop is six inches, your stalks should be seven inches from the bottom of the seed head to the end).

Tie two wheat stalks together right under the seed head with raffia, forming a "V" shape with the stalks. Repeat this step with all the wheat stalks. Don't cut the excess raffia off after you tie them together.

Lay out all five pairs of stalks on a table, arranging them in a rough pentagram shape with the seed heads as the points and the stems forming the rest of the star. If it helps, you can draw a five-pointed star on a piece of paper to help position them. When the "V" shapes are arranged into a pentagram, each star point will have two seed heads and two stem ends overlapping each other. When you have the star arranged and you're happy with it, tie the seed heads and the stem heads together using the raffia that is already attached to the seed heads. You can still adjust the star after tying them if you need to. Make adjustments by gently sliding the wheat stems back and forth through the tied raffia until they are right where you want them.

Place the hoop on top of the star, lining up one point of the star at the top where the hanging loop is. The knot where the seed heads are tied together should line up with the knot to hang the pentagram, so the seed heads will extend past the hoop, and the star will be on the inside. Starting with the top, use the same raffia ties to

attach the star onto the hoop. Make sure you tie double knots so it will be secure. You can then manipulate the wheat stalks slightly to make sure you're happy with the look of your new wheat pentagram. Trim off any excess raffia and you're ready to hang it.

All One Family

Dallas Jennifer Cobb

THE FIRST OF THREE harvest festivals, the greater sabbat of Lammas celebrates grains and marks the beginning of the harvest season. Also called Lughnasadh after the god Lugh, Lammas is a time to think about our hopes and fears. We remember Lugh, the Sun God, because it is on this day that he lays down his life for the sake of harvest. Lammas is both a time to celebrate and a time to mourn and remember.

Lammas is a festival honoring both fire and water. Fire symbolizes our survival in the physical world, providing warmth, cooking, protection, and the bright spark of imagination and intelligence. The sun is central to the growth and ripening of the crops. Fire was traditionally used to bake breads, make preserves, and bubble the cauldron to make fermented drinks like cider and ale. Water symbolizes our survival in the emotional and psychic worlds. It provides healing, transportation, and hydration for humans, animals, and crops.

Harvest time means endings. Lugh is cut down like the grains and descends into the earth and into the womb of the Goddess, preparing to be reborn. The God sacrifices himself for the greater good, knowing he will be transformed.

While we enjoy the harvest of early fruits and berries, grains, and vegetables, we also start to think ahead to winter. Days are growing ever shorter, and there is a cooling at night. The sun sets earlier and it is suddenly dark.

Even if we live in a city, we contemplate storing some of our abundant crops away. People buy seasonal produce and "put it up." In rural areas, pickling and making jams augment what can be frozen. Because of the duality of Lammas, celebrating harvest and mourning the loss of the God, it is a good time to both count our blessings and share with those in need. When we put up our fruit and vegetables, it is easy to get into the Lammas spirit of sharing by sending a jar of harvest riches to family, friends, or neighbors.

We think about sacrifice and recognize we must begin to prepare ourselves for what lies ahead. Our teens start to think about going back to school, and they begin the task of preparing themselves for that big transition. They realize that they will soon have to sacrifice their "freedom."

The sobering reality of school and the creep of the darkness is enough to inspire a fantastic feast, one that reminds us to really enjoy all that we are blessed with, even as we look ahead to what is guaranteed.

Practice: Feast on Life

One of the easiest ways to celebrate Lammas with your teens is to plan a feast that incorporates both fire and water. It could be a big beach celebration that involves swimming, sunshine, and beach volleyball, or a barn dance with twinkling lights, cold drinks, and a corn roast. If you live in the city, maybe you will simply plan a community picnic in a local park enjoying the sun and a juicy watermelon. Make the gathering a potluck and suggest local harvest as the theme.

Because we are celebrating abundance, let your teens bring a friend with them. In the ideal world, you can gather with your friends, other families with similar-aged kids, and the teens.

This summer I had the pleasure of gathering with three other families. We met at the beach in the afternoon. With lawn chairs, beach toys, and tons of food, we were equipped to enjoy sun, water, and sand.

There was a combined total of ten teens and kids aged 7 to 14. Despite the age differences, they played well together, enjoying noisy games of tag and Marco Polo in the warm water. The adults lazed on the beach while enjoying conversations, laughter, and the chance to watch our teens being kids for a while.

When several families come together, there is always an abundance of food. Because I live in a rich agricultural area, I took burgers, sweet corn, and a home-baked blueberry pie, all produced locally. Other people brought roasted chicken, new potato salad, grilled zucchini and summer squash, coleslaw, fresh rye bread, two kinds of local cheese, maple grilled peaches, fresh raspberries with whipped cream, and locally produced wine. The feast was truly a feast of local agricultural abundance and the richness that evolves when families and friends come together.

After dinner, most of the moms played in the water with the kids. I was thankful to have some fun time with my daughter. I got to enjoy some "kid time," knowing that this too is coming to an end as she grows into a young woman.

The park warden warned us that the sun goes down quickly at this time of year, so we packed up all our stuff while we had light. Then, calling the kids out of the water, we stood on the shore as the sun slipped down over the horizon, and suddenly it was dark.

Stretching out the celebration, we went back to one family's farm. The adults sat around the bonfire talking, laughing, drinking wine, and singing along to the strummed guitar. The kids gobbled s'mores, and then they went bravely into the dark vineyard to play "manhunt."

There is so much to teach our teens. But if I can teach my daughter to be present, appreciate her friends, share the bounty, and enjoy the good times, I've given her the gifts of Lammas. Recognizing that we are rich with family, friends, sustenance, and joy, we have what's needed to survive the dark times ahead.

And without having to coax, teach, or tell, I know my daughter got the lesson.

Lammas Ritual

JD Hortwort

SOME RITUALS ARE SERIOUS of purpose. Lughnasadh, for our group, isn't heavy or long. After a day of games, the ritual sets the stage for the dinner and bardic circle that happen after the circle is opened.

If at all possible, Lughnasadh should be held outside. It is, after all, a harvest festival. It would be hard to pick a more appropriate time to be outside than Lughnasadh, except for Beltane at the start of the growing season in most of the northern hemisphere.

This ritual calls for establishing quarters. For the directions, we will be calling to the four cities and the bards or druids who instructed the Tuatha De Danann in their magickal arts. We use representations of the four treasures from those cities: a spear, a sword, a cauldron, and a large stone. These aren't required but are nice to have if you can gather them.

Items Needed
Altar table
Candles: gold and white
Basket of assorted flours and grains
Seasonally appropriate cakes and ale
Sage and cedar (smudging herbs)

Aspersing water (pure or rain water with a few drops of cedar oil)

Anointing oil (light oil with a few drops of rosemary essential oil)

Participants will be asked to sit for a portion of the ritual and should bring a towel or blanket, if desired. They should also be advised to bring a story, poem, song, or other material to share at the bardic circle at the end of the day.

Four people are assigned to call quarters. Two are assigned to smudge and asperse participants as they enter the circle. The High Priest/Druid and High Priestess/Druidess will conduct the ritual and call the deities. The Crone or eldest female will cast a circle once all participants have been anointed.

Call to Circle

As participants approach the circle area, they are smudged—"By fire and air, I purify you"—and aspersed—"By water and earth, I purify you." The individuals doing the smudging and aspersing cleanse each other and prepare to enter the circle. The High Priestess anoints each person as they come to circle, asking, "Do you come of your own free will?"

Once all are assembled, the Crone casts a circle in the tradition of the group.

At this point, the quarters are called beginning in the east.

East: (If a spear is available, raise it.) *We call to Esras in the city of Gorias from which comes the Spear of Lugh. No warrior who went to battle with it could fail. No enemy could stand against it. Esras, be with us and guard us for this, our Lughnasadh ritual today.*

South: (If a sword is available, raise it.) *We call to Uscias in the city of Findias from which comes the Sword of Nuadu. No enemy could escape its edge. No warrior could stand against he who wielded it. Uscias, be with us and guard us for this, our Lughnasadh ritual today.*

West: (If a cauldron is available, hold it.) *We call to Semias in the city of Murias from which comes the Cauldron of the Dagda, the Good Father. Bountiful, overflowing, no one ever came away from it unsatisfied. Semias, be with us and guard us for this, our Lughnasadh ritual today.*

North: (If there is a stone available, stand on it.) *We call to Morfessa of the city of Falias from which comes the Lia Fail, stone of destiny. Stone of sovereignty that knows the worth of leaders. Morfessa, be with us and guard us for this, our Lughnasadh ritual today.*

High Priest: *Welcome Lugh, Lámhfhada, Lugh of the Long Arm, Samhildánach, Lugh of the many skills, High King of the Tuatha De Danann. Be with us as you were with the Tuatha in days of old. Join us for our Lughnasadh ritual today.* (Light the gold candle.)

High Priestess: *Welcome Tailtiu, Earth mother, Goddess of the Harvest and foster mother of Lugh. We welcome you at first harvest. Join us for our Lughnasadh ritual today.* (Light the white candle.)

Participants settle down in the circle.

High Priest: *Today, we celebrate Lugh, sun god, warrior, bard, hunter, leader, artist, and smith. There are many stories to tell of Lugh, but today we will talk of how he came to Tara. As a young man, Lugh journeyed to Tara in search of his heritage. Son of the Tuatha and of the Formorians, he had been fostered by Tailtiu until he could bear arms.*

But not everyone could enter Tara. At the gates, Lugh was stopped and asked why he should be allowed to enter. Lugh told the gatekeeper he was a skilled warrior. The gatekeeper replied that Tara already had skilled warriors. Lugh spoke of his skill as a blacksmith. He was again told that Tara had blacksmiths.

One after another, Lugh listed his many talents as an artist, a hunter, a bard, and more. Each time he was rebuked.

At last, Lugh looked at the gatekeeper and asked, "Is there any one man in Tara who can do all these things as I can?' The gatekeeper said no and let Lugh enter the city.

We learn from this not only to develop our talents but to also be persistent in our pursuit of our goals, our dreams. We must not be turned away from the gate when we are in our rights to enter. Be strong. Stand your ground. Secure your dream.

High Priestess: *Today is also the day we honor Tailtiu, foster mother to Lugh. Tailtiu was the last queen of the Fir Bolg, but she was also an earth goddess. In order to provide for her people, she cleared a great tract of land, roots and all, so that it could be farmed. Her effort was so great, it caused her death.*

Just as the grain falls before the reaper, Tailtiu fell in service to her people. At this harvest season, we celebrate the bounty of the fields. Even in these modern times, we look forward to the harvest, even if we are not mowing the grain or picking the corn. Even in our satisfaction in our bounty, we know it doesn't come without sacrifice. (Picks up the basket of grain.)

We have a basket of grain. I am going to pass it around the circle, and I ask each of you to give your energy to it. Think of the things you have to be thankful for since we last met. When you have finished filling the basket with positive energy, pass it to the person next to you.

Everyone remains in silent meditation while the basket is passed around the circle. When the basket comes back to the **High Priestess**, she says:

Lady Tailtiu, Earth goddess, Goddess of the harvest. We thank you for your sacrifice and ask that you bless this grain. After this ritual and before our next gathering at the Fall Equinox, one of our members will bake it into a hearty bread that we may reap the bounty you have granted.

Next, cakes and ale are shared. When this is done, the deities are thanked by the **High Priest** and **Priestess**. They are invited to stay for the remainder of the festivities. Each of the druids are thanked and released in reverse order.

The circle is opened and the group leaves the circle area for a pot luck dinner. After dinner comes drumming, singing, story telling, and fellowship in the bardic circle.

Notes

Notes

Mabon

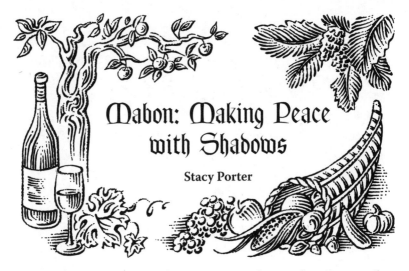

Mabon: Making Peace with Shadows

Stacy Porter

THE APPROACH OF FALL always gave me a burst of excitement that was very quickly followed by a surge of sadness. As a child, I loved sweet corn, harvesting when summer was technically over, and shopping for school supplies. I loved freshly sharpened pencils and notebooks with blank lined pages just waiting to be filled with stories of unicorns and witches. Ultimately, however, they would be used for math homework. The sun would no longer greet me in the morning, peeking through the lush green trees. Instead, the mornings would be filled with fog, as if even the universe was in despair over us having to wait for the school bus.

Mabon, also known as the autumn equinox, is the day when the daylight and night are equal in length, right before we begin our slow descent into darkness as the earth begins to die a little bit every day. The air gets cooler, the leaves lose their vibrant green color and begin to tumble down onto the earth's floor, and the nights get longer.

The earth, just like every living being, dies and in doing so she becomes a mirror for one of our greatest fears as mortals. Death, unknown troubles, and danger are what many see in the darkness. We hide from it instead of embracing mystery, while labeling all that we don't know to be something that's bad.

As the earth turns cold and the nights get longer, we are reminded of loss and sadness. The Ancients viewed the harvests as both a time to reap the rewards of their hard work and also as a time of rest and preparation for the hard times to come.

There are many myths surrounding the beginning of fall. My favorite is a story of both love and loss. While most connect the myth of Persephone with Hades, the Lord of the Underworld, to me her story is really about her relationship with her mother, Demeter, the goddess of earth and grain.

For most of her life, Persephone had been sheltered by her mother from the harshness of the world and the eye of men, but one day, she caught the eye of Hades, and he plucked her from the land of the living, abducting her and forcing her to live in the land of the dead. While she was missing, her mother wandered the earth. Lost in grief and rage, she would not let any of the crops grow. The earth became cold and lifeless, reflecting the ache and emptiness Demeter felt. It was because of this protest that Zeus, the god of the sky and thunder and ruler of Olympus, was forced to intervene and return Persephone to her mother's side. However, while Persephone was in the Underworld, she was tricked into eating three pomegranate seeds that bound her to the Underworld forever. She then had to spend a third of the year with Hades as his wife and queen of his realm. Since that time, Demeter mourns her daughter every year until spring when she is returned and the earth may once again bloom with life.

This proves that dark times are always followed by the light. Even when the gods walked this earth, shadows chased us, playing their games and cackling at our expense. But we must look to Demeter as an example during our troubled times. Even when she was lost in her own grief, she took control. She blackmailed the most powerful of the gods and forced him to right what had been wronged. There is always a choice. There is always a way through even the darkest of times. The trick is to not run from the problem but to face it and, like Demeter did, fight back. This does not mean we should throw punches or make a hoodoo doll for all of the cheerleaders giving us a hard time, but we do need to be actively involved in the troubling situation. We need to take charge of our lives. We need to take our power back.

✼

These days, it is very easy to get separated from reality, from our peers and society, and from ourselves. We are living in such a fast-paced environment that we have to run and juggle a dozen things at a time just to try and keep up. Our focus has turned to material gain and outer successes while still trying to put food on the table and clothes on our backs. To survive, we have to stay ahead of everyone else, or that's what we've been led to believe.

In Buddhism, it is said that we fidget and keep moving and pushing forward because we are afraid. We are afraid of being left behind and forgotten. We are afraid of losing out. We are afraid of ourselves and our inner truth and light.

Our lives revolve around fear. What we all really need is to slow down, which is what autumn is all about. Perhaps that's why we're so afraid of it.

Like bears that hibernate through the winter, we too need to give our bodies and minds time to heal from our hard work. That state of rest and stillness can be frightening to many people because they've been racing through most of their lives and are unfamiliar with all that silence brings.

We don't all have the means to take a monthlong holiday or fly south for the winter, but we can take a few minutes every day to tune back in to ourselves and what is important.

We can sit and quietly reflect as we drink our morning tea or coffee, or we can simply take the time to make a nourishing meal for ourselves or our whole family. Sit on the meditation pillow, write in a journal every day, or take a walk outside to breathe some fresh air.

One of the things I like to incorporate into my daily spiritual practice is yoga.

Yoga means union. It is literally the union of the mind, body, and spirit in moving meditation. Each breath carries us to the next pose, getting us out of our heads and into our souls by bringing our focus away from thoughts and into the body.

I first started practicing yoga in college when I was battling a particular brutal episode of insomnia, which is unfortunately something I have suffered from most of my life. The stress of exams had made it worse, and I started sneaking a minute here and a minute there to breathe and sweat it all out on my yoga mat. It was in those moments that time seemed to stop. My monkey-mind would shut up. I found that even in the midst of chaos, in a dorm room at a time of heightened stress (midterms), peace could be found. I didn't have to wait until it was all over. I could live in the light even when I was surrounded by darkness.

That is life.

In my yoga practice, I was taught that our fears aren't real because love is the only truth. That is very difficult to remember, especially when the evils of the world are shoved in our faces whenever we turn on the news. There has always been darkness, but now that we can reach every corner of the earth with just a click of a button (or just a few minutes scrolling through Twitter), it is very easy to get lost in it.

We have been taught to look for the bad in people. We've grown skeptical of miracles and now question everyone's motives. I spent some time in Russia where it is culturally frowned upon to smile at strangers because it makes them think you're going to con them. We have grown to be distrustful and paranoid.

Nowadays, parents walk their kids on leashes in the mall and run background checks on their babysitters. We live in a constant state of fear of our neighbors and of the unknown. Not even the vegetables are safe if you factor in GMOs.

It would be very easy for us to cover our eyes and hide in the safety of our own homes. In fact, with everything that goes on, it actually makes sense for us to start separating ourselves from the rest of the world. I think that's why so many people get addicted to the internet. Why go out in the scary world when you can hide behind a screen?

Living in a dream world or book, movie, or game is a choice readily at our fingertips, but is that really living? Is that really fulfilling our purpose? We only have a moment here; we shouldn't waste it.

There will never be a perfect time to be happy. We may trick ourselves into believing that's true by telling ourselves that we'll be happy once we're financially secure or when we've found that perfect partner, but we all know that perfect doesn't exist.

People spend their whole lifetime waiting for something great to happen to them when they could be making those great things happen for themselves. Life is waiting for us to show up for ourselves and fear is what gets in our way.

Fear is an illusion created by reliving pain from our past and by projecting that fear into our future. We create these scenarios of what could be. We ask ourselves a lot of what-ifs. We bring pain from the past into the future and petrify our present lives. Fear is what stops us from living.

In yoga, we are taught that long and conscious inhales create space and that long and deep exhales help us move into that new space. This is true for the body and also for the mind. Fear gets its power by leading us far into the future where no one can really know what's going to happen. There are too many variables, and that is what scares us. But when we bring our focus into this very moment, like yoga and meditation teaches us, we take away the power that fear has and give it back to ourselves.

Our world is full of darkness and light, hate and love. There cannot be one without the other, for this world is made up of opposites that must balance each other out. All we can do is be conscious. We can be aware of the problems. Once we see a problem for what it truly is, not the what-ifs or could-bes that our ego tricks us with, the problem will no longer have any power over us. Truth cancels out fear because it is the reality, where fear is the illusion.

We always find what we look for. When we go searching for the bad, we will surely find it. The same goes for the good. Approach every day, every situation, and every conversation with an open mind and heart and you will be surprised at the joy you will experience. This does not make the bad things in the world disappear, but it does make the light in the world shine brighter. If enough of us choose to be the light and live our lives without fear, we will be able to chase away the darkness and create a much more magical and beautiful world for everyone.

When we step fully into our power by letting go of our fears and past, we may finally be able to truly experience life.

The world we live in can be full of darkness and pain, but it is also rich with magic and love. Every breath we take is a blessing, giving us more moments to live and to make a difference in our own lives, the lives of those close to us, and the whole world around us. Our fear can either paralyze us, holding us in a box, or it can ignite us, pushing us forward on our path. Remember to breathe deeply and steadily, for our breath is a reminder of our greatest purpose: to live.

Cosmic Sway

April Elliott Kent

THE GREAT WHEEL TURNS toward autumn in the northern hemisphere when the Sun enters Libra, the sign of balance. Day and night are equal in length at the equinox, each resting on opposite sides of perfectly balanced scales, the symbol for Libra.

Libra's scales are also scales of justice and fairness. The farmer, at autumn's harvest, reaps what he's sown. When it's time to sell his crops, he negotiates a price based not only on how well he has tended his farm but how well others have tended theirs—and how well nature has treated them all.

This is the time of year to evaluate the fruits of your year's labors so far. If you have goals to meet before the calendar year is over, you will have to evaluate what is feasible. Libra is the sign of partnership, and you may decide you will need to enjoin others to help you.

There are many contentious planetary aspects throughout this Mabon season, so we shouldn't expect all matters to proceed smoothly. Making an effort to treat others well and meet challenges with good faith and fairness will be rewarded, even though you may not see those rewards until the wheel turns to Samhain.

Full Moon in Aries—October 5, 2017

The Aries Full Moon is in challenging aspect to Pluto, and while all the outer planets (Uranus, Neptune, Pluto) indicate change, Pluto's changes can be the most sobering. Aries is an individualistic sign, and the Full Moon here shines a light on both the strengths and weaknesses of that approach. But Pluto times are best suited to those who downplay their individual objectives in favor of societal well-being. If you seek personal power during Pluto times, you may gain it—but it is likely to eventually backfire on you.

Venus and Mars, still together in Virgo, oppose Neptune (Sep. 24 and 29) and square Saturn (Oct. 5 and 8) in the Full Moon chart. This is one of those times when it's necessary to confront what is real in our personal relationships and what is not. It's also important to remember that both compassion and hard work are needed to make a relationship successful. If you have been fooling yourself about your relationship, or if the relationship is too much work for too little return, this Full Moon will bring clarifying revelations.

Jupiter in Scorpio—Oct. 10, 2017–Nov. 8, 2018

Traditional astrologers called Jupiter "The Great Benefic" and considered its influence uniformly positive. I wouldn't go that far, personally. But I do consider Jupiter a great teacher and life coach, one that encourages you to stretch yourself and take chances and explore new experiences.

Jupiter takes twelve years to move through the entire zodiac, spending about one year in each sign. On October 10, Jupiter will enter Scorpio and stay in that sign through November 8, 2018. While it is there, Jupiter asks that we grow in wisdom and generosity in the area of sharing. Some of us share too easily and with the wrong people. Some of us struggle with sharing our resources for fear of being exploited by others who want to take from us.

Jupiter asks us to consider the best way to share, suggesting to err on the side of trust, optimism, and generosity. Do not throw out experience and judgment altogether; use them to decide who deserves your trust, and then share with them whole heartedly.

Jupiter's most recent passage through Scorpio was between October 25, 2005, and November 23, 2006. Take a look back at that period of your life and remember in hindsight where you experienced significant personal growth. That's where you will be doing some more advanced work this time around. Here are some ideas about the areas where you will be asked to stretch and evolve in the coming year. Read the section for your Sun sign or Ascendant.

Aries—shared resources, intimacy, working through psychological issues, inheritance, insurance, taxes

Taurus—equal partnerships, marriage, closest friends, negotiation, enemies and rivals, fairness and justice

Gemini—health, work, coworkers, routines and habits, rituals, unequal relationships

Cancer—creative projects, recreation, games and hobbies, children, love affairs

Leo—home, houses, family, women, food, history, genealogy

Virgo—siblings, neighbors, communication, learning and acquiring practical skills, short trips

Libra—earnings, possessions, contentment, security, confidence

Scorpio—independence, personality, appearance, immediate environment, identity

Sagittarius—retreat, spiritual inquiry, confinement due to illness, hidden matters, introspection

Capricorn—friendship, social networks, future goals, earnings from your career, building a legacy

Aquarius—career, reputation, ambition, mentorship, authority figures

Pisces—long journeys, higher learning, religion and beliefs, adventure, performance

Libra New Moon—October 19, 2017

With the Sun and Moon in an exact opposition to Uranus, the Libra New Moon is another lunation that emphasizes change. Uranus changes are sudden and unexpected, like the tornado that sweeps up little Dorothy Gale from Kansas and deposits her in the fascinating Land of Oz!

Wherever you're stuck, Uranus wants to liberate you. He's like a renegade cowboy who sneaks to the jail in the middle of the night to break you out. But the more you have been stuck, the more dramatic the change must be to free yourself.

Venus is square Pluto in this New Moon chart, so relationships must weather some tests and confront some uncomfortable truths. And Mars square Saturn is a sort of "pounding your head against a brick wall" aspect when we often expend too much energy trying to move an immovable object. All this obsessive power from Venus and Mars is at odds with the New Moon's theme of change and liberation. Try to keep your eyes open and remain conscious of what you're doing and why it may not be working. Think about whether the time has come to move on.

Setting Intentions for the New Moon

Each sign can be expressed in both positive and negative ways.

The waxing phases of the New Moon cycle (between the New and Full Moons) provide the best opportunities for launching projects and setting intentions, particularly related to the sign of the New Moon. For the Libra New Moon, set intentions for better relationships, fairness and justice, living a more balanced life, and experiencing satisfaction in your artistic projects.

The waning phases of this cycle (between the Nov. 3 Full Moon the Nov. 18 Scorpio New Moon) are best suited to releasing some of the shadow tendencies of the New Moon sign. For Libra, this includes any tendency toward vanity, unhealthy competition, and indecisiveness. This can also be the time when you may need to let go of relationships that are not bringing you happiness.

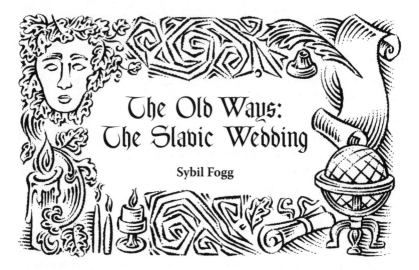

The Old Ways: The Slavic Wedding

Sybil Fogg

MABON IS THE SECOND harvest, the autumnal equinox, a time many pagans associate with balance. In old Poland, September was the most common month for marriage. Perhaps it was the beautiful shift of seasons when the day's light is balanced with the night's darkness. Perhaps it was the fall leaves changing from dewy green to amber hues. Maybe it was because the joining of two in love represents the most important balance of all.

There is an old myth that humans once had four arms, four legs, two heads, and two hearts. These early humans were so content and filled with love that they neglected worship of the gods. This made the king of the gods and goddesses so jealous that he struck them with lightning, splitting them all into two and scattering them across the planet. Humans were depressed and fueled with a desire to find their other half—their one true love. If we are so lucky to find our other half, we often want to consecrate the event with a ceremony bonding us back together. This is why marriage is sacred.

The month of September hallmarked the end of the harvest season in Poland. Given the back-breaking work of gathering the year's yield, it is not surprising that the season culminated in great celebrations, marriage often being the largest festivity. This is a good time to honor Lado and Lada, the god and goddess of marriage, happy unions, and pleasure. It was customary for a bride and groom to present offerings to Lado and Lada to ensure a successful union. Polish weddings were a lengthy celebration. Most marriages in the old days were arranged. The engagement period was called *Oswiadczyny*, *Zareczyny*, or *Zrekowiny* and consisted of both sets of parents "officially meeting." This would be a small gathering in either the groom's or the bride's family household. After that, invitations were sent out. It was considered an ill omen if any member of the village was left out of the merriment. In this way, a wedding was indeed a communal festival since all were invited to gather and celebrate. Traditional foods included *barszcz czerwony* (Polish beet soup), *bigos* (hunter's stew), *kopytka* (dumplings), *pierogi* (dough pockets), roasted meats and vegetables, potatoes with gravy, meat pastries, torte, and fruit bars. Traditional Polish drinks like vodka and wine were also served. The wedding revelries often lasted three days.

An important tradition of the Polish wedding is the *Oczepiny* ceremony (the unveiling and capping). This ritual still takes place in many Polish weddings. It still harkens back to the old ways and marks the transitions from maiden to matron for Polish women. Traditionally, the single women surround the bride, and the maid of honor stands behind the bride and lifts the wedding *welon* (veil) from the bride's head. After this, married women surround the bride and pin the *czepek* (cap) to the her head. After this ritual, the bride is considered to officially be a married woman.

A long time ago, the veil was a gift to the bride from her god-mother. It was kept and held in sacred regard, worn for special oc-casions, including the bride's funeral.

As the couple left the ceremony, the bride would toss straw to the young boys and girls surrounding the wedding party. It was be-lieved that whomever the straw touched would marry first. Which-ever bridesmaid touched the bride first was believed to find marriage within that year. Guests would also throw small coins to the couple or shower them with grains, usually millet, to insure a financially prosperous future.

During the wedding party, guests would circle around the bride for one more chance to dance with her. Money was given as payment for this dance. Bills were often pinned to the bride's dress or placed in a basket to be sent off with the couple to help them start their lives together, or the money could be used on their honeymoon.

❧

Paraskeva-Piatnitsa may have replaced Lada after the arrival of Christianity in Russia. Paraskeva-Piatnitsa was often depicted as a tall, thin woman with long flaxen hair who governed spinning, harvest, and other "womanly" duties. She was traditionally worshipped on Fridays and would be invoked in October when young women would gather to make a veil in her honor. Women celebrated Paraskeva-Piatnitsa on Fridays by abandoning their weaving and spinning for "orgies pagan enough to be denounced by church councils" (Hilton 142).

Russian marriage traditions included the winding of the bride's hair: The matchmakers would divide the bride's hair into two braids, a symbol of wedlock. A *kika* (a complex headdress of a Russian matron) or a *povoinik* (a kerchief worn by married women of the peasant class) would be placed along with the bridal veil. Several items were often scattered around the bride and groom to ensure happiness and success. Traditional items included hops being tossed over the couple to bring happiness, fur coats offered for a rich life, and straw mattresses with the seams left open in hope for easy birth.

It was a tradition in Lithuania for the bride and groom to make their way through blockades of flowers from the ceremony to their home, where they would be impeded by the last garland of flowers. Friends of the groom would be responsible for "buying" the couple's way with candy and whiskey. Traditionally, the couple's parents met them at the door laden with bread, salt, and wine glasses that were filled with water ("Customs of Lithuania").

Many Slavic fairy tales involve maidens marrying snakes. In fact, snakes were so sacred to the ancient Slavic cultures that it was considered sacrilegious to kill one. The Latvian black snake goddess, Melna čūska, was said to have laid the cosmic egg. Her consort was the grass snake god Zalktis (his Lithuanian name was Zaltys). Together, they represented fertility of the body and soul. It was considered lucky to have a snake reside in the home, and if one turned up, it was often given a place of honor to reside by the hearth. While the snake was present, good fortune would come to the family. If the morals of the family began to break down, the snake would leave. If a maiden or lad came across a snake, it prophesied an upcoming marriage. If a married woman or man encountered a snake, an impending pregnancy or birth was in the works.

Although Mabon is often considered a Celtic holiday, the celebration of the start of fall circles the world. September is becoming a popular wedding month in the West; why not incorporate some Slavic traditions in the wedding ceremonies? Leave something out for Lado and Lada and do not disturb snakes that cross your path. They are simply trying to soak up a little more heat as the sun wanes and gives way to winter. And who knows, their visit might bring a bit of luck.

Bibliography

"Customs of Lithuania," accessed August 9, 2015. http://www.sepc.lt /softlanding/index.php?option=com_content&view=article&id =55&Itemid=61.

Gogol, Nikolai. *Dead Souls.* Christopher English, trans. New York: Oxford University Press, 1998.

Hilton, Alison. *Russian Folk Art.* Bloomington: Indiana University Press, 1995.

Hodorowicz Knab, Sophie. *Polish Customs, Traditions, & Folklore.* New York: Hippocrene Books, Inc., 1993.

Mandelstam-Balzer, Marjorie, ed. *Russian Traditional Culture: Religion, Gender, and Customary Law.* New York: M.E. Sharpe Inc., 1992.

"Polish Wedding Traditions," *Meet the Slavs,* accessed August 10, 2015. http://meettheslavs.com/polish-wedding-traditions/.

Taylor, Bron, ed. *The Encyclopedia of Religion and Nature: A–J.,* Volume 1. London: Continuum, 2008.

Terletski, Michael. "Old Russian Wedding Ceremony," *Russian Crafts,* accessed August 11, 2015. http://russian-crafts.com /russiantraditions/old-wedding-ceremony.html.

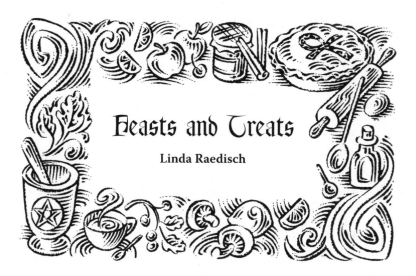

Feasts and Treats

Linda Raedisch

THE MOON IS BIG and bright tonight! Some Westerners see a face, others see green cheese. The Chinese see a beautiful lady or a rabbit pounding rice in a mortar. I see a bowl brimming with rice porridge.

Congee

I have been told that congee or "rice gruel" is only for sick people. I have also been told it is only for breakfast. In our house, it's the ultimate comfort food, and comfort foods are good any time of the day. If you really are sick, you might want to stick with the basic recipe with a chunk of chicken breast thrown in, but congee is only as bland as you want it to be. Feel free to add cubed raw sweet potato, any kind of meat, fresh loofah (it looks like a cucumber), shiitake mushrooms, or sweet Chinese sausage to your brew. In this recipe, I have suggested sliced hard-boiled eggs for a topping, but the more traditional choice is the emerald green "thousand-year-old egg" that you can find in the dry goods section of any Chinese grocery store.

I make congee in my rice cooker, but I find it tastes best the next day, thinned with water and reheated on the stove.

Prep time: 10 minutes
Cook time: 60 minutes
Servings: 4

½ cup white short grain or "sushi" rice
4 cups water
1 teaspoon salt
Small dash sesame oil
Large dash Chinese cooking wine
Dash black pepper
Fresh ginger root (about an inch long section, peeled and minced)
2 whole scallions, minus roots, minced
Sliced hard boiled eggs (optional)
Pork sung (fried, dried pork: looks and tastes like pig-flavored cotton candy) (optional)

Drop all ingredients (except eggs and pork sung) in large pot and bring to boil. Once boiled, reduce heat, cover, and simmer for 60 minutes. Serve hot in bowls and top with either sliced eggs, pork sung, or both if desired. (If you like extra heat, add more ginger or pepper; if not, add less.)

Chrysanthemum Tartlets

If you're a previous celebrant of the moon festival, I know what you're thinking: where are the moon cakes? Moon cakes—molded pastries filled with sweet red bean, lotus, or green tea filling and then stamped with beautiful designs—are certainly at the heart of my own family's lackadaisical Moon Festival celebrations, but we buy them at the Chinese grocery store and will continue to do so until someone bestows a set of wooden moon cake molds upon me.

My chrysanthemum tartlets are a variant of the more usual Hong Kong egg tarts that are a part of the typical Sunday morning dim sum experience. Because we are using phyllo dough for our crust, the overlapping golden leaves will give these egg tarts the appearance of golden chrysanthemums.

Prep time: 50 minutes
Bake time: 15–21 minutes
Servings: 8

½ stick (4 tablespoons) butter

¼ cup white sugar

⅓ cup hot water

2 eggs

2 brimming tablespoons evaporated milk

¼ teaspoon vanilla

8 ounces phyllo dough or 1 roll phyllo dough, thawed (half of a 16-ounce package)

Pastry brush

8 cup muffin pan

Heat butter in small pot until melted. Keep watch: don't let it burn! Use pastry brush to grease muffin pan with a little of the melted butter. Set pan and butter aside.

Put sugar in medium sized bowl, pour hot water over it, and stir until dissolved. Set aside to cool.

In another medium bowl, whisk eggs, evaporated milk, and vanilla until well mixed. Pour sugar water into egg mixture and whisk again until slightly frothy, about 4 minutes. (Don't put the sugar water bowl in the sink yet!) Pour mixture through sieve back into sugar water bowl. This is to make the filling smooth. Let rest at room temperature while you prepare the pastry cups.

Unroll your thawed phyllo dough. (If you forgot to thaw the dough before embarking on this journey, that's okay; the filling will keep.) Using a sharp knife or scissors, cut dough into 3-inch squares. (This is for 2½-inch diameter muffin cups. If your muffin pan has smaller or larger cups, you will have to cut slightly smaller or larger squares.) Keep phyllo squares covered with a clean, damp kitchen towel while you work.

Gently push first square of phyllo into first muffin cup, brushing with a little butter. Continue layering butter and phyllo until you have 10 squares of phyllo in the cup. Neatness doesn't really count, but be sure not to press too hard; you want phyllo to remain light and flaky. Repeat with remaining muffin cups. (Find a good station on the radio—this is going to take a while!) When you are about halfway finished, preheat oven to 350 degrees F.

Fill phyllo cups evenly with egg filling and bake for 15–21 minutes or until toothpick inserted in center comes out clean.

Let cool a few minutes before lifting tarts from pan. Serve warm.

Chrysanthemum Tea

Many of us celebrate fall by arranging cut chrysanthemums in vases around the house and putting potted ones by the door. But you can also drink them! In order to make chrysanthemum tea, you are going to have to make a trip to your Asian or Chinese grocery store. There are over 1 billion Chinese speakers in the world. That means over 1 billion Chinese eaters, so trust me when I tell you there's an Asian grocery store near you. The following exotic ingredients should be found in the tea aisle.

Prep time: 5 minutes, if you don't count the shopping
Brew time: 5 minutes
Servings: 4

1 cup dried chrysanthemum flowers—yellow, white, wild, etc.
4 tablespoons rock sugar
4–6 pieces dried licorice (looks like wood chips)
4½ cups boiling water
Teapot
Sieve

Put chrysanthemums, sugar, and licorice in tea pot. Pour in boiling water. Let steep 5 minutes. Pour through sieve into cups. If it's hot out, you can strain the tea into a pitcher and chill for 1 hour before serving.

Crafty Crafts

Mickie Mueller

MABON IS A TIME of harvest when we focus on abundance and the blessings we've had over the year. It's a really good time to express our gratitude. The thing about gratitude is that the more you appreciate what you have, the more the universe blesses you.

Gratitude Hoop

A gratitude hoop is a really easy craft project and a lovely way to mindfully recognize all that you're grateful for; it's part ritual, part decoration, and all Mabon. Hang this meaningful decoration over your dining table as you celebrate the fall harvest or hang it on the wall as part of your autumn décor.

Time to complete: less than an hour
Cost: $8 to $12

Supplies

9-inch grapevine wreath
Hot glue and a glue gun
Autumn garland (check the dollar store)
Twine
Autumn-colored ribbon (several colors wide enough to write on)
Permanent fine-tip marker

Lay the wreath flat on the table and arrange the fall garland until you're happy with how it looks. Trim any excess garland with a pair of wire clippers. Carefully attach the garland to the wreath with your hot glue gun. Glue about an inch at a time, holding the garland in place long enough for the glue to set, and then move on to the next section until the entire garland is attached.

Now, decide where you want to hang it. If you want to dangle it horizontally over your dining table or porch awning, cut four even pieces of twine a little bit longer than the length you want to hang it. Tie the pieces of twine to each quarter section of the wreath. With the wreath flat on the table, garland side up, gather the twine together and tie the ends together so they are even and the right length for the wreath to hang horizontally. Now you can hang it wherever you wish.

Cut several different fall shades of ribbon, such as reds, yellows, oranges, and olive green, into strips about a foot and a half to two feet long. Using a fine tip permanent marker, write something that you're grateful for on each ribbon; it can be successes of the previous year, people you love, blessings of opportunities, guidance of deities or spirit guides, promotions at work, or anything at all that's a blessing in your life. Feed the ends of each ribbon through a vine underneath the gratitude hoop so they dangle down. You can tie them off or pull them halfway through the vine so they don't need to be tied, depending upon your preference. If you wish to make your gratitude hoop part of a group gathering, write one or two statements of gratitude and hang them on the hoop to get it started, and then display the rest of the ribbons and marker so other people at the gathering can add things they're grateful for.

For those who either can't or don't want to display the hoop as a mobile, it can be hung as a wreath on a wall or door with the gratitude ribbons dangling along the bottom.

Apples and Acorns Prosperity Broom

Another kind of magic in the air during the season of Mabon is the energy of prosperity we enjoy during the second harvest. This prosperity broom hung near your door uses acorn bells and dried apple pentacles to sweep prosperity into your life.

Time to complete: 1 hour (6 hours or so to dry the apples)
Cost: $8 to $12

Supplies
Apples
1 tablespoon of salt dissolved in one cup of lemon juice
A craft-store cinnamon broom
Hot glue and glue gun
Acorn caps (for free on a hiking trip or in the park)
Small gold jingle bells to fit your acorn caps
Shallow dish of rice

Twine
Autumn ribbon
Optional: fall leaves or silk flowers

Cutting the apples horizontally, cut slices about a quarter inch thick. You can carefully use a sharp knife or you can get nice even slices if you have a mandolin slicer wide enough for the apple. Be sure to take proper precautions when using a knife or mandolin slicer. Choose the best slices that show the star in the middle, and place the slices in a bowl with the lemon juice and salt mixture. Let them soak for about thirty minutes or so. The salt and lemon juice mixture helps the apples keep their color better while they dry.

Plug in your hot glue gun and let it heat up. Once it's ready, place the acorn caps upside down in the bowl of rice so they don't tip over. Fill one cap about halfway with hot glue and immediately put the top of the bell into the cap. Now turn the acorn bell over in the rice so that the cap is on top until the glue cools completely. Repeat with the rest of the acorn caps.

Cut one length of twine about six inches long for each acorn. Tie the ends together to turn them into loops. Put a dot of hot glue on the top of an acorn cap and glue the tied end of the loop to it. Repeat this with all the acorns.

By now your apple slices should be done soaking—blot them dry with a paper towel. Place a wire cooling rack on top of a cookie sheet and lay the apple slices on top. Put them in the oven and let them bake for six hours at 150 degrees F, turning them over every two hours. When they're done, take them out of the oven and allow them to cool. Poke a hole at the top of each apple pentacle and run twine through for hanging.

All you have to do now is decorate your broom. Wrap some of your fall ribbon around the handle; you can either attach the ribbon with hot glue or by just tying it. Attach the apple slices and acorn bells in a pleasing arrangement. You can secure them by tying them to a broom bristle on the front of the broom with a ribbon, or you can run the loop that you added through the broom bristles into the back of the broom and tie the loop to the bristles in the back. You may also attach them to the front of the broom using hot glue. Be creative and have fun while making it uniquely yours. You can also add real or silk fall leaves if you wish. Once you have it exactly how you want it, hang it on your front door so it chimes lightly every time the door is opened, bringing in prosperity. This is also a great Mabon ritual broom.

All One Family

Dallas Jennifer Cobb

THE SECOND OF THE three harvest festivals is the lesser sabbat of Mabon. Mabon is also known as Pagan Thanksgiving, Harvest Home, and autumn equinox. "Equinox" comes from the Latin *aequus* (equal) and *nox* (night). Day and night are equal length at the equator, and the earth's northern and southern hemispheres get equal amounts of light and darkness.

We hover in time and space, momentarily in balance. With the pause, we look around and inventory our abundance. We count our blessings. Then with a tick of time the Wheel of the Year moves and soon we will know the spread of darkness. After the moment of balance, the dark will now overtake the light.

We give thanks for crops that are harvested, and while enjoying the abundance, we observe the cycle of decline. If we look a long way forward, we are aware of the potential for rebirth, long after the symbolic death.

Our kids have been back in school for a while now, and hopefully they are settling into a routine. By Mabon they have gone beyond the joy of shiny new shoes and fashionable new clothes. They are no longer excited by new teachers, reunification with old friends, or the delight of making new friends. Now the darkness is creeping into their daily lives: homework, looming midterms, exhaustion from the long days, and the dread of their increased responsibilities.

The excitement may be gone, but they still have to go to school each day. The days grow shorter and darker, but the alarm clock continues to ring at the same time, drawing them up from their dreams to the reality world of responsibilities, homework, and part-time jobs.

Mabon comes at a good time. The opportunity to celebrate and feast allows us to connect with our teens, celebrating their smooth transition back to school. Sometimes our words of praise, even for the smallest achievements, can make a huge difference for our kids, off-setting the dread they might be feeling. And for those who might be slipping behind at school, our attention now could be the very act that helps them find their way back to a routine that supports their success at school.

On Mabon, prepare a feast of seasonal foods like baked squash and potatoes, a roasted chicken or turkey, pumpkin pie, or homemade bread. As you eat, make merry. For this is the time of thanksgiving. And when your bellies are full, gather together for a seasonal ritual.

Practice: Facing Fears

Gather your teens tonight and ask them to help you in the evening when it is dark. Tell them you don't want to do this alone because you are afraid and need their help. Our kids often see us simply as Mom or Dad: reliable, committed, and invincible. It is good for them to see us as human beings too, and letting them know that we too have fears can make it possible for them to admit their own.

Go around your home turning on every light, reminding them of Demeter and Persephone. By now they know the story and you won't have to recount it in detail:

Each year, Persephone must leave her mother and journey down into the dark of Hades. Before she leaves Demeter, Persephone feasts on the magnificence of the light-filled world: the fruits, flowers, love, and care of her mother. Tonight, let us illuminate our joys, successes, achievements, and creations. We need to know the "light of life."

Ask your teens to list a few good things that they are "harvesting" right now. Maybe it's rugby or soccer season, which are in full swing, or a growing understanding of the periodic table of elements. It could be late-season ever-bearing raspberries, or that pumpkin that finally grew big enough to decorate the front step. Make sure that each of you come up with a few good things. And when everyone has identified something good, affirm:

We are rich and abundant. Filled with love and light.

Now move through the house and turn off the lights, one after another, saying:

The darkness is growing. And soon it will overtake the light. The nights will stretch long, into the cold, mean winter. Just as Persephone journeys to the heart of the earth, this is the time when we move more inside. When it is dark without, we turn to the light within.

With all the lights out, pause, standing quietly in the dark. Say:

Our true harvest lies within us. We are safe, secure, nurtured, and supported. We enjoy the shelter of this home and democracy in this country. Even in the bleak darkness, we shall fear not. For we remember the eternal cycle: birth, growth, decline, death, decomposition, and rebirth.

Turn to look at your teens and remind them:

You are your truest source of support, belonging, and acceptance. And you are your own fierce mother Demeter…but also remember that I love you. Regardless. Forever.

Now, ask your teenagers to turn with you.

Let us face our own shadows, and let us take the first steps. Like Persephone, we walk alone into the dark. Let us each walk alone, in silence, to our rooms and spend a few moments in the dark there. And when you are ready, and when you have faced your fears, turn on the lights in your small rooms and be reminded of the myriad lights inside you.

Heading in different directions, slowly walk away from one another and through your home. Claim the darkness, claim the space, claim your power, and utter Persephone's prayer:

We have waxed into the fullness of life,
and waned into darkness.
May we be renewed to tranquility and wisdom.

Mabon Ritual: Honor the Shadows

Stacy Porter

MABON IS OFTEN REFERRED to as the Witches' Thanksgiving. It is a harvest festival where we reap the rewards of our labor. To some, this might mean having a great feast with the crops collected from the fields or a table full of favorite dishes that are prepared with love. However, Mabon also has strong ties to the Underworld. It is the first day of autumn and, until the wheel turns at Yule, the nights will be getting longer and the air will be getting colder as the earth descends into darkness.

Instead of being afraid of all that darkness means, I invite you to take time to reflect on the obstacles and struggles you have faced in the past and give thanks for where you are today.

One does not truly have to be out of the dark to be thankful for the light in their life. Simply acknowledge that every step you take is guiding you to a better place. Also remember that there is no such thing as perfection. There is only progress. There is only love.

You are not defined by your past, but you would not be who you are or where you are now without it. This ritual is meant to honor those dark times. It can be a very emotional ritual, but the intention is to cleanse yourself of the pain, so you are only left with the lessons learned. The goal is to love where you have come from, so you can truly appreciate how far you have come on your path.

Now, it's almost time for tea!

Preparing the Ritual

As children, we see tea parties as a beautiful event where we don tiaras and pretty feather boas. Sometimes we would be hosting our teddy bears, or perhaps some friends would come over and we'd play pretend.

As adults, tea has become a source of ultimate comfort. It is often served to offer people a distraction during awkward social situations since it's nice to have something to hold and stir when times get tough. There is something truly wonderful about having a warm mug in your hands as you curl up and read a good book. There are thousands of teas dedicated to helping people relax, soothe their worries, and help them sleep.

This ritual is designed to be private and quiet. It is very personal and can lead to a very emotional response as we are diving into the past. It can of course be modified for a group, if desired. It can be an intimate ritual that you do on your own (perhaps you dust off those teddy bears and invite them into your circle), or it can be done with your coven (with tiaras and feather boas).

Notes: It's best to do this ritual at dawn at the first light of the new day or at dusk at the last light of the day.

Wear black, brown, burgundy, deep orange, or purple to honor the darkness. You can dress in formal wear or pajamas—whatever you are most comfortable in!

I recommend reading through the entire ritual before starting. This will help the ritual go smoothly.

Items Needed
Sage smudge stick
Matches
Freshly boiled water

Your favorite tea (like an herbal tea—chamomile or lavender)

Three teacups or mugs: one for you, one for the Goddess, and one for the God

Table for altar

Candles for the quarters: red, blue, green, yellow, and white

Salt water mixture

Optional: teddy bears, plastic tiaras, and feather boas to bring some fun into the circle (You can also use a journal for notes during your ritual reflection)

Before you begin, light the sage and let the smoke cleanse as you enter your sacred space. This will clear you of all stagnant energies and give you the opportunity to start the ritual with a clear mind and open heart.

Now prepare your altar and your tea, and sit somewhere where you are comfortable. This can be on your meditation pillow, at your kitchen table, or outside. Be sure that you will be able to sit up straight, with a tall spine and open chest.

The Reflection Ritual

Cast the circle by walking the perimeter of your sacred space clockwise while using a sacred tool to draw it in the air. This tool can either be an athame, sword, or your fingertip. In my instructions, I'll be using a fingertip, but please use any tool you feel comfortable with.

On the first rotation, keep your fingertip pointed at the ground while saying:

By the power of my hand, I cast this mighty circle round. From earth to sky and sky to ground.

On the second rotation, keep your fingertip pointed out at the height of your shoulder while saying:

It shall stand strong and sound, a protection shield for those that it does surround.

On the third and final rotation, keep your fingertip pointed up at the sky, solidifying your cone of power while imagining a white glow encompassing your sacred space.

Once you have completed the circle, stomp the ground and declare:

In perfect love and perfect trust, this circle is sealed.

Invoke the Quarters

Sometimes covens create altars for each quarter, but you can just have a candle for each one. Start in the east. Light each candle while you summon the quarter's energy.

East (light yellow candle): *I call the power of the East, the element of air, to enter this sacred space and open my mind with a gentle breeze. Bring communication, compassion, and understanding. Hail and welcome.*

South (light red candle): *I call the power of the South, the element of fire, to enter this sacred circle and fuel my inner fire. Bring passion, warmth, and creativity. Hail and welcome.*

West (light blue candle): *I call the power of the West, the element of water, to enter this sacred ring and cleanse my body and mind. Bring intention, healing, and clarity. Hail and welcome.*

North (light green candle): *I call the power of the North, the element of earth, to enter this sacred ground and protect us in this hour. Bring balance, stability, and strength. Hail and welcome.*

Center (light white candle): *In this hour, lost in time and space, it is our past we wish to face. Stand with us now, the force and the form, at this time when we are reborn. Demeter and Persephone, hail and welcome.*

Note: You may, of course, use any god and goddess that you connect to in your personal practice.

Ritual

Pour the tea, and as the steam rises out of the cups and into the air, say:

It's in the heat where passion burns,
It's in the fire where emotion churns.
It's in my heart where pain dwells,
It's in my mind where anger swells.
It's in my soul where light shines,
It's in this hour where love and fate align.

At this time, allow your thoughts to wander. Think back to when you've been hurt or when you have done the hurting. Think back to when you've been lost or confused. Think back to when you've truly felt the darkness.

This can be a painful process at first, but allow the tears to come, for they are a true cleanse, straight from your soul. Let the salt water stream down your face and wash away the pain.

Keep your eyes closed and the work internal as you dip your fingertips into the salt water mixture and say:

By the water that is her blood and the earth that is her body, my spirit is now ready to come home.

Touch the salt water to your forehead, to your lips, to your throat, to your heart, and to your belly.

Sip your tea and visualize any negativity you've held on to about your past literally being cleansed. You can never lose your past, but you can try and see it with clearer eyes. You are here today because of the path you walked yesterday. Embrace what happened. Embrace who you are today.

When you're ready, say:

Playing with fire, fighting with fate.
I cut the wire, I release the hate.
My past is over, but my future is clear.

I claim my power and disown my fear.
Thankful for freedom, grateful for love.
So mote it be, below and above.

From this moment on, stop concerning yourself with what was and instead focus on what is. Focus on what you can do at this moment to live a life that serves you and the greater good.

Close the spell with these lines:

By the magick that has been spun, in perfect love with harm to none, this Mabon spell is done.

Close the Quarters

Do not blow the candles out as you close the quarters. Walk the circle counterclockwise, dismissing the elements in the opposite order you called them.

Start at **North:** *Mighty Earth, thank you for this transformation. Hail and farewell.*

To the West: *Gentle West, thank you for this healing. Hail and farewell.*

To the South: *Powerful South, thank you for this reawakening. Hail and farewell.*

To the East: *Truthful East, thank you for this inner knowing. Hail and farewell.*

Then close your circle by walking counterclockwise and imagine that your hand or tool is sweeping up the wall of the light. Once you are back at **North,** say:

This circle is open, but never broken. Clear the air, as my words are spoken. Merry meet, merry part, and may we meet again.

Clap your hands to dispel the energy you've swept up and give yourself a few moments to ground and center. You can sit and meditate formally, or you can physically touch some earth, whether it's salt, a plant, or the actual ground. Visualize yourself offering the excess energy to the Great Mother. Clear yourself of what was and embody the moment.

As you leave the circle, once again light the sage and let the smoke wash over you. This will cleanse you of the feelings and energies you felt within the ritual, and it will allow you to have a fresh start, leaving the past behind you.

Allow the candles to burn in a safe place until they go out on their own. When they are out, bury any remaining wax and take down the altar. Be sure to pour the tea from the God and the Goddess cups onto the earth for their pleasure.

You are a beautiful light in the darkness, and remember that the past is out, the present is clear, and the future is open.

Happy Mabon. Happy Witches' Thanksgiving!

Notes

Notes

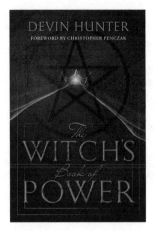

The Witch's Tools Series

With illustrations by Mickie Mueller and contributors from throughout the witchy world, *The Witch's Tools* series delves into the fascinating history, symbolism, and modern uses of various tools, from the athame to the wand. With a variety of spells, rituals, and methods for creating or personalizing each tool, the books in the series present a wealth of knowledge that every age and kind of witch can use.

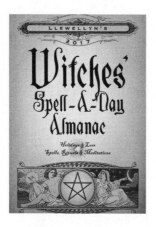

Notes

Notes